Northwest Historical Series
XVII

AN ENSLAVED SHASTA GIRL

The Shasta and Pit River Indians were the greatest source of slaves for lower Plateau tribes who traded them at The Dalles for horses and other things. Acquiring the horse in the early 19th century, the Klamaths raided these two groups . An important consequence of the raids was an emerging Klamath aristocracy at about the time the practice was prohibited by the U.S. government. *Courtesy, Stark Museum of Art, Orange, Texas. Neg. #31.78/57 WWC 57.*

Indian Slavery
in the
Pacific Northwest

by
ROBERT H. RUBY
and
JOHN A. BROWN

with a foreword by
JAY MILLER
The Newberry Library, Chicago

THE ARTHUR H. CLARK COMPANY
Spokane, Washington
1993

LIBRARY OF CONGRESS CATALOG CARD NUMBER 93-31861
ISBN 0-87062-225-0

The Arthur H. Clark Company
P.O. Box 14707
Spokane, WA 99214

Library of Congress Cataloging-in-Publication Data

Ruby, Robert H.
    Indian slavery in the Pacific Northwest / by Robert H. Ruby and John A. Brown :
with a foreword by Jay Miller.
        p.   cm. — (Northwest historical series ; 17)
    Includes bibliographical references and index.
    ISBN 0-87062-225-0 : $37.50
    1. Indians of North America—Northwest Coast of North America—Slaves,
Ownership of. 2. Indians of North America—Northwest, Pacific—Slaves, Ownership of.   I. Brown, John Arthur.   II. Title.   III. Series.
E78.N78R83   1993
979.5'00497—dc20   93-31861
                                                                                    CIP

Contents

Illustrations and Maps

Foreword

Slavery is an uncomfortable subject for Americans, who pride themselves on living in the land of the free. That "peculiar institution" was, nonetheless, part of American history until legally ended by the Civil War. The strains, however, are still with us, expressed through stereotypes of race and geographical origins so pervasive in the New World, where Europe, Africa, and other continents have left their imprints.

While Europeans and Africans met as equals in the Old World, they came to the Americas as master or slave, drawn from many cultures and expressing many personalities and perspectives. Yet these are not reflected in the documents. Instead, we have the records of a business venture—a triangular trade of goods, rum, and slaves—written by shippers and traders. Almost all of our documents come from Europeans, except for exceptional instances when slaves learned to write narratives and confessionals. Our only other sources are oral traditions carried on by the families of freed slaves, but these are meager.

Similarly, for native America, we have only Euro-American records about indigenous slavery, which Ruby and Brown have commendably discussed in terms of an intertribal swirl with a vortex among the Chinook, the great traders of the lower Columbia River and the subject of another of their books.

The existing accounts of native slavery of the Northwest were also written by whites and need to be treated with caution, if not actually judged to be prejudiced. In the primary documents, observers may not have understood or condoned what they were seeing. For the scholarly analyses, the intellectual fashions of the time may have influenced the conclusions. In the case of the famous study of Northwest Coast slavery by Julia Averkieva, her work had to conform to the Marxist ideology of Russia, where she was born, educated, and sentenced to internal exile for her wide-ranging interests.

As with most topics dealing with Native America, the sheer volume and diversity of the sources allow us to gain a common understanding of the subject. For native slavery, alas, we have no accounts by slaves themselves, and only occasional mention of them in native oral traditions. It is their unspoken voice, therefore, that needs to be kept in mind as you read this book. In lieu of primary documents presenting an insider view of slavery, the best available source is the anthropological record, both on specific tribes and from a comparative perspective.

Long before white and black foreigners settled in the New World, indigenous growth created societies of great complexity. Particularly distinctive among these were the communities of the northwestern portion of the continent of North America, where coastal people recognized ranked gradations consisting of nobles, a freeborn majority, and, beyond the pale, a residual category of slaves.

As war captives yanked from their own societies, debtors who forfeited their lives, or the children of slaves, these individuals held in slavery were fellow natives, at least until a few Europeans were also taken as slaves. Given the varied cultural practices of the coast, however, many slaves appeared different from other members of the community. Along the southern coast, freeborn people had shaped heads, molded as infants in cradleboards. Northern peoples had unmodified heads. Thus, southern captives in the north were marked by broad faces and angular skulls. Similarly, northern slaves among the southern tribes were distinguished by their naturally rounded heads. Other less flattering stereotypes about regional differences among slaves, are provided by Ruby and Brown in quoted extracts from journals and letters.

The relationship between capture and slavery was complex. Sometimes, after a slave raid, captive women revealed their noble status by their comportment, and they were taken as wives by chiefly raiders. By a polite fiction, they were not regarded as having been slaves, but coerced visitors. In other cases, such nobles were ransomed by their natal households, and cleansed of the captive stigma by an elaborate give-away (a potlatch) on their return.

Those who remained slaves, however, were further set apart by their lack of personal or social identity. Among the Salish, slaves were known only by the term for their natal tribe, never by a distinctive name. Even the word meaning a slave was itself used as an insult, suggesting that someone was worthless. Such reference did not mean that someone was lazy or no-account, because slaves worked harder at the same economic pursuits than anyone else of their age and gender. Rather, slaves had nothing worthwhile of their own, and, thus, no way to express generosity. It was by sharing that reputations and worth were established in the community, confirming heredity rights or fostering upward mobility.

In special cases in the north, a noble would gain added prestige by giving away life—killing a slave—at a public occasion to signify what a precious commodity life was. Usually, the victim was a slave specially traded because slaves of the household were regarded too fondly to be sacrificed. In some instances, however, slaves were expected to take risks on behalf of their master and his or her family.

In other instances, slaves took risks on their own initiative, earning community rewards even after death. Among the Tsimshian, the name of a slave who drowned while killing the particularly haughty and murderous chief who had been his master is now regarded as having chiefly rank. In gratitude for his sacrifice, the community began the process of elevating his name to its present exalted status by lavish potlatching. Other slaves were given their freedom among the Tsimshian because they were such superb artists that their efforts attracted fame and regard for their households. In these and other cases, therefore, initiative and ability on the part of slaves earned them the reward of freedom.

In one famous instance, however, this was not the case. The Tsimshian high chief Legaix decided to stage his own death and resurrection. He sent envoys throughout the coast looking for a slave who looked like himself. One was found among the Tlingit, brought to Legaix with great secrecy, and hidden in the community. At a large gathering, the slave, dressed in Legaix's chiefly attire, walked to the beach, where he was obviously killed. Later, at a special ritual, Tsimshian chiefs revived Legaix from the dead, proving his special powers.

Equally wondrous were many of the stories of first contact between Europeans and Natives, when slaves played a significant part because they were selected by the leaders to eat and drink what the sailors offered. When none of them died, although several seemed to come close to death after filling up on grog, new staples like coffee, sugar, flour, and molasses were added to the native diet.

In the Northwest, then, slavery was not an easy way of life but it was preferable to the alternative—death. If food was scarce, it is likely that slaves were last to be fed, but since the food quest was their major activity, they could always snack on the so-called slave foods while collecting provisions for the household. These eatables were less tasty and glamorous, but they kept body and soul alive.

It was at death that the stigma of slavery was revealed in full form. Usually, slaves were neither mourned in public nor accorded burial, except in the most perfunctory and haphazard way. Mostly, their bodies were simply cast into the sea or forest. While interpretation is problematic in the absence of verbatim accounts, it seems likely that slaves were thus discarded because they no longer had a homeland. Either because they were captives or they were born into slavery, they knew only the homes of their masters. Unless they could enter the appropriate afterworld, they had no hope of rebirth or reincarnation.

Throughout the Northwest, the land of the dead was believed to be located below that of the living, mirroring it in every way except that seasons, tides, and time were reversed between them. Often, the templates which became infant bodies lived in a section of the underworld, waiting to be born or reborn among the living. Given the strong parallelisms between the land, the living, and the dead, it becomes clear just how far outside this system slaves were located. They were truly ungrounded. By remaining alive in foreign territory, they forfeited links to their homeland, their ancestors, and their own afterworld. This was the real tragedy of being a slave.

And yet, all was not lost. When northwestern slaves were freed by the same Emancipation Proclamation issued by Abraham Lincoln to entitle black slaves in the South, some of the most successful native entrepreneurs were former slaves, who continued to apply the same degree of hard work to their tasks but now for their own benefit, as illustrated by the success of John Kettle at Suquamish who sent shellfish to Seattle.

Though an uneasy subject, slavery is an important one. Scholars have applied countless theories and models to its many manifestations around the world. Yet all must rely on basic observer descriptions to test their suspicions. The bringing together of such data is a significant contribution of this volume on slavery; many details from myriad sources are now between the same covers. Admittedly, the observers were whites and the times were characterized by great stress, along with what I suspect was greater cruelty, but the records stand on their own. For this, Ruby and Brown are to be commended.

JAY MILLER
The Newberry Library
Chicago, Illinois

Preface

In over three decades of researching Indians of the Pacific Northwest region we have been made aware of the many interesting aspects of their history and culture. Many of these we "flagged," planning a return for more in-depth study. One of these "flagged" topics was Indian slavery which, unlike the slavery of black America, has hitherto been little known or understood by both scholars and the public at large. When we began delving into the subject of Pacific Northwestern Indian slavery we discovered that source materials pertaining to it were more sparse than we had anticipated. Possibly this was because anthropology, on which we had hoped to heavily rely in our study, matured only when slavery in the region was in decline; or perhaps because the practice appears to have been of little concern to both early observer-scholars as well as to those in more recent time. Literary sources were also meager and the common form of obtaining information, the interview, was lacking since descendants of slaves discussed the servitude of their ancestry in hushed tones or not at all.

Scholars hitherto have tended to suppress subrational forces at work in Native American history. This may have stemmed not only from their belief in the inherent goodness of man, but also from a reaction to early accounts of Indian ancestry which stressed its sanguinity more than its positive accomplishments, and in which early times the equally sanguinary exploits of white conquerors were ignored. American Indians today resent the stereotyped characterizing of their ancestry as "warlike." Yet, it must be said that to achieve a well-rounded picture of Indian history one must be aware that subrational forces militated against peace and bliss long before conflict with white men. Events such as the culture-altering trauma of the Columbian discovery of America, whose Cinquecento is celebrated at the time of this writing, only added to the early Americans' unhappiness, precipitating a stronger belief in a happier future life. Some might argue, however, that the Indians' happiness in the here and now called for a similar life in the hereafter. Yet, attention must be given to Voltaire's dictum that history is that of silken slippers descending the stairway of time to the accompaniment of hobnail boots ascending from below.

Laying aside the fact that the subjects of this study, Pacific Northwestern Indian slaves, were taken from and to Indian communities mostly by violence, the fact remains that such was an expression of man's inhumanity to his fellow man. Lest vaunted Western Civilization boast of its silken slipper accomplishments, it must be remembered that until recent times slavery was practiced in and by its so-called civilized nations, falling short of their achieving their long-sought age of millennial happiness. Moreover, Indian slavery, especially in highly structured Pacific Northwestern native communities, reveals, as it does in previous similar complex cultures, that such servitude was an important part of their existence.

Since slavery and its trade are inexorably intertwined, we have, wherever possible, combined discussion of the practices under the single term, "slavery." Lest we be open to criticism, we have taken the liberty of identifying native groups as tribes when, in fact, their political structure was minimal, unlike that of tribes elsewhere in America. Thus, we use the term "tribe" as one would use "world" for earth.

Despite limitations in our researches as cited above, we are grateful to those scholars who have boldly conducted studies of Pacific Northwestern Indian slavery. Since black slavery in the American South is so well known, observers of Indian slavery in the Pacific Northwest, sympathizing with eastern reformers, often graphically detailed its excesses. We trust from their accounts we have sifted out the truth from a subject of interest to use, which we now incorporate within the written word.

We wish to acknowledge the assistance of our consultants, Dr. Robert T. Boyd and Dr. Donald Mitchell, and our cartographer, Louise Drew.

ROBERT H. RUBY Moses Lake, Wash.
JOHN A. BROWN Wenatchee, Wash.

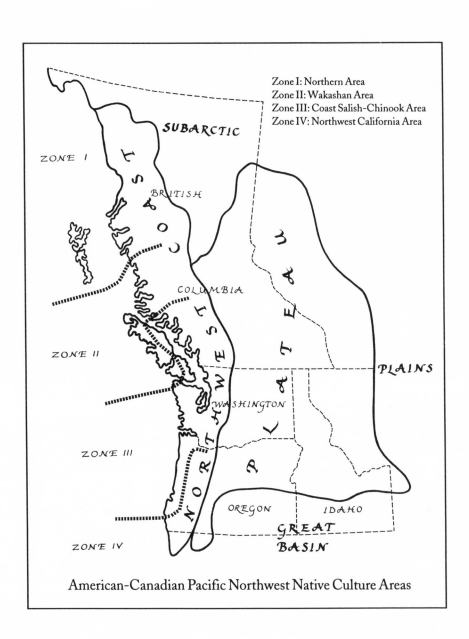

Zone I: Northern Area
Zone II: Wakashan Area
Zone III: Coast Salish-Chinook Area
Zone IV: Northwest California Area

SUBARCTIC

ZONE I

BRITISH

COLUMBIA

ZONE II

PLATEAU

PLAINS

WASHINGTON

NORTHWEST

ZONE III

OREGON   IDAHO

GREAT

ZONE IV   BASIN

American-Canadian Pacific Northwest Native Culture Areas

1

Introduction

The mere mention of the word "slave" generally brings to mind a person of African descent. Yet Native Americans in the Pacific Northwest were enslaved long before whites came to the New World. Slavery among the indigenous peoples of the Pacific Northwest appears to have originated spontaneously in the area over many years, probably centuries ago, without input or influence from outside the area. The practice accelerated, however, with the arrival of Euro-Americans involved in the coastal fur trade.

These native societies which practiced slavery were located in the American-Canadian Pacific Northwest, a region encompassing roughly Washington, Oregon, Idaho, western Montana and the northwestern tip of California, as well as the southern and western portions of British Columbia. Within this region were two cultural areas: (1) The Northwest (Pacific) Coast Cultural Area, a littoral trough extending southerly from Yakutat Bay near the Alaska-British Columbia border to Trinidad Bay in northern California, and bounded on its east by the coastal ranges of British Columbia and the Cascade Mountains; and (2) the Plateau Cultural Area lying between the coastal ranges and Cascades and the Rocky Mountains, extending southerly from the lower half of British-Columbia to southern Oregon.

When Euro-Americans reached the Pacific Northwest in the latter half of the 18th century they found slavery already existing among its coastal natives. An intriguing question arises: "How long before this white contact did slavery exist in the region?" The practice appears to have originated spontaneously among matrilineal clans of the northern extremity of the area under study—just one of four such slave clusters.

Because of diverse elements in the cultural development within the Northwest Coast area, anthropologists have subdivided it into sub-areas or zones. There are several variations of the divisions, but they are similar. We use herein anthropologist Philip Drucker's titles and delineation of the four zones (see map page 20).[1] Of the Northern zone were Tlingits, Haidas, Tsimshians and Haislas (the latter formerly Wakashan-speaking Northern Kwakiutls) who conducted summertime raids in the Wakashan zone to the south, enslaving Kwakiutl and Nootkan captives. Wakashan zonal peoples occupied a stretch of the British Columbia mainland where lived Kwakiutls (now known officially as Kwakwaka'wakw), Salish-speaking Bella Coolas (now known officially as Nuxalk), Nootkas (Nu-chah-multh-aht) of Vancouver Island and Makahs of the northwestern tip of Washington. This second cultural zone was composed of all groups of the Wakashan linguistic family and one group of the Coast Salish.

Anthropologist Joseph G. Jorgensen states that by historic times Tlingits raided as far south as Puget Sound.[2] During those times Northern peoples preferred captives of the Wakashan zonal upper class, whose heads had been deformed by binding when infants. Originating the widely disseminated Winter ceremonial, the Wakashans were the northernmost peoples to practice head deformation.

---

[1]Philip Drucker, "Sources of Northwest Coast Culture," *New Interpretations of Aboriginal American Culture History,* 66. Recently anthropologists have detached each end of the Northwest Coast cultural area excluding the Eyaks living north of the Tlingits, and in the south, the Tolowas. Wayne Suttles, "Introduction." In Wayne Suttles, ed., *Handbook of North American Indians Northwest Coast* 7, pp. 5, 9. Among the Eyaks slavery varied as compared with that of other Northern Indians. Joan B. Townsend writes of rather complex social structures among Aleuts of the Alaskan Pacific Rim into which the Eyaks fitted, with societies which had developed mixed forms of slavery such as that "within a familial rather than a full class system." Ranking varied in degrees with incipient stratification, where, as among the other four groups in the north, it was a very pronounced system. See Townsend, "Pre-contact Political Organization and Slavery in Aleut Societies." Because of this variation in the practice of slavery from that of the remainder of peoples on the Northern zone we have excluded them from this writing. However, since the practice of debt slavery among Tolowas was like that of others in northwestern California, we include them herein.

[2]Joseph G. Jorgensen, *Western Indians,* 246.

A flattened head such as this woman's was a mark of beauty in certain tribes. Such deformation was practiced along the lower Columbia River, the coast of Washington State and less frequently in the Sound and Straits. These tribes dealt in human bondage, enslaving round-headed natives. Likewise, they were victims of enslavement to British Columbia coastal peoples who did not flatten heads. The flattening was the result of pressure applied to an infant's forehead and occiput. *Courtesy, Smithsonian Institution. Neg. #3084.*

Archaeologists claim that Wakashan head deformation was practiced 2500 years B.P.[3] If it were practiced among affluent peoples of British Columbia, it would have been about 1500 years after Wakashan speakers migrated to the coast. In that pre-cranial modification period Wakashans progressed from a full-time subsistence society to one of accumulative excess which created the right setting for a sharp differentiation of property rights dividing chiefs and wealthy persons from commoners. The question arises: "Since Northern peoples did not deform their infants' heads, how then does it follow that if they raided for slaves among head-deforming peoples, no such skeletal remains have been found in this Northern zone?" Slaves there were given no funerary attention, but cast into sea or forest for predatory animals to feed upon. In other instances thralls were buried deeply in house post holes where their remains escape discovery.

With minor exceptions head deformation was limited to peoples of two zones extending southerly from among Wakashan speakers to Chinookan speakers along the lower Columbia River. The practice was limited among Oregon coastal peoples, and rarely found among those of the Plateau. At contact the greatest center of the practice was among Chinooks at the mouth of the Columbia River. Drucker designates natives of the Coast Salish-Chinook zone as those living east and south of Wakashan speakers along various straits between Canada and the United States and of Puget Sound, and extending along the Washington coast and three quarters of the way down the Oregon coast.

When the supply of slaves reaching the Northern zone was insufficient, the need for them increased. Wakashans then undoubtedly sought peoples to enslave and trade to the Northerners. This trade in slaves reached ever further south, reaching Chinooks at the mouth of the Columbia River and

[3]Jerome S. Cybulski, "Human Biology." In Wayne Suttles, ed., *Handbook of North American Indians Northwest Coast*, 55-56.

making them important slave suppliers in this second Pacific Northwestern slave cluster. Geography was important in the Chinooks' rise as slaveholder-traders, since they held a strategic intermediary position among Pacific Northwestern Coastal peoples thus giving them control of the flow of slaves and other trade items between the two cultural areas.

Likewise, at the beginning of historic times head-deformed Chinook chiefs and wealthy persons were distinctly separated from their commoners and slaves, the latters' rounded heads signifying their lowly position. The Chinooks were also the southernmost practitioners of the highly competitive potlatch ceremonial. This ceremonial required wealth such as slave chattel which, in masters' minds, was scarcely distinguishable from other items of wealth obtained from land and sea.

The primary means of procuring slaves from Chinooks was not in raiding, but in trading. The Chinooks acquired slaves from those who raided for captives. Originally Northern zonal peoples acquired slaves from Wakashan speakers and eventually from peoples as far south as Puget Sound, the furthest extent of their raidings. In time, these Wakashans purchased captives from further south who had been traded from one native group to another and sold by Chinooks to Northern peoples. Whether this trading was due entirely to increasing economic wealth or to a lessening of plunderings of these Northern peoples is speculative. Yet, according to Ruth Kirk, the human commodities acquired through trade or other means served as a basic part of the economic foundation on which Northwest Coast culture was built.

A third slave cluster was in the southernmost sub-area of Coastal culture, that which Drucker terms the Northwest California zone located at the tips of southwestern Oregon and northwestern California among Athapaskan-speaking Tututnis and others including Yuroks, Hupas and Wiyots. Slavery in this zone differed from that in others in that most enslavement was for debt in which men and women alike were retained in their captors' communities and not exported to the north. Their servitude could encompass lifelong confinement, or in shorter periods when debts were repaid or worked off. Such entry into slavery contrasted with that to the north where, thanks to pride and purse of masters, slaves could experience premature death.

A semi-arid cultural area, the Plateau's place in the slave trade was established after the arrival of the horse at mid-18th century, and the coming of Euro-American fur traders just prior to the 19th century. The fourth cluster of Indian slavery lay in south-central Oregon in Klamath Indian homelands. This cluster has the distinction of having evolved in historic times. Raiding in the Plateau at the beginning of the historical period, to avenge warrior deaths, to poach, to gain territory or to acquire booty, was primarily an economic objective for most Plateau peoples. The Klamaths were an exception since it would be well over a half-century before they took on horse culture which extended their aggressive activities. Jorgensen defines economic booty "as all chattels that could be carried [off the battlefields]..."[4] At contact the Klamaths were horseless, for they acquired this new beast of burden only after the dawn of the 19th century, and it quickly and drastically altered their booty-taking to include captives from the battlefields which were enslaved. By mid-19th century their acquisition in wealth from trading slaves enabled certain tribesmen to produce separate property rights leaving commoners and slaves to perform menial tasks.

It had been the practice of other Plateau peoples to raid for captives, most of whom were not sold into slavery, but were still denied their freedom and ability to move about at will. Brought to victors' camps, they were subjected to humbling harassment, degradation and abuse. In time, however, they gained their freedom and frequently married into their captor's tribe, usually after having been adopted.

---

[4]Ruth Kirk, *Tradition and Change on the Northwest Coast,* 45; Jorgensen, *Western Indians,* 246.

Repercussions of the coming of horse culture spread from the   Plateau to coastal peoples such as Chinooks who, as noted, traded for the Plateau captives in a trading chain stretching easterly to entrepôts like The Dalles of the Columbia River, from which captives were shipped downstream as potential trade items.

Following the coming of the horse to the Plateau, Euro-American fur traders came to the Pacific Northwest. Natives in various cultural zones acquired items of manufacture from these newcomers, including clothing and decoration to cover and adorn their bodies, new food for their dietary, and metal for tools with which to lighten their work. Where formerly such imports were limited to native use, an increasing Euro-American trade enabled native entrepreneurs to acquire even more goods and thus, even more things to exchange for slaves and, in cyclical fashion, to acquire even more goods. After mid-19th century this circle was disrupted both by a declining fur trade and the coming of white settlers with different economic patterns in their dominant culture. With such revolutionary changes slave masters found themselves in a new milieu, their slaves becoming thanes rather than things. Lingering long afterwards, however, was the stigmatic legacy of slavery bearing out the native saying, "Once a slave, always a slave."

This demeaning attitude is reflected in the names given slaves in various tribes. Interpretations of the word "slave" universally carry the same connotation of inferiority. The Klamaths, for instance, equated their word, *lugsh* (from *luk-tha*), with the English "to carry a load," since slaves carried burdens among that tribe. Yuroks called slaves, the extremely poor and bastards "people without rights." The Yakima word for slave, *as-wan-nee,* was the equivalent of "insignificant."[5]

An early authority on American slavery, William Christie

---

[5]Frederick Webb, ed. *Handbook of American Indians North of Mexico* 2, p. 598; W.W. Elmendorf and A.L. Kroeber, *The Structure of Twana Culture with Comparative Notes on the Structure of Yurok Culture*, 307n.; Lucullus V. McWhorter, "The Dreamer Religion of the Yakima Indians." Ms. 1519, no. 1.

MacLeod, states that in the Northwest Coast cultural area there was more active and voluminous inter-tribal trade than among other native groups on the North American continent, with the slave traffic seemingly following longer, more regular and deep cut social channels than trade in other commodities. MacLeod's assessment is confirmed by anthropologist Leland Donald, who states that "Nowhere else in North America do we find slavery important either numerically or productively."[6] By contrast, until more recent times slavery was practiced with less frequency among natives east of the Cascade Mountains across the Columbia Plateau to the Rocky Mountains.

Summarizing the various aspects of Pacific Northwestern Indian slavery MacLeod writes:

> [It] was a practice widespread on the North American northwest coast, a region where slavery was of such greater economic importance than elsewhere in the Americas. Not satisfied merely with breeding slaves, or enslaving captives in the ordinary course of wars of blood revenge, groups all along the coast and adjacent plateau frequently made offensive war expeditions against weaker groups, primarily with the object of getting captives to sell in the intertribal slave trade... *The data available on prices in connection with the data on the percentage of the slaves to the total population,* distinctly suggests that slavery on the northwest coast among the natives was of nearly as much economic importance to them as was slavery to the plantation regions of the United states before the Civil War.[7]

When slavery is mentioned today, that of blacks in pre-Civil War times more often comes to mind than does that of enslaved Native Americans. Other than being chattel of masters and representing substantial investment of these owners, black slaves in the American South were purchased in owner to owner transactions or en masse at auction blocs. Indian-acquired slaves were sometimes obtained individually, but more often were combined by those purchasing them. Examples of this were slaves brought to Pacific Northwest-

---

[6]William Christie MacLeod, "Economic Aspects of Indigenous American Slavery," 645; Leland Donald, "Was Nuu-chah-nulth-aht (Nootka) Society Based on Slave Labor?" 116.
[7]MacLeod, "Economic Aspects of Indigenous American Slavery," 642, 649.

ern slave marts like The Dalles of the Columbia River, most of whom were adult women and some children. In similar situations black families were often broken up, becoming slaves of various buyers. Such also occurred among Indian slaves, but there were instances in which masters sought to bring marriage partners together. In many instances Indian families consisted primarily of wives and other women sold into slavery, for most often their men had been killed in raids in which these female captives were taken. Where large families were encouraged among black slaves to increase the work force, no evidence suggests that a similar policy was adopted in Indian communities.[8] In the American South black women were sexually exploited by white men as evidenced by large numbers of mulattoes who remained enslaved.[9] The absence of a color line between Pacific Northwestern owners and their slaves did not lessen the rigid relationships between the two. Offspring from such unions spent their lives in enslavement.

Punishment of Indian slaves frequently involved death whether they were miscreant or not. Punishment of black slaves often involved whipping. Such action no doubt resulted at times from owners' anger, revenge or lust, but positive incentives were primarily the masters' "powerful instrument" to control. Deaths did result from outbursts of such passion, but usually were stopped short of such extremity. On the other hand, slaves of the Kwakiutls forfeited their lives to masters as victims of a calculated policy of displaying extravagance in ceremonials, or as gifts to intimidate or upstage rival noblemen.

Such action among native masters in a highly structured competitive society was regarded as a practical means of expressing ostentation. In the American South practicality and utility were considered, for the death of each slave represented economic loss to masters. In fact, the death penalty

---

[8]Robert William Fogel and Stanley L. Engerman, *Time on the Cross: The Economics of American Negro Slavery*, 85.
[9]Ibid., 132-33.

was often commuted to whippings and exportation so as to recover "a substantial part of the value of a slave that would have been lost through his execution."[10] Plantation owners "were generally concerned about losing slaves or impairing their health through the neglect or real illness."[11] Unlike blacks in the South, no hospitals or physicians attended to the physical welfare of Indian slaves. Moreover, evidence of shamans attending to needs of an ill Indian slave appear to be lacking, for as Peter Farb points out, "To all intents and purposes [a slave],…had been a dead man from the moment he allowed himself to be captured; killing him a few years later merely represented a delay in the execution of the sentence."[12] Where black slaves were sometimes punished by a denial of food, Indian slaves were denied such sustenance more from neglect than as corporal punishment. There were ample incidents of black slaves escaping confinement, later recaptured and punished at the whipping post. There were fewer instances of Indian slaves escaping. Since many of them had come long distances, it was difficult for them to return to their original homes. In some Indian communities slaves were punished by having the soles of their feet slashed, a practice in keeping with the short-fuse violence among masters who often put slaves to death, sometimes at the hands of slave lackeys. There was a practicality in the sole-slitting, since it rendered victims unable to escape their confinement. Sometimes slaves were beaten for running away and other offenses.

It has been estimated that a quarter of black slaves were engaged in managerial, professional or both skilled and unskilled tasks.[13] From the ranks of black skilled labor arose leaders who enforced behavior in slave quarters, negotiating with masters on behalf of slaves. Indian slaves, however, composed an undifferentiated group lacking rights, privi-

---

[10]Ibid., 144-47.
[11]Ibid., 119-120.
[12]Peter Farb, *Man's Rise to Civilization as Shown By the Indians of North America*, 142.
[13]Fogel and Engerman, *Time on the Cross*, 147; ibid., 40.

leges and property ownership. They performed menial tasks, sometimes becoming involved in those requiring skill, let alone certain semi-skilled functions. Such slaves were entirely at the disposal and mercy of masters to help validate the latters' position of rank and wealth.

Indian slavery was primarily intraracial, with only a few exceptions such as foreign seamen-traders whom natives captured in fights or rescued from shipwrecks. Black slavery was also intraracial at its roots. In the initial African stage of the black slave chain other blacks captured those of their own race for enslavement in the New World.

Among whites, servitude was not strictly racial. Some whites were brought from the Old World (England, Scotland and Ireland) in servitude to landowners in colonial times. Even blacks coming to eastern America in 1619 were indentured and freed in the same way that whites worked off terms of their indenture. This soon changed, however, when white landowners wanted more new people of their own race to populate the land and legislated to limit terms of indenture which served to encourage their immigration. Such legislation specified that blacks be kept in perpetual enslavement. In 1663, Maryland enacted a law that all blacks coming into the colony would be perpetual slaves, as would be their children.[14]

Some Indian slavery, although not stemming from pigmentation, did stem from bodily configuration, especially in those cultures in which head deformation was more highly prized than heads which were round. There was also gender discrimination. Women and children were more often enslaved rather than adult males, as evidenced by the fact that in raiding Indian villages, these males were often

---

[14]Stanley M. Elkins, *Slavery*, 38-40. Eastern agriculturalists flirted with the idea of enslaving indigenous peoples. Various tribes captured Indians of other tribes and then sold them to whites to work the land. The use by whites of Indians as slaves in eastern United States virtually failed. Indians in their own environment followed basically nonhorticultural subsistence patterns. On the other hand, blacks came from an agrarian society in Africa. Enslaved Indians in eastern America escaped or died in captivity. In instances where they were forced to labor, they "preferred death to servitude." Elkins, *Slavery*, 94n.

destroyed. To have destroyed black males would have resulted in a reduced work force for heavy labor in slaveholding
communities.

Those who defended black slavery cited portions of the
Bible, claiming Ham's descendants would be punished by
servitude because of his indiscretions with his father, Noah.
There was a belief, especially in the American South, that
blacks were an inferior people. At the extremity of this bias
was the supposition that they were actually people of "darkness," somewhat reminiscent of the earlier belief that Indians, like the earth, were under a Divine curse. Much white
attitude toward slavery was based on the myth of superior
and inferior classes and persons within races. This is not to
say that such group discrimination did not exist among
Pacific Northwestern Indians, but Indian slavery appears
more often to have been based on elements of cyclical
revenge resulting from conflict, rather than from color or
appearance. Not unimportant were breaches in native proto-
col, resulting in feelings of hostility and retribution. An
example is recorded by George Gibbs, a mid-19th century
ethnologist, involving a native account of a great feast at
which a guest criticized the cooking of fish. Disgusted at
such ill-manners, the hosts sought to punish their rude guest
by proposing to enslave him so he would perpetually have to
pay for his insulting behavior.[15]

Then too, stratification in Pacific Northwestern Indian
society did much to set classes off against each other. The
anthropologist, Erna Gunther, has described this stratification as "distinguished from the rest of America by its unusual
social structure, and by the lack of definite political organization."[16] Upper classes or nobility were composed of head
men, who, in some cases, excelled in physical prowess for
having performed great feats. Important requisites for membership in the class, however, were birth, wealth and posi-

---

[15]George Gibbs, *Tribes of Western Washington and Northwestern Oregon* 1, Pt. 2, p. 188.
The origin of slavery is told in a Twana legend as recorded by Edward S. Curtis in his *The
North American Indian* 9, 161-62.

[16]Erna Gunther, "The Indian Background of Washington History," 198.

INTRODUCTION   33

tion. Below them were the freemen, the commoners, and
below them, the slaves. These came mostly from other native
groups, especially distant ones.

Class distinctions between southern black slaves and masters are not as well known as might be surmised. This is especially true of relations between masters and the "house slave"
who was often treated almost as a family member. Field
slaves on large plantations were subjected to demands of
hard-driving and hard-driven overseers standing between
them and their masters. Most Pacific Northwestern slaves
could be termed "house slaves," since they lived in close proximity with masters, but they were not as well treated as many
of their southern counterparts. The common factor in both
black and Indian slavery was the victims' status as chattel, a
largely hereditary condition.

Like Afro-American slavery, which intensified with tech-
nological developments such as the cotton gin, that of Pacific
Northwestern Indians was strongly influenced by importation of goods of the Industrial Revolution. As Leland Donald has pointed out, the demand for such goods sustained the
need to supply the coffers of native acquisitors with enslaved
merchandised captives, an important source of their bargaining wealth especially during the 18th and 19th century fur
trading era.[17] Although Indian slaves performed tasks for
their masters, as did their black counterparts, such work,
albeit technical in some instances, was primarily menial.
Unlike southern slaves working on large plantations and on
numerous smaller farmsteads, those in the Pacific Northwest
performed no agricultural work since they, like their masters,
subsisted by hunting, fishing and gathering. Thus, their
function was to serve masters for show, and suffer abuse as
ostentatious objects for possession and display much in the
manner that we display rare paintings and precious gems.

In contact times Pacific Northwestern slaves composed
roughly a quarter of native populations with some variation
in this number among native groups (see Chapter 11 herein).

---

[17]Leland Donald, "The Slave Trade on the Northwest Coast of North America," 152.

In some instances southern slave populations approximated that of non-slaves. Suicides were frequent among slaves of African origin, especially during their mid-passage to America, but apparently there is no record of Pacific Northwest Indian slave suicides which, of course, does not mean that such did not occur. Where black slaves were important in cultural cross-fertilization, contributing to American society in numerous fields including music, dance and folklore, Indian slaves similarly brought to captor peoples cultural elements, especially those of a spiritual-material nature. For example, anthropologist George Peter Murdock writes that among the Haidas in the north, the spirit performances associated with house-building potlatches "are expressly stated to have been borrowed in the main from the Bellabella through the medium of slaves captured from that tribe."[18] By the same token, in rare instances when slaves returned to their own people, they brought with them certain cultural elements of their erstwhile owners.

In native Pacific Northwestern communities, especially those of the coastal region, no rationale existed for "have nots" to challenge the "haves" since both slave and free persons were "haves" in the sense that they subsisted together, albeit unevenly, on the bounties of a beneficent nature. As in the South, despite exceptional incidents like the abortive 1831 Nat Turner revolt, Pacific Northwestern Indian slaves apparently did not revolt against masters. The overlords exerted not only physical, but social control over them in a ranking system made possible by what Charles N. Bishop suggests was the relative abundance of certain raw material resources to trade for non-local items. Although not essential to the natives' survival, these various resources and abundant materials enabled specific groups to control harvests and exchange them with the outside for non-local products, thus enhancing owners' wealth and dominant position.[19]

---

[18]George Peter Murdock, "Kinship and Social Behavior Among the Haida," 6.

[19]Charles A. Bishop, "Limiting Access to Limited Goods: The Origins of Stratification in Interior British Columbia," 150.

In 1865, two years after the Emancipation Proclamation, several southern tribes convened at Fort Smith, Arkansas, where they signed treaties providing for peace, and abolition of enslavement of persons of African and American Indian descent. A decade earlier, however, several tribes in northwestern Washington Territory signed similar treaties with its governor, Isaac Stevens, and his party.[20] It seems incongruous for the treaties to have anti-slavery clauses when at the very same time the United States permitted slavery of blacks in the South. Apparently there are no records extant explaining the rationale of this anti-slavery stance; nor is there record of the negotiators' official instructions regarding the matter. Only the following is found in records of the National Archives: "It was deemed absolutely necessary that Slavery among the Indians in this Territory should cease, because it is a direct consequence of war upon neighboring Tribes, which by Treaty is prohibited." Comments Governor Stevens' biographer, Kent D. Richards, "This [quote] is taken from the minutes of the commission that Stevens had put together to formulate the Puget Sound treaties (Gibbs, Doty—who as secretary wrote the above,—Simons, Shaw, and Goldsborough). They may have discussed the issue, but there seems to

---

[20]Tribes identified as Shoshonean-speaking "Snakes" also signed antislavery pacts. Felix S. Cohen, *Handbook of Federal Indian Law*, 181 and n. From the 1619 importation of slaves into the Virginia colony the Cherokees, Creeks, and Choctaws came into possession of runaway black slaves. Before being forced into the Indian Territory in 1830-1833, these tribes dealt in such black slaves and because of the lucrative nature of that commerce, took to buying these refugees, some of whom they took with them into what is now Oklahoma. During the initial phase of the Civil War these Indians had a vested interest in the Southern cause. In early October 1861, at the beginning of the war, part of the Osages, Seminoles, Shawnees and Quapaws signed treaties with the Confederacy as did the Cherokees on October 7, 1861. William G. McLoughlin writes that all southern tribes practiced slavery and, that they allied with the Confederacy, and "seeking desperately to maintain a social status above that of Negroes, had rapidly developed the same attitude toward them as [did]...white[s]." The United States, which had provided protection of Cherokees, Choctaws, Chicasaws and Creeks, withdrew its troops. Few tribesmen retained their loyalty to the Union, most having espoused the Confederate cause. Yet, influenced by the Emancipation Proclamation (January 1, 1863) the Cherokee Nation severed ties with the Confederacy and abolished slavery. The subsequent 13th Amendment, which prohibited slavery in the United States, included persons of African and American and mixed descent. Julie Philips, "Black Slavery Among the American Indians," 613; William G. McLoughlin, "The Choctaw Slave Burning: A Crisis in Mission Work Among the Indians," 124-26; Cohen, *Handbook of Federal Indian Law*, 181-82.

be no record of it nor mention of the slavery issue elsewhere by any of these men."[21]

When United States President James Polk recommended territorial status for Oregon, legislators, apparently unaware of or unconcerned for its Indian slaves, delayed action, hoping to open Oregon to black slavery. Following considerable controversy the territory was designated in 1848 as slave free.[22] Considered for statehood in 1857, it remained with the citizens to vote on the issue. Since their constitution made no reference to such servitude, a two-question proposi-

---

[21]"Records of the Proceedings of the Commission to Hold Treaties with Indian Tribes in Washington Territory and the Blackfoot Country, December 26, 1854," *Records of the Washington Superintendency of Indian Affairs, 1853-1874, No. 5, Roll 26;* Kent D. Richards, to authors, March 3, 1993. Professor Richards further comments:

"It is my impression that a large number, perhaps majority, of settlers were sympathetic to slavery or at least to the Southern states and the Constitutional guarantee of slavery in those states. On the other hand, no one either in the territory or at the national level believed that a northern territory like Washington would become a slave state. Of course, Douglas' Kansas-Nebraska Act of 1854 opened the possibility, at least in theory, that any territory could vote slavery up or down, but it does not seem to have arisen as an issue in Washington. My comment [in previous communication] that 'This seems to be a clever way of avoiding the direct question of slavery in the territories' is a reference to the Kansas-Nebraska Act which Stevens was obviously aware of since he was in Washington, D.C., at about the time it passed and the weeks thereafter, and in fact probably was in direct contact with Douglas during that period.

"It is only supposition on my part, but it is likely that Stevens or any other politician in the territory did not want to take a direct stand on slavery in the territories. Thus, they could say that slavery among the tribes was prohibited because they acquired them through war which was prohibited. It is a way of ending slavery, which I think Stevens and his commission saw as an evil, but avoiding the political hot potato of the Kansas-Nebraska Act and in fact avoiding the whole political question of the Constitutionality of slavery. The people in the territories had other more pressing issues they had to deal with, and it was only when the Civil War actually started, or perhaps during the 1860 election, that they were forced to take a stand as pro-North or pro-South."

In a letter transmitting the Medicine Creek Treaty to the Commissioner of Indian Affairs Isaac Stevens made only the following comments: "Article 8th stipulates that the Indian parties to the Treaty shall keep peace with the neighboring Tribes, and article 11 that they shall free all slaves now held by them and not purchase or acquire others hereafter. Article 11 is a direct consequence of the stipulation referred to in article 8, slavery being the result of war and the most prolific cause of difficulty and vice with the Indians on the Sound." Isaac Stevens to Commissioner of Indian Affairs George Manypenny, December 30, 1854, *Records of the Bureau of Indian Affairs, Documents Relating to the Negotiation of Ratified and Unratified Treaties with Various Tribes of Indians, 1801-69, Microcopy T-494, Roll 5.*

[22]There were about thirty blacks in the Oregon Territory at this time. Lieut. Neil M. Howison, *Report,* February 1, 1848 (30 Cong., 1 sess., *House Misc. Docs. no. 29*), Serial 523, 1848, p. 15.

tion was submitted to them for ratification. As a result of the voting slavery was rejected 7727 to 2645, and free blacks were to be excluded, 8640 to 1081.[23] Provisions for exclusion would not be removed until November 2, 1926.

Most Oregonians drew between themselves and their Indian neighbors a line over which they stepped to exploit rather than to regulate. Their low-key response to black slavery may have been linked to their similar reaction to Indians, whom they considered as being "outside the Pale" with little political-economic clout. This, in essence, was both cause and effect of Indian disenfranchisement and lack of civil rights. For years these transplanted Oregonians left concern for Indians to other whites of reforming bent. These immigrants were little concerned with the welfare of Indians, let alone, for their slaves. In the May 1839 issue of *The Oregonian, And Indian's Advocate,* is an histrionic editorial describing the dichotomy of the "Noble Redman" on the one hand and his "Ignoble Slave" on the other.[24]

The coming of settlers to the Pacific Northwest, especially to Oregon, on the heels of traders coincided with the declining slavery in the region. Unlike the freeing of black slaves in the South, slavery's decline among Indians in the Pacific Northwest came less from concern for the slaves' welfare by sympathetic whites, and even less from manumission; instead, it came from loss of status by slaveowners due to a changing socio-economic system, brought on to a great extent as a product of acculturation. The ghost of Indian slavery, however, remained to haunt descendants of slaves even to the present-day stigmatizing its victims.

Information available today concerning Pacific Northwestern Indian slavery is based in Euro-American expansion which took its mercantilist, religious, adventurous peoples to one corner of the globe hidden away on western shores of

---

[23]Dorothy O. Johansen and Charles M. Gates, *Empire of the Columbia,* 262.

[24]"Editorial," subtitled "The Boston Quarterly Review and Our Indian Policy," appears in *The Oregonian and Indian's Advocate* 1, no. 8 (May, 1839), 251. It was excerpted from the April (1839) issue of the *Boston Quarterly Review.*

upper western North America. It is from this exploratory expansion that slavery in this region came under scrutiny. The cast of characters in the general expansion ranged from lordly popes, such as one of the 16th century who arbitrated international law for all western civilization, pontificating that North American Indians as seen by Columbus were not Christian and their properties thus subject to confiscation, to the humble friars and deckhands playing their own roles in the discoveries.

Indian slavery in the Pacific Northwest , especially that of post-contact times, is more clearly understood today than in the 18th and 19th centuries. Early white men to the region had more on their minds than understanding and explaining native cultural practices including slavery. However, anthropologists, on the basis of what records are extant, give some inkling of the characteristics of Indian slavery. Ironically, shortly after these non-Indians appeared on the scene, Indian slavery went into decline, leaving but a short period during which first-hand observations could be made. It may also be that during this brief period moralisms against such slavery would have been more critical had such practices not continued in British and American societies, for not until 1832 was slavery abolished in Britain, and not until the post-Civil War period in the United States.

The principal geographic area in which groups observed Indian slavery was the lower Columbia River where traders, seamen, missionaries, and settlers gathered to a greater extent than elsewhere in the region. Their accounts provide what information we have on the region's Indian slavery. Indian eye-witness accounts of slavery are few. What information we might obtain about the much longer prehistoric slave period will have to await the archaeologists' spade.

2
The Chinook Slave Cluster

Includes data on other societies besides Chinook

Although Pacific Northwestern Indian slavery originated among northernmost tribes of the area, it was most intensely practiced in historic times among Chinookan peoples at the mouth of the Columbia River. This was primarily due to the proficiency of the Indians in that region with trade-barter. Moreover, their strategic geographic position allowed them to control traffic between coast and hinterland.

The Chinookan speakers occupied both shores of the Columbia River for 185 miles from The Dalles downstream to the Pacific Ocean. The turbulent Dalles anchoring the eastern end of this slave complex is discussed in an ensuing chapter. Like The Dalles, the Columbia-Pacific confluence in lands of the Chinooks was a breaking point in the exchange of various products. The bounties of land, sea and river could have adequately provided subsistence for these natives; yet, their drive to acquire additional goods created a socio-economic environment conducive to commerce. The coming of Euro-American traders to their shores in the late 18th and early 19th centuries enabled them to further ply skills long honed before the coming of these white strangers. As middlemen between natives of vast regions to their north, south and east the Chinooks cannily bartered and bantered, taking ample profits in the exchange. Many goods, human or otherwise from points as distant as California and Alaska, reached their destinations only after the Chinooks received heavy duties for their passage. Highly-prized items, especially Nootkan dentalia (hiqua) or shell money, were traded southerly and westerly in exchange for slaves and other products brought by natives from every direction.[1]

---

[1]Philip Drucker, *Indians of the Northwest Coast*, 12, 13.

The extent to which Chinooks and other Pacific Coastal peoples accumulated goods and other properties depended not only on their trading skills, but on the productivity of their environment. Unlike natives of prairie and plateau, who measured wealth in such items as skins and horses, the Chinooks in their deeply wooded country and broken shorelines measured theirs in things like canoes and slaves. Whether living in one of the Chinooks' populous winter villages or more likely in transit, slaves benefitted from Chinook opulence, but only in a secondhand way.

Complex rules of inheritance and status by which Chinook slaves were held were established for their masters.[2] Chattel were a ready means of exchange, for they were traded, especially before white contact, for dentalia, and after contact, for guns and other white men's goods. Slaves also served their masters as indemnifaction for debt[3] and as wedding presents,[4] called the "bride price." In one type of bride price transaction the family of the prospective groom sent a messenger to the family of the girl they chose on behalf of their son. The messenger took a gift along, and if it was a slave, the messenger led the slave by the hand. Presents bestowed were commensurate with the wealth of the girl's family. Were such overtures accepted, the usual practice was for the groom's parents to send gifts to those of the bride.[5] The wealthier the family involved, the greater the proffered gifts not only in slaves, but in beads, copper bracelets, dentalia and other items.[6] An example of this type of gift transaction occurred north of the Columbia River at the Hudson's Bay Company's Fort Nisqually on the southern reaches of Puget Sound. At that place on February 18, 1838, the family of a Coast Salish Skykomish male presented that of a

---

[2]James Arneson, "Property Concepts of 19th Century Oregon Indians," 422.

[3]Robert H. Ruby and John A. Brown, The Chinook Indians: Traders of the Lower Columbia River, 9, 10.

[4]Ibid., 29.

[5]Curtis, The North American Indian 8, p. 90.

[6]Gabriel Franchère, Narrative of a Voyage to the Northwest Coast of America in the Years 1811, 1812, 1813, and 1814 or the First American Settlement on the Pacific, 254.

Chehalis girl eight guns, ten mountain goat skins and a slave. In return, the girl's people presented the groom's family a similar amount.[7] Up the Columbia River to the east the three slaves which an Upper Chinookan Wishram family brought to a girl's parents were a greater number than those held by the average family of that native group.[8] Chinook Chief She-lathwell received a record bride price at his daughter's betrothal to Chinook Chief Telemmecks—twenty slaves, twenty sea otter skins, a canoe and twenty leather cuirasses called *clamons*. It was also a practice for owners to buy mates for their slaves when the latter reached a marriageable age, such transactions increasing the owners' "stable" of slaves.[9]

It has been claimed that aversion to physical work among native male aristocracy contributed to its espousal of slavery as a substitute for their own labor. The accumulation of wealth by this aristocracy by whatever means was both cause and effect of its acquisition of slaves. The potlatch ceremonials stemmed from the accumulation of excess wealth which Chinookan and other coastal societies acquired, and these ceremonies apparently had more meaning than survival itself. Discussed more fully below, it may be pointed out here that slaves were an important commodity among items given at these ostentatious displays of wealth. To those unfamiliar with potlatches they appear to be generous exercises, but like Potemkin villages, were false fronts of pride. The Chinooks' practice of potlatching, adopted at contact times, was held with less ceremony, meaning and meanness than those held among the Northern Indians.[10] Among the Chinooks'

---

[7]Clarence B. Bagley, ed., "Journal of Occurrences at Nisqually House, 1833-1835," p. 160.

[8]Leslie Spier and Edward Sapir, *Wishram Ethnography Linguistic Relationship and Territory*, 223.

[9]T.C. Elliott, "The Journal of the Ship Ruby," 277; Verne F. Ray, *Lower Chinook Ethnographic Notes*, 53.

[10]The potlatch ceremonial diffused south to the Quinault around 1800 and Comcomly may have brought it to Chinooks, the southernmost practitioners of the ceremonials. The practice "had fallen into disuse" in western Washington and Oregon at 1850 according to anthropologists Douglas Cole and David Darling. This was before the practice of slavery started a downhill slide. "History of the Early Period," in Wayne Suttles, ed., *Handbook of North American Indians Northwest Coast*, 7, 133.

neighbors to their north, the Quileutes, is found an explanation of the potlatch in a legend involving a slave: a slave of
Golden Eagle, Bluejay watched daily as the Whale tribe pursued a strange bird which, in turn, invited other birds to what
became their first potlatch.[11]

In other native legendry are found situations involving
slaves. In one, a slave girl of the Clatsops, the Chinooks' near
neighbors to their south across the Columbia River, went
huckleberrying with her mistresses. When they laughed and
imitated thunder in a lightning storm, Thunderbird avenged
their insulting response by killing the entire berry picking
camp except one youth.[12] Legendry of the Tillamooks, who
lived south of the Clatsops on the Pacific Coast, tells of
Crane who went shopping for good slaves only to discover
that his purchases turned out to be of inferior quality.[13] Such
accounts reveal the importance of animals to natives, and the
human qualities given them by storytellers. Like human
slaves, also acquired through warfare, purchase, or trickery,
the actions of animal slaves stemmed from real-life situations. In such legendry are also found responses of retribution and disillusion as well as warnings and lessons to be
learned.

Following the Pacific Northwestern coastal pattern of
social stratification, the Chinooks were composed of differing groups of greater or lesser status. The numbers of their
upper class of chiefs, shamans, warriors and business persons, especially prosperous traders, were small compared
with those of other Chinookan freemen, the commoners.[14]
Chinook upper class persons were important in both commerce and combat, but in the latter, less so with time. The
rapid increase in commerce from contact time caused a

---

[11]Manuel J. Andrade, *Quileute Texts*, 171.

[12]Ibid., 231. Creatures dangerous to man were feared for their supernatural powers.
Making fun of them was thus fraught with dangers. Like the Clatsops, who were avenged
by Thunderbird, elderly slaves among Haidas of the Northern Indians were said to have
been lured away by the Bear People because they made fun of bears. Cottie Burland, *North
American Indian Mythology*, 34.

[13]Elizabeth Derr Jacobs, *Nehalem Tillamook Tales*, 64.

[14]Ray, *Lower Chinook Ethnographic Notes*, 48.

greater distinction of the wealthy from commoners and slaves. In Coast Salish communities to the north class structure was weaker according to anthropologist Wayne Suttles, who suggests that "except for the former slaves, social class was more a myth than a reality."[15]

It should be noted that in the remarks which follow concerning the rigid distinction between Chinook noble and servile classes there were exceptions as in all native slaveholding communities. Chinook upper class persons were said to have loathed associating with those of lesser class, forbidding their children to play together.[16] Masters were also said to have communicated with slaves through intermediaries and reproved these slaves for noticing strangers.[17] They were also said to have encouraged their slaves to thievery, maintaining that their own regal persons were above such practices.[18] Dealt with impersonally and offhandedly by the upper class, obsequious thralls associated more often with masters than with persons of their own class.[19] Consequently, unions between masters and slaves did occur, producing "half-slave" offspring who were usually kept in slavery, reminiscent of the mulatto births in the ante bellum South. Only offspring of free Indians were free persons.

Upper class "hands off" policy toward slaves was followed throughout the Coast. In such manner the Chinooks, disassociating themselves physically from slaves, were said to have touched neither live nor dead slave bodies. In practice such

---

[15]Wayne F. Suttles, *Coast Salish Essays,* 5.

[16]On the other hand, some tribal chiefs used young male slaves as companions for the male youngsters.

[17]Elsie Frances Dennis, "Indian Slavery in Pacific Northwest," 288.

[18]Chinook and Clatsop slave owners encouraged their slaves to acts of thievery. These owners, however, remained aloof from carrying out such practices. Jesse E. Douglas, "Matthews' Adventures on the Columbia, A Pacific Coast Fur Company Document," 120.

[19]Anthropologist Philip Drucker, writing of Northwest Coast culture area native society, states that in the natives' view it "consisted of the freemen of a particular group." He writes further that slaves, "like the natives' dogs, or better still, like canoes and sea otter skins and blankets, were elements of the social configuration but had no active part to play in group life. Their participation was purely passive, like that of a stage-prop carried on and off the boards by the real actors. Their principal significance was to serve as foils for the high and mighty, impressing the inequality of status on native consciousness." "Rank, Wealth, and Kinship in Northwest Coast Society," 56.

was not always the case since there was divergence between principle and practice. The Canadian artist, Paul Kane, sketching in the Pacific Northwest near mid-19th century, while on Vancouver Island beach, came upon the dead body of a woman he had seen but a few days earlier walking about "in perfect health." On inquiring of the slave's mistress about her unconcern for this victim now carrion for birds of prey, the woman made light of the death, stating that the slave had no right to a burial. When Kane responded that the victim was as good a person as she, this chieftain's daughter, angered by the insult to her social status, took down her lodge and moved on.[20]

With the coming of white merchants the Chinook economy increasingly shifted from an Indian to Indian relationship to that of Indian to white. Unfamiliar initially with the natives' class structure, but unhampered by it, white merchants learned to deal with Chinook nobility and commoners alike. These commoners, having withstood the rigors of trading with whites so as not to be disadvantaged by them, and having acquired the means and managerial skills by which to obtain and display wealth with which to purchase slaves, were able to rise to the top of Chinook society. This enabled them, during famines, to appropriate food from their erstwhile commoner class. One means by which Kwakiutl nobility to the north sustained themselves and their families, especially in famine times, was by selling young girls into slavery. In extreme cases Coast Salish speakers were also known to have sold their children into slavery in exchange for food.

Chinook slaves were said to have gained their freedom through exercising shamanist powers, the attainment of which on spirit quests was apparently not denied these novitiates. As a rule married slaves were permitted to purchase their freedom, although early 19th century accounts of Chi-

---

[20]Paul Kane, "Incidents of Travel on the North-West Coast, Vancouver's Island, Oregon, &c. &c.," 276.

nookan couples attaining theirs can be overstressed.[21] One
Chinook slave couple gained freedom and group adoption in
an unusual way when a twenty-year-old female, purchased
and brought to a village at the mouth of the Columbia River,
was separated from her husband. In desperation she twice
tried to commit suicide by drowning, but was restrained from
doing so by being tied to a tree. A chief's wife recognized
words of the unfortunate woman, for the wife had learned
them from a male slave brought to the village two years earlier. Speaking to the woman in that language, the chief's wife
learned that the woman and a male slave of her own chieftain
husband had been married and then separated when
enslaved. Consequently, the two were permitted to purchase
their freedom and be adopted into the tribe.[22]

Since many, if not most, slaves came from varying distances from a patchwork of tribes, they were forced to learn
the languages of their owners. Linguistic and geographic
separation from their various homelands were twin barriers
making it difficult for them to escape back to those places.
Slaves in the vicinity of their kinsman also faced trouble, for
their careless or unintentioned remarks that a freeman's relative was a slave might cause the freeman to seek revenge on
these slaves eventuating in their deaths.

Bondsmen from differing cultural groups bore differing
physical characteristics. Silas Smith, who lived among Chinooks and Clatsops and whose father, Solomon, came to the
West in the early 1830s with the American trader, Nathaniel
Wyeth, noted such differences among their slaves:

> These tribes held as slave members from the various tribes inhabit-
> ing the region north of the Straits of Juan de Fuca to nearly the
> Alaskan border, and also from those of Southern Oregon and
> Northern California, including the Rogue River Indians, Shastas,
> Klamaths, Modocs, and occasionally some from the Snakes.
> Almost every leading family held from one to half a dozen slaves,

---

[21]Andrew P. Vayda, "A Re-examination of Northwest Coast Economic Systems," 621;
Ray, *Lower Chinook Ethnographic Notes*, 53.
[22]Dennis, "Indian Slavery in Pacific Northwest," 78.

and some of the chiefs having even many more. Among these slaves, gathered in this promiscuous way from these various sources, it would be nothing strange to find a good many who would be bandy-legged and otherwise ill-shaped; and the earlier writers observing these, and not making the proper inquiries as to where they originally belonged, it was noted down by them that the Chinooks and other Indians on the lower Columbia were bow-legged, which statement is ever afterward reiterated by writers who are not themselves informed on the facts by personal observation. It is not denied here that occasionally some of these people were crooked-limbed, but the rule was the other way—that they usually had well-formed extremities.[23]

The Indians of the Northern Zone of the northwest coast cultural area (hereafter called the Northern Indians) were so intrigued with head deformation that they wanted the so-called flat-headed slaves; conversely, peoples practicing deformation preferred round-headed slaves.[24] Not only primitive, but so-called civilized peoples the world over altered their physical size and shape to conform to whatever style and custom suited the fancy of the simple and sophisticated alike. Head deformation was thus joined by other body alterations in other peoples. Northern Indians such as the Tlingits of Norfolk Sound and Haidas of the Queen Charlotte Islands had their own body deformation—wood or stone labrets pressed by a bar across gums to make horn-like protrusions appear from upper lip perforations. The privilege of wearing such ornamentation was reserved for free women among these people.[25] Tlingit women also wore shell and bone ornaments in earlobes and nasal septums, which custom was reserved for free persons of that gender.

Head deformation involved the upward shaping of foreheads from noses to crowns making eyes appear exoph-

---

[23]Silas B. Smith, "Primitive Customs and Religious Beliefs of the Indians of the Pacific Coast," 257-58.

[24]MacLeod, "Economic Aspects of Indigenous American Slavery," 645.

[25]Richard J. Cleveland, *A Narrative of Voyages and Commercial Enterprises*, 19. Other types of body mutilation in other ethnic groups involved enlarging lower lips to hold discs, perforating ears to hold drumshaped objects, elongating earlobes with weighty pieces, pinching feet to permit persons to wear baby-sized shoes, squeezing waists to fit cinched-in hourglass corsets.

thalmic. The practice in the Pacific Northwest was more persistent and extensive among Chinooks than among other peoples practicing head deformation. Only free persons were allowed to deform heads of their offspring.

Alexander Ross, a Nor'wester of the North West Company, noted one or two instances in which half-slave children of favorite female slaves and fathered by slaveowners were permitted to have deformed heads.[26] The Astorian-Nor'wester, Ross Cox, observed that sometimes slaves adopted by families were permitted to marry into native groups, and their children by undergoing the deformation process "melt down into the great mass of the community."[27]

As the practice distanced itself to the north from the Chinooks only noble families submitted their infants to the process which for them as for the Chinooks served to distinguish them from round-headed slaves. The deformity thus subjected those with malformed heads to enslavement by British Columbia coastal peoples who preferred them to those whose heads were round. Enslaved northern natives did not make good slaves because of their warlike nature. Conversely, docile and industrious ones from the Oregon country to the south were considered better slave material. Head deformed peoples did not enslave those whose heads were similarly altered. Thus, their nobility would be assured they would not be mistaken for slaves in both the now and the hereafter. Cox observed that "all their slaves have round heads; and accordingly every child of a bondsman, who is not adopted by the tribe, inherits not only his father's degradation, but his parental rotundity of cranium."[28]

Deformation of infants' heads began at birth and continued from three months to a year and sometimes longer according to whites who observed the practice.[29] Infants

---

[26]Alexander Ross, *Adventures of the First Settlers on the Oregon or Columbia River*, 99-100.

[27]Ross Cox, *Adventures on the Columbia River* 1, p. 306.

[28]William Graham Sumner, *Folkways*, 270; Cox, *Adventures on the Columbia River* 1, p. 303.

[29]Ruby and Brown, *The Chinook Indians*, 47-49.

were strapped to cradles, the simplest being pieces of boards or planks around which subjects were laid supine with heads slightly raised by pieces of wood buffered by moss or bandages. Wood or leather straps, laid across the infants' foreheads, were anchored down to the planks with strings which were increasingly tightened as the head-molding process continued. Infants were confined to their cocoon-like prisons until the process was complete.[30]

Unlike Chinooks, who perfected the process before white contact, Siuslaw Indians to the south apparently began it shortly before mid-19th century.[31] Unskilled in the practice Siuslaw mothers killed so many infants that their men put a stop to it. It has been speculated that Siuslaws adopted the practice following a disastrous raid on them by Columbia River Indians who did not raid head-deformed tribesmen for slaves. In response, the Siuslaws killed some of the raiding party. To replace their stock of women captured and enslaved in such raids, the Siuslaws went among natives of southwestern Oregon's Umpqua River seeking wives since in the Siuslaws' words these natives were "most like the Siuslaws."[32]

Outward from the centric Chinook country, Indian agents would find it hard to stop head deformation, especially among peoples whose declension from imported diseases was less severe than that among Chinookan peoples. To the north among Coast Salish Skokomish and Chehalis peoples an agency physician, D.N. Egbert, Jr., as late as August 31, 1870, would report undertaking an aggressive campaign to stop the head alteration process during an eleven-month period sparing eight infants from the practice.[33]

Clallams along the Strait of Juan de Fuca were said to have told inquirers that their deity, Nukimatt, had ordered heads

---

[30]Hubert Howe Bancroft, *The Native Races of the Pacific States of North America* 1: *Wild Tribes*, 226. An early settler stated that many times he had seen infants carried on their mothers' backs while having their heads flattened. T.M. Ramsdell, "Indians of Oregon." Ms. 852.

[31]Harold Mackey, "Suislaw Head Flattening," 173.

[32]Ibid.

[33]*Records of the Washington Superintendency of Indian Affairs, 1853-1874, No. 5, Roll 13.*

altered to make the people more handsome. Such belief seemed incredible to white persons who found round heads far more handsome.[34] The practice was initially forbidden half-blood children of white men whose activities with native women had obviously gone far beyond mere inquiry.[35] When infants of free Chinook women and white fathers in fur company employ, and those of other white men in the region, became subjects for head-altering, domestic troubles ensued when the fathers insisted that their wives not deform their childrens' heads. Marital complications also arose when free Indian fathers objected to deforming heads of infants born to slave wives.[36]

The process was prevalent not only among lower Columbia peoples at contact, but among those at its northernmost locus among Wakashan-speaking Bella Bellas and Coast Salish Bella Coolas. It was also practiced by most peoples in the Wakashan zone among whom the process varied from that of the Chinooks. It also occurred among peoples of the Coast Salish-Chinookan zone, such as the Suislaws along the Oregon coast below the Clatsops and Tillamooks of that region who also flattened heads.[37]

From the Chinooks the practice extended up the Columbia among peoples as Cathlamet, Clatskanie and Cowlitz Indians; southerly among Tualatin peoples of the Willamette River valley; and easterly among natives to The Dalles. Shortly upstream from there it was occasionally practiced among Cayuses and Wallawallas. Among those noting its presence among the latter in the early 1840s were members of the United States Naval Expedition under command

[34]Gibbs, *Tribes of Western Washington and Northwestern Oregon* 1, Pt. 2, p. 211.

[35]Ibid. Some native mothers killed their offspring of white fathers who would not permit the deforming practice, considering death a lesser evil than an unflattened head. Frederick Merk, ed., *Fur Trade and Empire George Simpson's Journal*, 101.

[36]In a fictional account, *Slave Wives of Nehalem*, 79-80, Claire Warner Churchill narrates complications among Tillamooks when enslaved aristocratic women unsuccessfully sought to flatten heads.

[37]There were various methods of deforming infants' heads. See Jerome S. Cybulski, "Human Biology." In Wayne Suttles, ed., *Handbook of North American Indians Northwest Coast* 7, pp. 52-53.

of Lieut. Charles Wilkes.[38] The practice was virtually nonexistent on Oregon's Umpqua River far to the south.

Although head deformation appeared pernicious to white men, far more so to them was infanticide practiced by Chinook women, especially when pregnancies resulted from liaisons between them and white mariners. In what was a common complaint a Clatsop woman revealed another reason for infanticide when she told a missionary that she killed her infants because she was poor and had no slaves to do her work.[39] It has been suggested that in impoverished households along the Oregon Coast, selling children into slavery in times of scarcity was the only "peaceful alternative" to infanticide.[40]

Rigors of slave life were apparent to Hudson's Bay Company Governor-in-Chief George Simpson, who observed them firsthand on a journey to the Columbia River in 1824-1825. Wrote Simpson:

> Slaves form the principal article of traffick on the whole of this Coast and constitute the greater part of their Riches; they are made to Fish, hunt, draw Wood & Water in short all the drudgery falls on them; they feed in common with the Family of their proprietors and intermarry with their own class, but lead a life of misery, indeed I conceive a Columbia Slave to be the most unfortunate Wretch in existence; the proprietors exercise the most absolute authority over them even to Life and Death and on the most triffling fault wound and maim them shockingly.[41]

It was incumbent on Chinook masters to put limits on harsh treatment of slaves, for they found them to be most important in securing their basic requirements of support. Alexander Ross, observing the Chinooks' trading proclivities ("Traffic in slaves and furs is their occupation."),[42] noted that

---

[38]Charles Wilkes, *Western America, Including California and Oregon,* 100.

[39]Daniel Lee and Joseph Frost, *Ten Years in Oregon,* 314. In a letter to the Reverend H.K.W. Perkins, February 27, 1840, Fort George clerk, James Birnie, stated that Indians around his post thought nothing of destroying their offspring, citing the example of a man who, declaring a child not his, ordered its mother to throw it into the river. This, she dutifully did, Birnie claimed, without thinking any more about it. W.P. Strickland, *History of the Missions of the Methodist Episcopal Church,* 139, 140.

[40]Suttles, *Coast Salish Essays,* 60.

[41]Merk, *Fur Trade and Empire,* 101.   [42]Ross, *Adventures of the First Settlers,* 87.

their "slaves do all the laborious work; and a Chinooke matron is constantly attended by two, three, or more slaves, who are on all occasions obsequious to her will. In trade and barter the women are as actively employed as the men, and it is as common to see the wife, followed by a train of slaves, trading at the factory, as her husband."[43] The wapatoo *(Sagittaria latifolia)* was a main staple of harvest and trade by Chinook women, as were basket and matting chief articles of their manufacture.

In some households slaves were allowed to sit at their masters' tables after the latter had eaten. In other instances food was thrown to them in the manner that it was thrown to dogs. Among Clallams of the Strait of Juan de Fuca slaves slept on the lower of two platforms in houses of masters whose families slept on upper platforms. Large slave families slept in separate huts behind masters' houses when there were too many persons to occupy the main dwelling. Slaves outside the main hut served to buffer and protect masters' houses. Slaves also slept on floors of their masters' houses. This was apparently to protect the masters, as slaves also buffered and protected them by sleeping outside the dwellings. Youngsters of the nobility were entertained by raising with poles roofs of slave huts.[44]

Slaves performed menial duties ranging from the less onerous such as paddling masters' canoes, to committing murder for them for wrongs committed against these overlords. Such wrongs ranged from spells cast on them and their families to humiliations to homicides.[45] Onerous duties also involved disposing of bodies of their dead and incapacitated fellow slaves. This involved dragging their bodies into the woods to be devoured by wild animals or by throwing them into the river. Dead slaves usually lay unburied and freemen never touched them.[46] Unlike other peoples where two or

---

[43]Ibid., 92.

[44]Erna Gunther, *Klallam Ethnography*, 184.

[45]Natives believed persons at great distance could cast spells on them. They also believed that foes or rivals could steal their personal power gained on spirit quests.

[46]Bancroft, *Wild Tribes*, 241, 248.

more slaves were killed at their masters' deaths, among Chinooks the number was usually limited to one. Breaking from tradition, the powerful one-eyed Chinook Chief Comcomly placed pistols in the hands of his two dead sons so they could protect themselves on their eternal journeys.[47] Child slaves, placed in burial canoes with noble children, suffered death so they could comfort them to the hereafter. Like their elders these children were denied entry to a heaven reserved for their masters. Some Puget Sound peoples believed that were slaves born within their communities they were eligible to enter the soul world, whereas persons enslaved from foreign peoples were denied such entry in the belief that they did not know how to make their way around in that world.[48]

Adult slaves were sometimes strangled with cords drawn about their necks and then lashed to their dead masters in face to face positions.[49] Sometimes they were left to die in this mode. Some had even been starved to death or killed before the tying. Bodies of the wealthy were wrapped in otter skins and placed in burial boxes in trees at the feet of which slaves were sometimes buried.[50] Slaves were among those attending funerals of their owners, but unlike them, did not have their hair shorn at such times to symbolize mourning, for it had already been shorn as a matter of custom. When Ross Cox reported slaves as participating in hair cutting of family mourners, he may not have known that slaves of the coast were continually and almost universally rift of their hair to mark their lowly status in life.[51]

---

[47]John Scouler, "Dr. John Scouler's Journal of a Voyage to N.W. America, Pt. 3," 277. In his "Early Followers of Captain Gray," 17, Howay cites Captain Charles Bishop who stated that the highest ranking Chinook chief was Tacum followed by Comcomly and Shelathwell. Comcomly has received the most "press" perhaps because his village was near the well-traversed entrance to the mouth of the Columbia River, and because of his friendliness and trade association with white men.

[48]"The Lost Tribes of the Chinooks and Clatsops," *Daily Astorian*, June 10, 1884, p. 3; Jay Miller, *Shamanic Odyssey, The Lushootseed Salish Journey to the Land of the Dead. Ballena Press Anthropological Papers no. 32*, p. 12.

[49]Elwood Evans, *History of the Pacific Northwest: Oregon and Washington 2*, p. 92.

[50]Curtis, *The North American Indian 9*, p. 87.

[51]Cox, *Adventures 1*, pp. 335-36. It was a fairly universal mourning practice among natives to cut their hair when deaths occurred in families. Men, who usually plucked facial

"Chinook Burial Grounds" an oil painting by John Mix Stanley. Upper class Chinook burials were conducted with much ceremony and ostentation. Favorite slaves of deceased noblemen, sacrificed to attend these masters in the other world, were often buried with them. *Courtesy, Founders Society Detroit Institute of the Arts, Detroit, Mich. Neg. #5543.*

U.P. (Julia) Averkieva quotes the Russian Veniaminov who wrote that to brand slaves Tlingits "made a red mark on the face and on the forehead of anyone destined for captivity, and they cut off the ear or some other part of the body of anyone they intended to kill."[52]

Differences between whites and Indians in the disposal of dead bodies were evident in an event occurring near the

hair, let it grow, exhibiting no ornaments for a specified time of mourning. Merk, *Fur Trade and Empire*, 100.

[52]U.P. Averkieva, in *Slavery Among the Indians of North America* (Thesis delivered, June 1935, to the U.S.S.R. Academy of Sciences, typescript copy of ms.), 109 cites the Russian missionary priest Innokentii (Ivan) Veniaminov who was in Russian America in the 1830s as reporting the branding of slaves among the Northern Indians in his "Notes on the Atkans, Aleuts and Kolosh…" 105.

North West Company post, Fort George, in Clatsop country. Clatsops were among those who had slaves carry dead slave bodies into the woods or throw them into the river. One day some Nor'westers discovered the body of a dead slave girl lying on the beach. Fearing that the Company's hogs might devour it they urged the Clatsops to bury it. Slaves were sent to perform the task which they did by tying a cord around its neck and dragging the naked corpse along the beach where they squeezed it into a hole with a paddle.[53] The Clatsops were not above equal cruelty to their live slaves, amusing themselves by dressing slave children in skins and making them dance, or by lashing them until blood ran down their legs, repeating the flagellation until satiated to resume it at some other time.[54] To the north, outside the Chinook vortex, during the winter of 1867-68 a slave received a more appropriate burial on a beach opposite Union City at the southern elbow-like bend of Hood Canal, a natural appendage of the Strait of Juan de Fuca which separates the American mainland from Vancouver Island. The burial followed Tyee Charley's shooting and killing one of his slaves, Port Townsend Kate or "Kitty," in the belief that she was about to poison him. The affair was investigated by the Indian agency as Charley feared it would be, which no doubt explains the reason for the burial.[55]

Fortunate were those slave children who were permitted the power quests of scions of the free and wealthy, for it qualified them for gaining the status of these groups unlike others who were deemed incapable of receiving things of the spirit. They were thus permitted to take post-death journeys, but, as noted, only to the boundaries of heaven. One slave in danger of journeying there prematurely was the property of Chi-

[53]Elliott Coues, ed., *New Light on the Early History of the Greater Northwest: The Manuscript Journals of Alexander Henry, Fur Trader of the Northwest Company, and of David Thompson, Official Geographer and Explorer of the Same Company, 1799-1814* II, 825-26. Hereafter cited as *Henry-Thompson Journals*.

[54]Martha Ann Minto, "Female Pioneering in Oregon." Ms. P-A 51.

[55]Statement of "Chehalis Jack," April 4, 1866, concerning the murder of "Kitty," a slave of "Tyee Charlie," *Records of the Washington Superintendency of Indian Affairs, No. 5, Roll 13*.

nook Chief Toke who lived north of the Columbia River at
Shoalwater (Willapa) Bay. The chief's daughter had requested him to supply her a slave to accompany her on her
heavenly journey. When the daughter died, the obliging
father tried to kill a slave who managed to escape. White settlers found the fleeing, half-starved woman in a forest. When
Toke sought to retrieve it, the settlers gave him a thrashing.[56]

In another incident Chinook Chief Elwahco shocked
white settlers by mistreating Dolly, one of many slaves
brought him by his wife, Jane.[57] Alluding to such events in
Lower Chinook country the Smithsonian Institution reported in an 1881 publication that until a few years previously
slaves had been killed or left to perish tied to their masters'
dead bodies.[58] White persons near the mouth of the Columbia River are credited with eliminating slavery in that area
according to an account in *The Pacific Monthly* (November-
December, 1901). A slave girl, about to be put to death,
escaped to a white family named Welch. The incident caused
such an "uproar" in the white community that a stop was put
to the "barbarous custom."[59]

Slaves served as interpreters for masters dealing with the
slaves' parent peoples.[60] Sometimes masters sold their slaves'
services as interpreters as when the Reverend Josiah Parrish
at mid-19th century did government work among Athapaskan speakers in southwestern Oregon. One whose services
he used was a Coquille slave stolen from his Athapaskan people about a decade earlier and later belonging to a Chinookan-speaking Wahkiakum Indian living a short distance
up the Columbia from the Chinooks. Parrish also took
another to interpret for him who had been purchased twen-

[56]H.A. Yarrow, *A Further Contribution to the Study of the Mortuary Customs of the North
American Indians,* 179.

[57]Ben I. Whealdon, "On Whealdon Hill (Ilwaco, Wash.) Eve of July 16, 1860." Ms. 50.
Mildred Colbert, a Chinook Indian, states that Jane was a slave wife, the daughter of a chief.
"Naming and Early Settlement of Ilwaco, Washington," 187, 191.

[58]Yarrow, *A Further Contribution to the Study of the Mortuary Customs of the North American Indians,* 179.

[59]"Historical Notes," 267.

[60]W.W. Oglesby, "The Calapoyas Indians." Ms. P-A 82.

ty-two years earlier from Athapaskan Tututni Indians, then sold to the Hudson's Bay Company and taken to Fort Vancouver (present-day Vancouver, Washington).[61]

In early times the Chinooks took slaves on raids. Sometimes their masters faced opponents in war-stance positions, but only for show to satisfy slights, grudges or complaints wherein the belligerents acted as though the battle were real. Their response in such instances was not unlike persons insisting that others apologize for some indignity. Adjustments were also made between contestants in which one made payment handing slaves over to another.[62] Noting this type of conflict between Chinooks and their Chehalis neighbors to their north, the Nor'wester, Alexander Henry, observed in 1814 that "no thirst for blood causes them to engage in war—merely a point of honor, to be satisfied by presents either in goods or slaves, or by blood; and this etiquette once settled, they are friends again."[63]

In other raids slaves and vengeful masters punished enemies by inflicting bodily pain and suffering on them, accompanied by plunder and booty-taking. In yet other raids persons were captured and returned to the victors' homelands as slaves. Of this type, M.A. Nattali in 1846 wrote:

> Feuds are frequent among them, but are not very deadly; thus totally differing from the warlike races in the vicinity of the Rocky Mountains, but, with the ferocity of the latter, if they fall upon an inferior force or village weekly defended, they slay all the men and carry off the women and children as slaves. They are mean and paltry warriors, and altogether inferior in heroic qualities to the truly equestrian savages of the buffalo plains.[64]

As the Chinooks fought mock battles rather than going on raids like certain other peoples, they depended on those others to supply them with slaves. Many of these thralls had been taken in raids only to be passed from people to people to

---

[61]Rev. Josiah L. Parrish, "Anecdotes of Intercourse with the Indians." Ms. P-A 59.
[62]Coues, *Henry-Thompson Journals* 2, p. 793.
[63]Ibid., 855.
[64]M.A. Nattali, *The Oregon Territory, Consisting of a Brief Description of the Country and Its Productions; and of the Habits and Manner of the Native Indian Tribes*, 51.

places far distant from the scene of their initial capture. Minimally involved in physical conflict to acquire slaves, the Chinooks were described by the historian, Hubert Howe Bancroft, as "always a commercial rather than a warlike people...[who were] excelled by none in their shrewdness in bargaining."[65]

Another fur trade account of native warfare involved Casino, a Columbia River chief living a short distance below Fort Vancouver. In 1814 he and his Kalapuya allies made war on the Cowlitz Indians. The latter were across the river from Casino's army and without firearms. After the chief's force fired aimlessly at them, the two sides parleyed. Casino would make no payment "nor give them any honorable reparation for the injury they had sustained"—which had precipitated the confrontation in the first place. The enemy managed to capture one of Casino's slaves for which he was paid but two blankets. Angered at this small reparation, he broke off negotiations. Alexander Henry, who recorded the incident, noted that the Cowlitz then plotted to attack Casino at night seeking revenge according to "savage custom," by planning to burn his village and destroy as many of its people as possible. Wrote Henry of this type of warfare, which was as much verbal as violent and as much bluster as battle: "spring is the season when all international disputes are adjusted, so as to allow full scope for the salmon fishery, to provide for the ensuing winter without molestation. They are not bloodthirsty; it is merely a point of honor. But when just reparation is refused, they are entitled to desperate measures; surprises and stratagems are then lawful."[66] After a confrontation between natives of the lower Willamette and the Nor'westers, a truce was effected between the two in which a chief, to help seal the transaction, offered the Nor'westers a slave as a token of good will.[67]

Other incidents involving fur men and Indians were ter-

[65]Bancroft, *Wild Tribes*, 238-39.
[66]Coues, *Henry-Thompson Journals* 2, p. 880.
[67]Alexander Ross, *The Fur Hunters of the Far West*, 76.

minated with neither side the clear victor. A case in point involved an expedition of Nor'westers and their native allies against the Watlalas of The Cascades of the Columbia River about 140 miles from its mouth.[68] Bad blood had existed between the two groups since an incident which the fur men and their allies regarded as theft, but which the Watlalas regarded as justifiable tolls for passage. (Ross termed a similar passage shortly upstream at The Dalles, a "general theatre of gambling and roguery.")[69] Responding to the plundering of a Nor'wester party at The Cascades a punitive expedition of nearly a hundred including canoe-paddling slaves headed upstream seeking vengeance. The Nor'westers expected trouble, although sometimes from fear or from haughty dignity Watlala freemen delegated slaves to return some of the goods which their masters had appropriated. The venture turned out to be what Ross termed an "inglorious expedition."[70] Successors of these Nor'westers, the men of the Hudson's Bay Company, believed they and their Astorian predecessors had lacked firmness at The Dalles-Cascades of the Columbia where turbulent natives and an equally turbulent nature conspired to make it difficult for fur men to traverse.

The Chinooks' reluctance to engage in combat made them susceptible to raids by their more bellicose neighbors such as the Quileutes to the north along the coast, and even by the Clatsops with whom they carried on petty raidings. These Clatsops were also raided by Quileutes. When pursued by five canoe-loads of Quileute warriors, a Clatsop youth warned his people of their coming, but they only laughed at him and neglected to prepare for hostilities; nevertheless in a pitched battle they managed to kill half the Quileutes who captured some of their children and threw them into the

---

[68]In his *The Fur Hunters of the Far West,* 13, Ross identified natives at The Cascades as the Cath-le-yack-e-yacks. Kenneth A. Spaulding, who edited the Ross volume, wrongly identifies them as the Echeloots. These people were the Wishrams of The Dalles area. Hodge identifies natives of The Cascades as the Cathlakacheckits. *Handbook of American Indians North of Mexico* 1, p. 216.

[69]Ross, *Adventures of the First Settlers,* 118.

[70]Ross, *The Fur Hunters of the Far West,* 15.

water hoping to retrieve them as slaves. The Clatsops avenged their attackers by killing their chief.[71]

Anthropologist Verne Ray states that one of his Chinook informants claimed that his people enslaved Quinaults north along the coast with whom in typical, but paradoxical, native fashion they also traded. Ray believes that the Chinooks took slaves from Quinaults less frequently than as narrated by his informant who boasted that they could have taken them "whenever they felt like it."[72] They felt that way more strongly in earlier times. According to a visiting ship's captain, his Chinook informants cited an example of their ancestors' aggression some time in the 1770s or 1780s. At that time a large combination of Chinookan warriors in a hundred large and small canoes were said to have journeyed "twenty days" up the Columbia to some great waterfall. Terminating their journey they destroyed a village, killing its men and returning to the lower Columbia with women and children captives whom they enslaved.[73] It was on such a raid, according to Quinault Indian agent, Charles Willoughby, that the Chinooks attacked a Columbia River village destroying half its houses and making off with a woman and child. The human booty would have been greater had the other villagers not fled for their lives into the forest.[74]

The ethnologist, George Gibbs, reported that a Hudson's Bay Company physician, William Fraser Tolmie, informed him that the course of the slave trade "has always been south to north," with one exception, namely that Cowlitz Indians

[71]Ray, *Lower Chinook Ethnographic Notes*, 62.

[72]Ibid., 52.

[73]Charles Bishop, "Commercial Journal Copy's of Letters and Accts. of Ship Ruby's voyage to N.W.T. coast of America and China, 1794, 5, 6." Typescript copy of Ms. A/A.20.5/R.82B, pp. 162-63. One can only speculate as to the destination of the Chinookan warriors. The waterfall may have been Kettle Falls of the Columbia shortly below the Canadian border; or it may have been that of the Spokane River, a Columbia tributary below Kettle Falls. The lake may have been Coeur d'Alene Lake from which flows the Spokane: or possibly it was Lake Pend Oreille from which flows the Pend Oreille River, another Columbia tributary. The destination, despite all of the above possibilities, is more likely to have been The Cascades of the Columbia; hence, the time-distance should not be taken literally.

[74]Charles Willoughby, "Indians of the Quinault Agency, Washington Territory," 269.

from the lower Columbia River forayed on Puget Sound from which they returned with captives to that river.[75] Were such the case, at least some of these human imports falling into Chinook hands would have been exported by them in trade to the north. Before and after the fur trade period the Northern Indians usually went no further south in their trade than to peoples of Puget Sound and to Makahs at Cape Flattery at the Strait of Juan de Fuca confluence with the Pacific Ocean. The Chinooks traveled as far north as the Quinaults along the coast for dried halibut, slaves, dugout canoes, whale oil and dentalia. After fur traders came with Euro-American imports, the Chinooks extended their excursions beyond the Quinaults to the Makahs, who then became the center of trade at the juncture with Northern Indian traders.[76]

After the American fur trader, Captain Robert Gray, crossed the treacherous Columbia River bar to establish trade with Chinooks at Bakers Bay on the Columbia right bank, several ships soon followed in the wake of his ship, the *Columbia Rediviva*. The Chinooks readily took to trading with crews of these vessels. Under Chief Comcomly's lead they discouraged non-Chinook traders from dealings with these crews near the mouth of the river and its environs, thus seeking to control the trade as well as that of the lower Columbia so that all goods would be provided them or at least, channeled through their hands. While the initial trade in slaves was south to north, they were, in time, traded up the Columbia, even reaching beyond the Rocky Mountains.[77]

---

[75]Gibbs, *Tribes of Western Washington and Northwestern Oregon* 1, Pt. 2, pp. 188-89.

[76]James G. Swan, *The Indians of Cape Flattery at the Entrance of the Strait of Fuca, Washington Territory*, 30-31.

[77]Because of the reputation of the Columbia River among prehistoric tribes east of the Rocky Mountains as a "highway" on which slaves were moved, it is believed to have been named by natives as the "River of Slaves," or "Slave's River"—in the Chippewa language *owah* or "river" and *waken* or "slave." Hence by combining the two it is rendered "river of slaves" by dropping the repeated syllable *wa*. Thus the original *owah waken* comes out in the manner of "Oregon." See Ruby and Brown, *The Chinook Indians*, 253-54n. With apparently less patriotism than poesy at a time of Anglo-American tensions, William Cullen Bryant in his *Thanatopsis* called the Columbia River the "Oregon" nearly three decades after its nam-

The Chinooks were poor fur gatherers, content to spend time and energy in diverse mercantilist activities using slaves to perform subsistence and household duties. From Chinook hands to those of white mariner-traders, furs passed outward to markets in China, eastern America and England in exchange for a host of things whose native counterparts were in many instances inferior to these imports. The Chinooks were not so entrenched in their lucrative trade monopoly that they were above retaliating against whites and Indians whom they believed threatened that monopoly.[78] Their efforts were directed to protecting their increasingly strategic mercantilist location. Once fur trader crews plied their coasts, goods passing through these Chinooks' hands appeared more frequently at Willamette Falls and The Dalles. At these places their fish, fish and whale oil, dentalia, olivella shells, wappatoo roots and slaves were exchanged for such items as skins, roots, grasses, and slaves coming increasingly from the southern interior. Along with native items the Chinooks traded for white men's goods which, although mostly in good demand, changed with their own changing tastes and fancies. Initial imports such as Jews' harps and intriguing gegaws gave way to more substantial articles—molasses, rice, rum, firearms, metal tools and utensils.

Shrewd Chinook traders may have been unaware of formally stated laws of economics, but they understood their workings, especially those of supply and demand which were conditioned not only by the plenty or scarcity of goods exchanged, but by their quantity and quality and desirability and by the times and locations of the exchanges. Sometimes when natives became satiated with products of Euro-Ameri-

---

ing for the District of Columbia by Captain Robert Gray. Gray is believed to be the first white man to enter the river, and his ship, the first American vessel to circumnavigate the globe. The name, "Oregon," was eventually applied not only to the river, but to the vast country of present-day Oregon and Washington, much of which lay within the Columbia River drainage area.

Slaves sold by Chinooks to tribes to the east fell into hands of Assiniboins and Chippeways who raided Flathead, Kutenai and Shoshoni Indians. See J.A. Meyers, "Oregon—River of the Slaves or River of the West."

[78]Merk, *Fur Trade and Empire*, 98.

can origin it took many imported articles to purchase even one slave. American and British traders would have soon learned that the native purchasers of their goods were not naive aboriginals, but sophisticated salesmen-customers despite their placing higher value on things purchased from these foreign traders than on things they sold them. An example of the Chinooks' discriminatory tastes was their awareness of inferior goods, even rum, purchased from John Jacob Astor's traders located across the Columbia from them at his namesake Fort Astoria (near present-day Astoria, Oregon).

In his canoe paddled by slaves, Comcomly frequently visited the fort. In 1813, during the War of 1812, the British assumed ownership of its operations renaming it "Fort George." Natives in the vicinity of the post feared that with its takeover its personnel would be captured and enslaved by its new owners,[79] apparently unaware that they were Nor'westers whom Astor brought down from Canada to manage his post because of their superiority to Americans in the fur business. Although Comcomly would have been pleased with the superiority of their goods to those of Astor, their stronger liquor proved umbrageous to him when one of his sons, drunkened by it, became the butt of slaves' ridicule. The ignominious event sent his slaves paddling him to the fort to complain to its personnel for offending his aristocratic dignity.[80]

Typical of native aristocratic extended families, Comcomly's was not above plotting nefarious acts, many of which were carried out by their liege subjects. On one occasion Comcomly placed two of his sons under the care of a neighboring shaman. Despite the latter's incantations, the two reportedly sickened and died. Another son, the vicious Casacas, ordered a slave to kill a shaman which assignment he duly carried out.[81] Among peoples of the Pacific Northwest

[79]Cox, *Adventures* 1, p. 268.
[80]Ibid., 321.
[81]Ruby and Brown, *The Chinook Indians*, 176.

the practice of killing those suspected of witchcraft or of stealing one's power provided ample employment for slaves in carrying out such lethal assignments.

The trade continued apace from the Chinook vortex despite such evil enterprises. A Hudson's Bay Company clerk, John Dunn, identified peoples south of the Chinooks only as the "original kidnappers" who sold their victims at a profit to Northerners who came down to purchase them (no doubt from middlemen).[82] In the ever changing sources and routes of trade the Chinooks also obtained slaves indirectly from the Columbia Plateau and easterly where they had been captured in wars and raidings. From such conflict, slaves from northern California were taken north to The Dalles and from there, through Chinookan hands, dispersed to Indians of Puget Sound and beyond along the Pacific Coast. Near mid-19th century Paul Kane noted that among Chinooks were slaves who had come from Shastas of southwestern Oregon and northwestern California. He did not explain which routes they traveled to their enslavement. They could have come via The Dalles, the Willamette Valley, or from lands of the Tillamooks through whose hands passed slaves from and along the Oregon coast.[83]

Slaves were a most important item traded to the Northern Indians in exchange for large seaworthy canoes by Nootkas. Chinooks also constructed canoes more easily than formerly when fire and primitive tools were used in their manufacture.

Natives had long settled their transportation problems. Needed now was a system of communication beyond local dialects, sign language and gestures in order to facilitate the Indian-white exchange of goods. Different groups speaking languages as varied as Chinookan, Coast Salish, Chimakuan and Wakashan with different price standards and trade practices necessitated a common trade language. Consequently, a

[82]John Dunn, *History of the Oregon Territory and British North-American Fur Trade*, 273.
[83]Paul Kane, *Wanderings of an Artist Among the Indians of North America*, 182.

lingua franca, the Chinook jargon, evolved with words added as necessity demanded. Theories as to its inception abound. One writer speculates that it sprang from protohistoric slave trade between Chinooks and natives of the British Columbia coast. He admits, however, that the Chinooks would not have undertaken direct long-distance trading expeditions to Nootkans of Vancouver Island, trading with them instead through middlemen along the way.[84] Chinook travel to the north was most irregular and infrequent, involving individuals or small groups.

Bearing the name "Chinook," the jargon was based on the simplified Chinook language, testifying to the importance of its namesake peoples in the trade. Among ingredients of the jargon were native words of Salish and Nootkan origin, and European words from the English and French, plus others based on onomatopoeia (e.g., "tum-tum" or heart). Despite its hodgepodge character, it was used not only along the coast, but into the interior and, in time, into the late 19th century when it was used by white settlers and government agents much as it had been previously used by fur traders, missionaries and settlers. All of them found it an awkward, but necessary means of communication. English and native languages proved more effective where precision was needed. Then the natives, some of whom were slaves and ex-slaves, were called upon to interpret.

The word "slave" appeared in the jargon as *elite* or *eliaty,* and as *elaidi, mistchimas,* or *cultis mischemus,* "nothing but a slave." The explorer, José Mariano Moziño, stated that the Nootkan *meschimes* was the word for commoners who, by their condition, were slaves. In his *Chinook...A History and Dictionary* (1935), Edward Thomas also listed, besides *elite,* the word *mistchimas* and its variants. Some early white men thought the latter word applied to slaves only. It may, in fact, have applied to Pacific Northwestern native commoners like those among the Nootkas who were forced to work for the nobility alongside slaves, differing from them only to the

---

[84]F.W. Howay, "Origin of the Chinook Jargon on the North West Coast," 41.

extent that as free persons they could leave their owners for other masters and mistresses.[85]

The influence of white men's goods in the native economy, to which the jargon contributed, helped advance highly visible native chieftain-masters such as Comcomly of the Chinooks, Casino of natives in the area of Fort Vancouver, Maquinna of the Nootkas or Sebassa of the Tsimshians.[86] Comcomly made his presence felt in white and native circles despite the demeaning words of Governor Simpson that "every Flat Head Indian who is possessed of a Slave considers himself a Chief."[87] Cox observed that possession of many slaves and wives gave chiefs more respect and greatness than it did authority.[88] Comcomly's chaffering shrewdness was well-known among whites and Indians despite his one-eyed blindness, the result of an arrow from the bow of an enemy "Shoshoni" from the interior. Comcomly avenged the act by dispatching a slave to bludgeon the attacker and inflict on him the coup de grace with a dagger.[89]

---

[85]Engstrand, "José Mariano Moziño," 19; Edward Harper Thomas, *Chinook: A History and Dictionary*, 166. The word for "slave" in the Haida language is *elaidi;* Alfred Selwyn, R.C., *Geographical Survey of Canada Report of Progress for 1878-79*, 132; Eugene E. Ruyle, "Slavery, Surplus, and Stratification on the Northwest Coast: The Ethnoenergetics of an Incipient Stratification System," 616. The Chinook jargon word is derived from the Haida language. The Methodist missionaries Daniel Lee and Joseph Frost used the Chinook jargon word, *eliaty,* for "slave" and *cultis mischemus,*for "nothing but a slave." *Ten Years in Oregon,* 321.

[86]Casino is generally identified as chief of Upper Chinookan speakers in the area of the mouth of the Willamette River. Coues, *Henry-Thompson Journals* 2, pp. 796-97. Later, after the Hudson's Bay Company located at Fort Vancouver, Casino appears to have moved north across the Columbia assuming leadership of its natives. Merk, *Fur Trade and Empire,* 123, 170. There he had a village near the Kalama River, a Columbia tributary. Franchère, *Narrative of a Voyage to the Northwest Coast of America,* 246. Charles Wilkes of the U.S. Naval Expedition, who visited the area in the early 1840s, wrote that Casino was leader of the Klickitats. *The Narrative of the United States Exploring Expedition, during the years 1838, 1839, 1840, 1841, and 1842,* IV, p. 369. Paul Kane also assigned the Klickitats as well as the Chinooks to Casino's leadership in his later years when his power was waning. *Wanderings of an Artist,* 173.

[87]Merk, *Fur Trade and Empire,* 97.

[88]Cox,*Adventures* 1, p. 321.

[89]Fred Lockley, "Chinooks and Others," *Oregon Sunday Journal,* June 23, 1929. In his letter to the Secretary of War, December 22, 1824, N.L. Sullivan stated that flatheaded Indians designated all peoples above the rapids (The Cascades and The Dalles of the Columbia) as "Shoeshoones." Douglas, "Matthews' Adventures on the Columbia," 120.

Less onerous were most chores in which slaves helped subsist their masters. The Chinook Chief Elwahco, whose slaves
initially performed only traditional chores such as fishing
and gathering, later hired them out to work for white settlers,
whose numbers increased as the 19th century progressed.[90]
Sometimes Chinookan speakers purchased slaves from
sailors visiting their shores. One who did so was Celiast
(Helen), the daughter of the important Clatsop Chief
Coboway, who purchased a Hawaiian girl whom she named
"Jessie Bill" after a sailor known simply as "Bill."[91] The
British Capt. George Vancouver in March 1792 returned to
the Sandwich (Hawaiian) Islands two other Hawaiian girls
abducted by Capt. James Baker of the British ship *Jenny*.
Baker denied knowledge of their presence aboard ship when
sailing from the Islands, contending that he had no intention
of selling them, assuring that he would return them to their
homes at the earliest opportunity.[92]

Slaves were surely aware of the results, if not the ulterior
motives of their masters' manipulations. These included
marrying off their daughters to important fur men. This was
done in order to reap the economic, and perhaps socio-politi-
cal advantage of such unions. These, in turn, enabled fur men
to develop better rapport with families of their women. The
marriage of Celiast to Soloman Smith exemplified such
inter-ethnic unions. Another was the marriage of Comcomly's daughter, Ilche (Moon Girl), to Duncan McDougall the
crusty chief trader at Fort Astoria. For his aristocratic bride
McDougall apparently dowered her people with no slaves,
but with such valuables as guns and blankets.[93]

Up the Columbia River Casino kept his slaves busy paddling him from one place to another. The report that he had a
hundred slaves[94] to do his bidding was no doubt exaggerated,

[90]Mildred Colbert, "Naming and Early Settlement of Ilwaco, Washington," 184;
Whealdon, "On Whealdon Hill (Ilwaco, Wash.) Eve of July 16, 1860," p. 21.

[91]Emma Gene Miller, *Clatsop County, Oregon: A History*, 57-58.

[92]Howay, "Early Followers of Captain Gray," 12.

[93]Ruby and Brown, *The Chinook Indians*, 144.

[94]John Mix Stanley, *Portraits of North American Indians*, 63.

as was that of his having ten wives. More accurate was the
report of his eighteen slaves and four children succumbing to
the intermittent fever, possibly malaria or some strain of
influenza first carried aboard ship to the lower Columbia
River in 1829, and the reduction of his household to but two
slaves.[95] Other reports of slave numbers of important chiefs
were Comcomly's three hundred when, in fact, Chinook
informants told Verne Ray that he owned but ten or twelve.
This, writes Ray, represented perhaps "a customary maximum." Exaggeration of the number of chieftains' slaves was
not unusual, for example the over one hundred slaves attributed to S'neet-lum, a Lower Skagit chief of Whidbey Island
in northern Puget Sound. A more accurate rendering of such
numbers was perhaps those of the Nootkan Chief Maquinna. According to British-born John R. Jewitt, a naturalized
citizen of the United States, for a time enslaved to that chief,
he had "nearly fifty, male and female slaves, in his house, a
number constituting about half its inhabitants..."[96]

Slave numbers owned by chiefs may have been exaggerated, but not accounts of their temperamentality. Like other
native royalty, Casino's feathers were easily ruffled when
insulted, but by the same token, becalmed by praise and adu-
lation. When Cowlitz Indians canoed to the mouth of the
Willamette to collect blood-feud money for an alleged
injury, he parleyed with them with little apparent success,
whereupon the Cowlitz managed to capture one of his slaves,
demanding only a couple of blankets for its return. Casino
was insulted not only by the demeaning nature of the
demand, but by such meagre compensation for the slave on
which he placed a higher value than did the Cowlitz. Evidence of intrigue among natives was seen in the fact that the
Cowlitz people brought along their own slaves to trade to
Casino's allies in an attempt to have them switch their alle-

[95]Kane, "Incidents of Travel on the North-West Coast," 273.
[96]A.G. Harvey, "Chief Comcomly's Skull," 162; Ray, *Lower Chinook Ethnographic
Notes*, 51; Victor J. Farrar, ed.; "Diary Kept by Colonel and Mrs. I.N. Ebey," 56; John R.
Jewitt, *Narrative of the Adventures and Sufferings of John R. Jewitt*, 73.

giance from him to them.[97] Such intrigue sometimes
involved Company traders from whom Casino obtained
enough sailor caps and jackets to dress his slaves in the best
British naval tradition. Comcomly once had his slaves paddle
him across the Columbia River to Fort George in full British
uniform.[98]

Casino's nefarious enterprises took him and his slave lackeys inside and outside their own circle. One time he reportedly led his people on a slave raid as far south as the Umpqua
country of southern Oregon, returning with two bright slave
lads whom they traded to Chief Factor Dr. John McLoughlin at Fort Vancouver.[99] Another time Casino held an assassin
for a year to have him dispatch enemies or other persons
obnoxious to him. The assassin, whose name was the equivalent of "Evil Genius," fell in love with one of Casino's wife
and ran off with her. Discovering her near the mouth of the
Cowlitz River, the vengeful chief shot her dead and then
concluded the dirty business by hiring an assassin to deal the
same fatal treatment to her lover.[100] Another time Casino
tried to destroy one of his wives in the belief that she had
invoked an evil mantra over one of his sons. His next evil
enterprise was the murder of a beautiful Chinook maiden,
Waskema, for refusing to marry his son.[101] (In native society
even refusal to pay bride-prices exposed prospective grooms
to dangers at the hands of fathers of the brides.) Furious at
the insult Casino dispatched two slaves to kill Waskema,
then residing at Fort William, Nathaniel Wyeth's fur post at
the mouth of the Willamette River. The slaves murdered the
young woman in a canoe and tossed her body into the river.[102]
Another time when Casino's son, Winatka, died, two young
slaves his age were weighed down and also thrown from a

[97]Coues, *Henry-Thompson Journals* 2, pp. 879-80.
[98]Roy F. Jones, *Wappato Indians Their History and Prehistory,* 90; Ruby and Brown, *The Chinook Indians,* 149.
[99]Samuel Clarke, *Pioneer Days of Oregon History* 1, p. 96.
[100]Kane, *Wanderings of an Artist,* 175-76.
[101]John K. Townsend, *Narrative of a Journey Across the Rocky Mountains, to the Columbia River,* 339-40.
[102]Ibid.

canoe into the river.[103] Casino even ordered one of his thralls to execute the desecrater of a grave.[104]

Casino's behavior became increasingly risky with Hudson's Bay Company people nearby, whites in the embryonic Willamette settlements across the Columbia River, and other whites passing through the area. Casino and Comcomly contested for control of the native fur trade along the lower Columbia to the concern of Company officials.

Unlike the declining inland beaver-based trade into which Casino and Comcomly were drawn, the maritime sea otter-dentalia-based trade continued. Dentalia, the tiny shells raked from bottoms of bays and inlets off Vancouver and Queen Charlotte islands and north to Sitka, were used to set rates in slave and fur exchanges.[105] Since many dentalia came from strategically located Nootkan sea beds, its natives set rates of exchange based on them.

Further north, rates were set by Haidas and Tlingits in whose sea bottoms these shells were also found. The standard number of dentalia was forty per fathom, the length of outstretched arms. After the inland fur trade began, a fathom equaled the value of a beaver skin. Were a fathom of thirty-nine of sufficient length, it was worth two beaver skins, and so on, increasing one beaver skin for every shell less than the standard number.[106] This apparent discrepancy in prices of lesser numbers of shells was due to traders not measuring their value in six-foot lengths as much as in the size of the dentalia of which they were composed. Thus, a string of sixty to a fathom was of less value and might not have been used in the trade.[107] Among Nootkas a slave might have brought five fathoms of dentalia, but among Yuroks on the southern edge of the trade, these shells were in such demand that a slave might have brought but one fathom.[108]

---

[103]Curtis, *The North American Indian* 8, p. 89.

[104]Kane, *Wanderings of an Artist*, 175-76.

[105]Dunn, *History of the Oregon Territory and British North-American Fur Trade*, 22.

[106]Kane, "Incidents of Travel on the North-West Coast," 276.

[107]Curtis, *The North American Indian* 9, p. 91.

[108]A.L. Kroeber, *Handbook of the Indians of California*, 24.

John Keast Lord, a naturalist visiting British Columbia and Vancouver Island around 1860, stated that twenty-five shells, placed together to the length of six feet, formed a dentalia cluster, purchasing a male or two female slaves.[109] After white contact dentalia were equated with European woolen blankets and horses. Other imported items were traded for slaves, but formed no stable standard of exchanges since values fluctuated widely depending on the natives' tastes. Even white men used dentalia in trading with various tribes.[110]

Some slaves passing through Chinook hands were enroute to the North.[111] They may have been destined for the interior since the Niska branch of Tsimshians (composed of four related language groups) of Nass River sold them to inland natives for furs. There were two open and honorable areas of commerce between the coast and the inland. Suttles concurs that the Chinooks had one of these monopolies in the trade. He cites the Tlingits in the north as having the edge over other tribes in the area with their trade with Athapaskans in the hinterland, as does anthropologist Leland Donald.[112]

In 1810, a male slave in Clatsop-Chinook country brought ten to twelve blankets in trade. A good male slave brought fifteen blankets, less than that for a female slave who in time became more expensive. Among Northern Indians at that time, a female slave brought thirty to seventy dentalia of

[109]John Keast Lord, *The Naturalist in Vancouver Island and British Columbia* 1, p. 22.

Leland Donald cites three sources which state that among Lower Chinooks, Quileutes and some Tlingit groups, female slaves were of less value than males. Three other sources indicate that among Quinaults and two other Salish groups, gender made no difference in determining slave value. Another of Donald's references states that women were more valuable. One of his sources states that in the Nootkan work force men were of greater value until the 1860s when female slaves were preferred because of their use as prostitutes. "The Slave Trade on the Northwest Coast," 146. Possibly women slaves were less difficult to control than their male counterparts; however, Donald finds that gender differences among Nootkas were not sharply defined since males performed women's tasks, slaves being used for any purpose demanded of them. "Was Nuu-chah-nulth-aht (Nootka Society) Based on Slave Labor?" 112.

[110]The Hudson's Bay Company tried to sell imitation dentalia of ivory to the natives, but they did not "take" to them. George B. Roberts, "Recollections of George B. Roberts." Ms. P-A 83.

[111]Dunn, *History of the Oregon Territory and British North-American Fur Trade*, 283.

[112]Philip Drucker, *Indians of the Northwest Coast*, 21; Suttles, *Coast Salish Essays*, 61.

standard size. A male slave brought seventy-five to a hundred.[113] Alexander Henry in 1814 noted that on the lower Columbia a sea lion was exchanged for a slave and a few assorted items.[114] In the 1830s the American naval lieutenant William A. Slacum noted that near the mouth of the Columbia the price of a slave ranged from eight to fifteen blankets, no doubt depending on the size, color, texture and general condition of these coverings. Slacum also noted that, unlike former times, a female slave brought higher prices than a male, with good slaves going for fifteen blankets.[115] Should a slave die within six months of purchase, he observed, the seller returned half the purchase price.[116]

Shortly after mid-19th century a white man rescued two Chinook slave boys slated to be killed on the death of their chieftain master. When trailed by four Chinooks seeking to retrieve them, the white man stated his wish to buy them for ten blankets each. When the Chinooks threatened him with knives he retreated to his cabin to fetch his revolver with which he threatened them. The Chinooks then accepted his order at a nearby store for the blankets, some of which they later cut into strips to cover the dead chief.[117] In 1842, a half-dozen years after Slacum was in the area, the price per slave was four or five blankets or two pounds of gunpowder.[118] One writer at the time noted that a male slave on the Pacific Coast was worth approximately four or five white woolen blankets either plain or gaudily striped, or, two pounds of gunpowder.[119] Female slaves in some instances fetched higher prices since they were in high demand by fur company personnel who took them as wives.[120]

[113]Ruby and Brown, *The Chinook Indians,* 116; Dennis, "Indian Slavery in Pacific Northwest," 184.

[114]Coues, *Henry-Thompson Journals,* 858.

[115]William Slacum, *Memorial of William A. Slacum Praying Compensation for his services in obtaining information in relation to the Settlements on the Oregon River,* 10.

[116]Ibid.

[117]James G. Strong, *Wah-Kee-Nah and Her People: The Curious Customs, Traditions, and Legends of the North American Indians,* 13-32.

[118]Ruby and Brown, *The Chinook Indians,* 191.

[119]Marguerite Eyer Wilbur, ed., *Duflot de Mofras, Travels on the Pacific Coast,* 185.

[120]Ruby and Brown, *The Chinook Indians,* 191.

The Tillamooks received less from Chinooks for the sale of female slaves who were unable to perform drudge work. When horses began appearing in their trade channels around 1830 the Tillamooks, who raided weaker tribes to the south, sold a good male slave for as much as a horse, i.e. from ten to twelve blankets according to sex, size and condition.[121] Female slaves brought less in exchange since the Tillamooks' only source of adult male slaves were those raised from childhood, unlike women who were captured as adults. Had buyers only nine blankets they would have been hard pressed to purchase a full grown, athletic slave. A good hunter slave fetched nine blankets, a gun, a quantity of powder and ball, a couple of dressed elkskins, tobacco, vermilion paint, a flat file and other articles.[122]

After Euro-Americans began suppressing slavery and its trade, prices of good slaves tended to escalate. Among Haidas prices rose to two hundred blankets or the equivalent of a thousand dollars per slave.[123] This contrasted sharply with prices of nearly a century earlier when the British trader Capt. John Meares found a young woman on the Pacific Coast who could be purchased for an axe and a quantity of glass beads.[124] Capt. Vancouver in 1792 was similarly offered children whose native owners wanted muskets and copper sheets for them.[125] Nowhere were Europeans such as Vancouver offered slaves for sale to as great an extent as by the Cowichans whom he met near the mouth of the Fraser River. An indication of the natives' demand at that early time for metals occurred years before Capt. Gray entered the Columbia River in 1792 when a Clatsop bought a slave for a piece of

---

[121]Lee and Frost, *Ten Years in Oregon*, 103.

[122]Dunn, *History of the Oregon Territory and British North-American Fur Trade*, 273.

[123]MacLeod, "Economic Aspects of Indigenous American Slavery," 649.

[124]John Meares, *An Introductory Narrative of a Voyage Performed in 1786, from Bengal, in the Ship Nootka. In Voyages Made in the Years 1788 and 1789, from China to the North West Coast of America* xxviii.

[125]George Vancouver, *A Voyage of Discovery to the North Pacific Ocean, and Round the World Under the Command of Captain George Vancouver* 2, p. 71; Edmond S. Meany, "A New Vancouver Journal," 134.

brass "two fingers wide" from a wrecked ship. In the 1850s an elderly Snohomish chief told George Gibbs that until the first ship came to Whidbey Island, a piece of iron as long as one's finger was worth two slaves. As metal objects became more plentiful it is doubtful that a similar rate of exchange would have prevailed for such small amounts.[126]

Slave values in the latter 19th century continued to be equated in blankets, but coins of the Euro-American monetary systems were also used. A new period was ushered in wherein prices alternated in the manner of a stock exchange, a reflection of changes in the natives' tastes and in Euro-American economies. In one dip of the economy in 1875 a female slave, purchased from Nisquallys, went for as low as two hundred dollars plus other properties.[127] Along the coast around mid-19th century forty to fifty blankets purchased a slave, but with the waning of slavery and a corresponding scarcity of its human commodity (c. the 1870s) there was a general escalation in prices to two hundred blankets per slave. A Hudson's Bay Company blanket selling for five dollars now meant that a slave could fetch a thousand dollars at the marketplace.[128]

On the basis of post mid-19th century reports Donald Mitchell presents a table of slave values in which those in some native markets fetched up to two hundred blankets which, as another scholar states, were "the most common and important item distributed..."[129] Mitchell and Leland Donald note that among the Northern Indians "slaves were themselves one of the traditional potlatch articles, but perhaps of greater importance in the 19th century, each slave

---

[126]Ella E. Clark, *Indian Legends of the Pacific Northwest*, 207; Gibbs, *Tribes of Western Oregon and Washington* 1, Pt. 2, p. 240.

[127]Ray, *Lower Chinook Ethnographic Notes*, 51.

[128]James G. Swan, *The Northwest Coast; or, Three Years' Residence in Washington Territory*, 166-67; Dunn, *History of the Oregon Territory and British North-American Fur Trade*, 273; Donald Mitchell and Leland Donald, "Some Economic Aspects of Tlingit, Haida, and Tsimshian Slavery," 69; Viola E. Garfield, *Tsimshian Clan and Society*, 29-30.

[129]Donald Mitchell, "Predatory Warfare, Social Status, and the North Pacific Slave Trade," 40; William H. Hodge, *The First Americans, Then and Now*, 407.

not a complete citation

could be converted into large quantities of blankets—and the distribution of these was increasingly the measure of a man's greatness."[130]

The exchange of slaves and furs for white men's blankets to wrap masters' imperial hides, and other precious commodities of status, brought these overlords pelf, pride and prominence. But the human exchanges, degradation and despair perpetuated by the trade in chattel resulted in a deadly triangle of white men, Indians and Indian slaves.

---

[130]Mitchell and Donald, "Some Economic Aspects," 30.

3
White Men and Indian Slavery: Involvement and Response

In the native slave scene white men played a vital role via the fur trade, purchasing native slaves not so much to put them to work as to use them in mutual bartering with other tribes in order to acquire furs. On the other hand natives captured and enslaved foreigners who came to their shores from England, Spain, Russia and America.

Two decades after Capt. Robert Gray sailed his ship, *Columbia Rediviva,* into a great river, naming it "Columbia's River" for the District of Columbia (and now shortened to Columbia River), a British Schooner named *Columbia* sailed along the Pacific Coast searching for furs. Built in Baltimore, she was owned by the North West Company and commanded by Capt. Anthony Robson and later, by a Capt. Jennings. Her first mate, Peter Corney, wrote: "I am sorry to say that the slave trade is carried on, on this coast, to a very great extent by the Americans. They buy slaves to the southward and take them to the northward, where they exchange them for the sea otter and other furs. If they cannot buy the slaves cheap, they make no scruple to carry them off by force."[1] It should be remembered that American slavers also carried on the trade in blacks since Congress made only feeble attempts to stop it. Early legislation attempting to curb that trade did not apply to the Pacific Northwest, which was not American territory until 1846.

Euro-American traders came to the Pacific Coast primarily to procure furs and hides for the China, New England and British Isles trade. In doing so their zeal for profits out-

---

[1] Peter Corney, *Early Voyages in the North Pacific 1813-1818,* p. 154.

weighed whatever humanitarian concerns they might have had for the natives. One infamous American trader whom Corney may have been referring to was George Washington Eayers (Eayrs, or Ayers), captain of the American ship *Mercury*, who contracted with Russian traders in the north to hunt sea otter southward from the Columbia River along the California coast. Under terms of his contract he was to use Aleut Indians whom the Russians had impressed into service. After the Russians withdrew these hunters from Eayers in 1810, he enslaved other natives to work for him. Three crewmen escaping from their oppressive captain remained for a year with Comcomly before being picked up by the American ship *Albatross*.[2] In their bitterness towards Eayers they undoubtedly fueled stories of his enslaving Indians, making other red men cautious in dealing with white traders. White traders likewise took special precautions to protect their ships and other properties from native traders.

Never one to do things on a small scale, Eayers enslaved natives in fell swoops. Seven of a dozen whom he snatched from Chinooks at the mouth of the Columbia River escaped by stealing a boat and making for shore.[3] The dastardly exploit became common knowledge among tribes up and down the river. Comcomly used the purloining to his advantage by warning tribesmen that were they to trade directly with whites at the lower Columbia, they too would be kidnapped. By this stratagem the crafty chief sought to retain his mercantilist leadership, buying furs from upriver natives and selling them to whites at inflated prices.

On one occasion Eayers sailed off with eleven unsuspecting Makah freemen when they boarded his ship to trade, and he also sailed off with others whom he purchased from natives near the mouth of the Columbia River.[4] Off islands near Drakes Bay just north of San Francisco he forced his

---

[2]Ibid.   [3]Ruby and Brown, *The Chinook Indians*, 116.

[4]It was Eayers' practice to sail off to some distant location with captive Indians, forcing them to labor without pay. After reading through a collection of Eayers' materials in the Los Angeles Public Library, researcher Winston Wutkee found but one instance in which Eayers admitted to having purchased a lad at the mouth of the Columbia River. Wutkee to authors, January 17, 1971.

captives to hunt seals for him. After they procured some hides he abandoned them, possibly because the nearest slave market was further north along the California coast. As the deserted natives made their way north along the coast eight were killed by natives, possibly Athapaskan Tututnis of southern Oregon. Tillamooks ransomed three of the refugees, one of whom the Chinooks brought to the Astorian Gabriel Franchère in 1811.[5] Another is recorded to have been too frightened to ever again board a ship off his native Makah coast for fear of being kidnapped.[6] The 1813 confiscation of Eayers ship as contraband during the War of 1812 spared the natives further enslavement of his hands during his seven years of nefarious activity.

Captain William Sturgis, an early fur trader in the region, revealed Eayers' opportunism to his fellow New Englanders. Recognizing the Pacific Coastal natives' wealth in captives, these New Englanders began buying slaves from natives amply supplied with them. The Yankees then sold them to others who had but a few. Sturgis also noted instances where chiefs were confined in irons, receiving their freedom from white slavers only on payment of heavy ransoms. Another slave trader of whom Sturgis may have been thinking was the captain of the *New Hazard* out of Salem, who purchased two slaves at Nahwitti on northern Vancouver Island, selling them three days later on the east coast of the Queen Charlottes, one for five skins and the other for three. Judge F.W. Howay, who devoted a lifetime of study to early New England traders on the Northwest Coast, wrote: "Slavery existed amongst the Indians of the Northwest Coast..." and, that in trading with these Indians, the white traders "were not averse to using slaves as a purchasing medium for skins."[7]

Of this traffic in human flesh Hudson's Bay Company Governor George Simpson observed that slaves were

[5]Eric Blinman, Elizabeth Colson, Robert Heizer, "A Makah Epic Journey," 157-59.
[6]Ibid.
[7]Charles G. Loring, "Memoir of the Hon. William Sturgis," 440-41; Stephen Reynolds, *The Voyage of the New Hazard to the Northwest Coast, Hawaii and China, 1810-1813,* p. 28; ibid., xv.

purchased for a mere trifle by the Americans from the Tribes about Cape Flattery, and the Straits of St. Jean de Fucca, and sold to the Northern Tribes at about 30 Beaver each, and some good looking female Slaves as high as 50. They are by those Tribes re-sold to the Tribes further North, and in the interior, as in that quarter an Indian ranks in point of consequence, according to the number of Slaves he possesses; in fact they are the principal circulating medium on this Coast.[8]

Among slaves which were reportedly taken by Russians in similar fashion were ten or twelve Nahwitti of a Kwakiutl subdivision in their northern Vancouver Island homeland. It is not known what became of these natives, but some historians credit their abduction with sparking the 1811 summer explosion which destroyed the *Tonquin,* a ship involved in Astorian-Russian trading. The tragic event occurred off Vancouver Island after the ship had disembarked men and equipment at the Astoria post on the Columbia River. Serving as interpreter aboard the *Tonquin* was the flat-headed half-blood Chinook named George Ramsay (Lamazu). After a two-year enslavement in the North he was ransomed by friends.[9]

Besides slaves, fur from the sea otter *(Enhydra lutris)* native to the North American Pacific Coast south to Alta California was an important item in a thriving trade. The powerful, mobile animal varied in length, reaching five feet including its short, flat tail which served as a rudder to guide it in the sea where it spent most of its time. Unlike the river otter, it ate no fish, but lived on sea urchins, clams, crabs, mussels and shellfish. Its soft, fine, dense fur varied in color from reddish brown to black interspersed with silver hair.

Off western Vancouver Island in Nootka Sound, an outfitting place for multinational white mariner-traders, the British Capt. James Cook in 1778 exchanged geegaws and a few metal pieces for lustrous sea otter pelts. White men thereafter sold a variety of goods for these furs which they took to China. There they were highly valued almost instantaneously. Although goods which the natives purchased fluctuated in value from time to time and from place to place, those of slaves and *clamons* (cuirasses or armour made from elk hide) which they traded for them remained fairly constant in the exchange process.

In early trading days Vancouver Island, as Cook discovered, was a good market place. It had thirty-seven Nootkan groups supplying goodly numbers of buyers of slaves and *clamons*. British and American traders, competing to capture the native markets, carried these commodities from tribe to tribe to exchange for furs. Robert Haswell, Captain Gray's first mate, visited Tatoosh Island at the tip of the Olympic Peninsula (northwestern Washington State) in March 1789. This was the land of the Makahs, ethnic relatives of the Nootkas who retained close trading ties with that tribe. He reported that in their eagerness to trade, the Makahs offered their own manufactured blankets (possibly of wool of dogs which they raised for shearing) "which weir realy curious[,] and children for sale." Natives had likewise offered their children to John Boit, also with Gray. Natives offered many children to Russian traders as well.[10]

In the early 1790s the Spanish had no difficulty acquiring Nootkan children, whom they took to Christianize in Mexico. The Nootkan practice of offering their children was so repulsive to the Spaniard, José Estéban Martinez, that it resulted in strained relations with Maquinna and with Kelekum, another Nootka chief who "had been accustomed to eating boys chosen from among prisoners taken by war parties and retained as slaves." One should be skeptical of Martinez' remarks since he was considered by his country-

---

[10]John Boit's Log of the Columbia—1790-1793," 280n; William Coxe, *Account of the Russian Discoveries Between Asia and America, to Which Are Added, the Conquest of Siberia, and the History of the Transactions and Commerce Between Russia and China,* 218. Thirty-six years after the offer of the blanket to Haswell, the Britisher, Dr. John Scouler, observed that from a little distance it was difficult to distinguish Makah dogs' hair blankets from those of European manufacture; Scouler, "Dr. John Scouler's Journal of a Voyage to N.W. America," 196.

men and foreigners as unreliable. Thinking such extremities had ceased by 1789, Martinez was sufficiently incensed to purchase the slave children for their own protection. John (Juan) Kendrick, Jr., the son of Captain John Kendrick, the American with Robert Gray on the coast also noted the reported practice of consuming slave children. The younger Kendrick had joined the Spanish explorers, leaving his father's employ and converting to Catholicism. With his new compatriots he reported being offered a hand and a piece of flesh from an enslaved four-year-old. When Martinez (in June 1789) purchased his first child, a young boy, the Nootkas asked if he was going to eat this one who had been christened "Esteban" after the Spanish commander. The answer would have been in the negative since he was taken to be Christianized. An eight-year-old girl was reportedly purchased for a pot and a frying pan, given a Christian name and with the lad and others, turned over to Franciscans for care and nurturing. Wrote an anonymous Franciscan as cited in Warren Cook, *Flood Tide of Empire* (1973):

> Macuina [Maquinna] ate the little boys among his enemies who had the misfortune to fall prisoner. For this purpose he tried to fatten them up first, and then when they were ready, got them all together in a circle (he did this some eight days before our people left that waterway), put himself in the middle with an instrument in hand, and looking at all the miserables with furious visage, decided which one was to serve as dish for his inhumane meal. Then, advancing upon the unhappy victim of his voracious appetite, he opened its abdomen at one blow, cut off the arms, and commenced devouring that innocent's raw flesh, bloodying himself as he satiated his barbarous appetite.[11]

In 1791 the Spanish commander, Alejandro Malaspina, put in at Nootka on returning from the North where he had sought the mythical Strait of Anian, believed to be a passage through North America. At this time Maquinna and other Nootka chiefs sold to Malaspina and a Spanish priest, Don Nicolas de Leura, "no fewer than twenty-two children of both sexes." Originally captured Kwakiutls from the main-

---

[11]Warren L. Cook, *Flood Tide of Empire*, 190, 309, 314, 351, 379.

land and northeastern Vancouver Island, three of these children escaped the Nootkas and found safety among the Spaniards, aware they were to be eaten by the nobility of that tribe or killed in ceremonious "detestable and horrible sacrifice." After three years in the area the Spanish commander, Don Francisco Eliza, departed Nootka with twenty slave children whom he acquired by trading copper pieces and Monterey (abalone) shells to the natives. During his three-year stay he reported no fewer than fifty-six children purchased at Nootka, Clayoquot Sound and the Strait of Juan de Fuca. Such transactions were not isolated incidents. In 1792, for instance, Lieut. Don Salvador Fidalgo received aboard the *San Carlos* some Nootkas who brought a child's hand which had been cooked, as they also brought other human extremities to other Spanish craft.

The Spanish appeared to have been deeply concerned about such cruelties imposed on native children, especially by the likes of Maquinna. Mention has been made of his method of selecting slave lads for eating. According to various accounts he regularly feasted on slaves—one every "moon," as reported by the early trader, John Meares. He would put them in a circle from which, blindfolded, he randomly selected a slave to be eaten. Then, according to Meares, he ceremoniously distributed body pieces of the thrall to attending chiefs. Meares' reliability has been questioned since he was widely discredited in his day. His account of misadventures were written for him by a ghost writer, William Combe. However, other accounts attest to this procedure in ceremonious decimations and distributions of body pieces to visiting chiefs. The Spanish explorer, Juan Bodega y Quadra, was among those noting Maquinna's cruelty. Bodega was more sensitive to the plight of slaves and other native underdogs in the Spanish exploration period of the latter 18th century along the Pacific Coast than were his 16th century conquistador predecessors in the New World. In fact, he threatened to kill Maquinna for his crimes. Such Spanish concern for Northern Indian slaves in this later era was evident as indicated above by the purchase of youngsters to be taken to Mexico for Christianizing. Slave children of both Kwakiutl and Tlingit origin were taken for that purpose, according to Bancroft.[12]

Perhaps none of Maquinna's white visitors were more shocked at his treatment of slaves than was Captain Péron, who visited the cavalier Nootka "king" in 1796. According to Péron, Maquinna claimed that a well-formed six-year-old child at his side was not his son and, that he planned to eat him for his evening meal. At this revelation Péron and his crew resolved to rescue the lad from his impending doom. After lengthy negotiations they were said to have purchased the youthful unfortunate for three fathoms of blue cloth, which material along with muskets and copper sheeting were much in demand by natives.[13]

Maquinna and his Nootkas were not alone in the child slave-selling business, for when Samuel Hill of the brig *Otter* out of Boston was in the Skidegate area of the east coast of the Queen Charlottes in 1811, Haida Chief Estakunah came aboard to trade four slaves, two boys and two girls. There is no indication that Hill purchased them, but the ship's carpenter, Samuel Furgerson, recorded in his journal that thirteen days later (February 19) Hill purchased from Estakunah "a fine boy about 10 years old" for fifteen *clamons*, four otter skins and two blankets.[14] In his personal account *Wah-Kee-Nah and Her People...* (1893), James C. Strong wrote that when the Nootkas were about to kill and bury a ten-year-old slave boy with a free person's son, he was purchased for five blankets and taken by his redeemer to the Columbia River.[15]

Another example of natives trying to sell their children is revealed in the accounts of Lewis and Clark, who wintered in

[12]Meares, *An Introductory Narrative,* 255-56; Edmond S. Meany, *A New Vancouver Journal on the Discovery of Puget Sound By a Member of the Chatham's Crew,* 39; Henry R. Wagner, *Spanish Explorations in the Strait of Juan De Fuca,* 34; Bancroft, *Wild Tribes,* 108.

[13]Capitaine Péron, *Memoirs du Capitaine Péron Sur ses Voyages* 2, p. 3.

[14]Samuel Furgerson, "Journal of a voyage from Boston to the North-West Coast of America, in the Brig *Otter,* Samuel Hill Commander, Kept by Samuel Furgerson, Ships Carpenter, March 31, 1809 to March 24, 1811." Entries, February 6 and 19, 1811. Ms. 207.

[15]Strong, *Wah-Kee-Nah and Her People,* 132-33.

Clatsop country in 1805-06. Although the two explorers commanded a military expedition, the Clatsops and Chinooks considered them primarily traders like most other white men who visited them. On February 28, 1806, the two were offered a ten-year-old boy for sale by the Clatsop Kuske-lar, who had acquired him from a Tillamook. The Tillamook, in turn, had captured him from a tribe at "a great distance" down the Oregon Coast. Asking price for the lad was a mere gun and a few beads.[16] According to Clatsop legendry, natives captured and enslaved two white men found near the south cape at the mouth of the Columbia River. Possibly they had survived a wrecked Spanish ship. One, a blacksmith, worked for the Clatsops making iron knives. Eventually the two were freed to make their way up the Columbia to The Cascades where they were said to have married native women and raised families.[17] Other details of their captivity and release by natives at the cape are sketchy. Village chiefs preempted the right to imprison others in similar unfortunate circumstances. Such persons were often passed back and forth among various tribes and, were no ransom available, kept as slaves.

The Lewis and Clark party dealt not only with Clatsop, Chinook and other tribal males, but with their opposite gender, especially Chinook women who increasingly took the initiative in trading and other more supine transactions with white men. Chinook males continued in management roles with their women performing the actual conduct of such affairs. One management activity of Chinook males involved letting out their women to prostitution. Under leadership of a Chinook madam known as the Princess of Wales, ten female slaves engaged in sexual promiscuities with white males, the remuneration from the affairs going to the employers of this pandering female. Most likely she was the one whom Lewis and Clark dubbed the "Old Baud."

---

[16]Reuben Gold Thwaites, ed., *Original Journals of Lewis and Clark Expedition, 1804-1806*, IV, 118, 120.

[17]Clarke, *Pioneer Days of Oregon History* 1, p. 159.

Thanks to her and her girls, the Corps of Discovery, as the expedition was called, soon discovered that it had been infected with the "venereal," a serious inconvenience for men already suffering the discomfiture of their dreary wintering place. Plagued by boredom, their long absence and distance from female companionship, and stimulated by the Chinook women's scanty clothing which revealed tatooed-limbs, the men succumbed to their charms. Attempting to meet the crisis caused by the women, Lewis and Clark administered the "mercury treatment." This, however, did not prevent the continuing visits and favors which the men continued to accept despite their increasing debility. To meet the problem of the loss of the expedition's tools, with which its members paid their courtesans, Lewis gave the men ribbons, not for good behavior, but rather with which to make their payments. He and Clark observed that nowhere among peoples visited on their long western journey had they seen such brazen female advances. Prostitution, which became common practice among slave-holding tribes, persisted well past mid-century. Before Clallams on the Strait of Juan de Fuca gave up their slaves, their chief, James Balch (Lord Jim), ran a prostitution ring, his female slaves pandering to both whites and Indians.[18]

For several years members of other expeditions had received sexual favors of women loaned out to them. In June 1791 natives as far north as Yakutat Bay offered Malaspina's crew "women [who] were slaves captured in warfare" for the purpose of prostitution. The following year the Northern Indians prostituted several slave women to Spanish sailors.[19] Slave women may have been offered to visitors as tokens of hospitality, but not insignificant in the practice among at least some natives was the profit motive. When Hudson's Bay Company Governor George Simpson, on a western journey in 1824-25, tried to stop the practice, the Chinooks complained of their possible loss of revenue. He recorded

[18]Ruby and Brown, *The Chinook Indians*, 97; Gunther, *Klallam Ethnography*, 264.
[19]Cook, *Flood Tide of Empire*, 309, 351.

that to keep that revenue flowing it was customary for female employers to charge proprietors "two or three times in the course of a Season and when they escape a violent Death they are brought to a premature end by Disease when they are left a prey to Dogs & Crows as they are denied the ordinary burial." Despite such a dire observation, Simpson believed his remonstrances to the natives to have been successful since chiefs responded in the manner of Casino who showed "his respect for the whites by kind treatment of his Slaves."[20]

Not all Chinook female slaves willingly served their overlords in prostitution. There were runaways. Those recaptured often met with mutilation for punishment, their feet being lacerated or burned on the soles or their ears being cut. Even were they to escape to their own people, they could not escape the stigma of having been slaves; yet, they would have escaped their former suffering from beatings or from having ashes thrown in their faces to amuse owners' families, a diversion among some peoples. Averkieva states that Tlingit slaves received varying degrees of punishment for repeated attempts to escape. For first attempts there was whipping; for second attempts, confinement in uncomfortable positions for long periods of time; for third attempts, calves of their legs cut; and for fourth attempts, death. There were also degrees of punishment for theft. Beatings followed first attempts; fingers cut from right hands for second attempts; and from left hands for third attempts; and for fourth attempts, death.[21]

Although prostitution was a new type of mercantilist venture to Chinook females at contact time, they had previously engaged in business activities including ownership of slaves and other properties. Under leadership of mistresses, they

---

[20]Merk, *Fur Trade and Empire*, 101. By this time Casino was subservient to personnel at Fort Vancouver. Although once exerting leadership among area Indians, changing times caused him to lose power and influence among them and white men.

[21]*Notices & Voyages of the Famed Quebec Mission to the Pacific Northwest*, 188; Curtis, *The North American Indian* 8, p. 89; Averkieva, *Slavery Among the Indians of North America*, 109-110. Taunting of slaves by Chinooks was no match for that of Assiniboins, who thrust lighted sticks in the faces of their captives and beat them severely when they tried to ward off such moves. F.H. Hunt, "Slavery Among the Indians of Northwest America," 283.

conducted a carrying business in their canoes. They were also permitted to retain income from other sources such as the production of baskets and other weavings, and from food harvested with slave help. When ships began visiting the nearby lower Columbia, younger women, led by older ones, became the preferred contact with white mariner-traders as they were with the Lewis and Clark party, associating and dealing with these male visitors more freely than did their men. This contact gave them greater facility in speaking English which, in turn, strengthened their role as primary traders. The prostitution which trapped their slave women was a by-product of this association. Explorer-fur traders introduced prostitution to coastal natives. By contrast, early Chinook women were virtuous prior to contact. White men must share with Chinook women the blame for introducing the practice. To the north on Vancouver Island, Nootkan men learned to prostitute slave girls for items of trade they wanted from whites. When these items were gone the women were no longer made available.[22]

Chinook males received remuneration from sexual activities of their women and slaves, permitting their women to solicit clients on their own. In former times female slaves accompanied daughters of the nobility to help them retain their chastity before marriage.[23] When unwanted pregnancies resulted from this type of mercantilism they were often terminated by abortions. Live births were terminated by infanticides.[24] One pregnancy not terminated was that of Chinook Chief Shelathwell's slave, who bore the child of Mr. William, first officer of the *Jenny*, which visited Bakers Bay on the lower Columbia in 1792.[25]

Relations between the Northern Indians and white mariner-traders often resulted in other troublesome situations. Such was the capture and enslavement by Maquinna's

[22]Douglas Cole and David Darling, "History of the Early Period," 130; Robin Fisher and Hugh Johnston, *Captain James Cook and His Times*, 95.

[23]Merk, *Fur Trade and Empire*, 99.

[24]Ruby and Brown, *The Chinook Indians*, 64.

[25]Elliott, "The Journal of the Ship Ruby," 267.

Maquinna, a Nootkan Chief, from a sketch by Spaniards visiting western Vancouver Island in the 18th century. A dealer in slaves, Maquinna also enslaved two white men whom he eventually sold in 1805 to American ship captain Samuel Hill, who rescued them and took them aboard his ship, *Lydia*.

Nootkas of John R. Jewitt, an armourer, and Mr. Thompson, a sailmaker and gunsmith, and the murder by Maquinna's people of the remaining crew of their American ship *Boston*. The two were saved perhaps because Thompson had a knack of repairing guns. When a gun given to Maquinna by the captain of the *Boston* broke down, the chief, in exchange for the repairing, spared the lives of his captives. During his confinement Jewitt got on better with the chief than did Thompson, who was contemptuous of natives. Maquinna was aware of this attitude, but in deference to Jewitt, who wanted the companionship of another Christian, spared Thompson's life whose services were apparently in less demand than were those of Jewitt.

In his *A Journal Kept at Nootka Sound* (1807), the first of two score publications narrating the captivity, Jewitt wrote of the many slaves in Maquinna's household.[26] Other chiefs whom Jewitt met in captivity had no more than a dozen, an indication of Maquinna's power and influence. Jewitt also

[26]Jewitt, *Narrative of the Adventures and Sufferings of John R. Jewitt*, 73.

noted that when one of the slaves died, they were thrown unceremoniously out the door of the house and taken by slaves who threw the body into the water. Such treatment caused him to ponder his own fate and that of his remains were he to die in captivity. One one occasion he accompanied the Nootkans on a slave-taking party. Unlike most of their owners who suffered defeat in the raid, the lives of the slaves were spared. In fact, Jewitt captured and enslaved four natives who served him as fishermen. As a slave, Jewitt's status was not unlike that of other Northwest Coast bondsmen who held slaves themselves.

When Vancouver Island chieftains wished to purchase slaves from other tribes they customarily sent emissaries splendidly attired in the down of a white bird. These emissaries understood their mission, advertising the articles with which they were willing to make payment. The Nootka Chief Wickananish of Clayoquot on western Vancouver Island wished to consummate such a purchase by offering for Jewitt four young male slaves, two highly ornamented canoes, many otter skins and fathoms of cloth. Despite this array of human and non-human items, Maquinna refused to exchange his prized slave, but did sell a small white boy from the murdered crew of the *Manchester*, which wrecked near Nootka. The tearful child soon sickened and died. After twenty-eight months of captivity Jewitt and Thompson were rescued by crewmen of the brig *Lydia*, who also rescued other enslaved white men.[27]

On November 1, 1808, the Russian ship *Sv. Nikolai* wrecked off the coast at the mouth of the Quillayute River on the northern Washington coast. Those aboard decided to make their way afoot southward along the Coast to Grays Harbor where another Russian vessel was scheduled to put in. The party consisted of fourteen Russians including Anna

---

[27]"Log-Book of the Brig Lydia on a Fur-Trading voyage from Boston to the Northwest Coast of America 1804-1805 With the Return Voyage By Way of the Sandwich Islands and Canton Aboard the Ships Atahualpa and Swift 1805-1807." Ms. S-213.

Petrovna, the wife of navigator Nikolai Bulygin, two female and five male Aleuts and Englishman John Williams, a Russian American Company employee. After fighting off natives for a week they had progressed no further to the south than the mouth of the Hoh River, a Pacific Ocean tributary. There they were harassed by Hoh, Quileute and Quinault Indians who sabotaged a boat some of them were using to ferry the Hoh River. Most of the party safely crossed, but four members, Anna, an Aleut wife of a Russian, a Russian male, and an Aleut male, were captured. In the manner of enslaved persons Anna was traded to the Makahs, and the Aleut woman was kept by the Hohs. The Russian male was traded to the Quinaults, and the Aleut, to the Quileutes. The rest of the party fled up the Hoh River. Along the way one wounded Russian was abandoned to ensure the safety of the others. Surviving spears and arrows which were fired at them, the party fled inland. There they built a blockhouse, giving them the distinction of being only the second temporary European settlers in what is now Washington State. They remained there through part of the winter, until February 8, 1809, laying plans to build and sail a craft down the coast to the Columbia River.

Returning to the mouth of the Hoh they again encountered natives who brought Anna down from the Makahs at the request of the party which sought to ransom her. They were stunned by her refusal to leave her captors to whom she had been traded as a slave.[28] Bulygin and four others surrendered to the Makahs on the spot since hungry and weary from struggling with natives and the elements they deemed it wiser to be enslaved than to continue their struggle for freedom. The decision gave Bulygin hopes of regaining Anna, who presumably had become infatuated with a Makah male. The remaining Russians attempted to escape the Hoh River to nearby Destruction Island in a dugout canoe, but when it capsized, they too were captured and enslaved by the natives.

---

[28]Kenneth N. Owens and Alton S. Donnelly, *The Wreck of the* Sv. Nikolai, 59.

Like other slaves they were traded from tribe to tribe or given as presents. Several were traded to the Makahs. Bulygin and Timofei Tarakanov, who left a narrative of their nearly two-year captivity, became slaves of a Makah chief who had Bulygin make toys to amuse young Makahs as well as make bowls for him, some of which were put up for sale.

In native fashion in which captive married men and women were permitted to join each other, Bulygin was traded to Anna's owner. But the chief who initially purchased him did so again. Subsequently, Anna's owner wanted Bulygin returned, offering the chief a little girl and fourteen feet of cloth for the exchange. Bulygin was finally returned to Anna's owner. Although the Russian captives were passed from tribe to tribe as saleable objects or gifts, they were, in the words of a student of their plight, "nothing but slaves, made to work interminably in all weather and given the worst of the food, usually revoltingly unfresh fish."[29]

Anna must have had second thoughts about the security she sought among the Makahs, for despairing of ever being rescued by passing ships, she committed suicide in August 1809. In death her body, like that of slaves, was thrown into the forest without burial.[30] Bulygin subsequently died of natural causes in February 1810. The natives made no attempt to kill adult males of the party although in native fashion they had tried to kill them before their enslavement.

On May 6, 1810, the *Lydia*, Capt. T.[J.] Brown commanding, entered the harbor at Neah Bay in Makah country. Aboard was one of the Russian party whom Brown had purchased at the Columbia River. The Russian had been traded to the Chinooks in that region. Brown ordered the Makahs and other natives to gather all of the Russian party for ransom. For the Englishman, two Aleut men, two Aleut women and eight Russians he paid five patterned blankets, thirty-five feet of woolen cloth, a locksmith's file, two steel knives, a

[29]Hector Chevigny, *Russian America: The Great Alaskan Venture, 1741-1867*, p. 145.
[30]Ibid., 146.

mirror, five packets of gunpowder and some small shot packets. When three natives, each bringing a Russian, wanted more ransom, Brown refused their demands. When they balked, he took a native hostage. The natives finally returned the Russians and accepted the original offer for the others. This accounted for fourteen of the party now no longer enslaved.[31]

Asians were also captured and enslaved by the natives. Through the centuries occasional disabled Japanese junks

---

[31]In Kenneth Owens' *The Wreck of the* Sv. Nikolai, p. 64, Timofei Tarakanov, an officer aboard the *Sv. Nikolai*, states that in his journal (one of two accounts of the wreck which Owens used in researching his volume), that it was Bolgusov whom Captain T.[J.] Brown had aboard the *Lydia* when she arrived in Neah Bay. It was Bolgusov who had been sold to mostly Chinook Indians on the Columbia River. Tarakanov names the thirteen rescued at Neah Bay, identifying Afanasii Valgusov as one of the eight Russians along with two Aleut men and two Aleut women. He also identifies those who died as five Russians and two Aleuts. This leaves one Aleut unaccounted for in Tarakanov's account. In his *Russian America*, p. 146, Chevigny states that Brown rescued one Afanassi Valgusov at the Columbia River, but may have confused Bolgusov and Valgusov. Chevigny also states, p. 146, that an Aleut, sold to Columbia River Indians, had been rescued the previous year by Capt. George Eayers of the *Mercury*. This may be the Aleut unaccounted for in Tarakanov's account; or did he include this with the two Aleut men who had died? Chevigny also states that Brown rescued thirteen more at Neah Bay (including Russians, two Aleut women and the Englishman). He states, pp. 146-47, that Brown ransomed the captives in the manner of that of Indian slaves. He recounts the death of seven of the party, but does not name them. Thus, the proportion of Aleut men and Russians is unspecified. Besides the Aleut rescued from the Columbia River, one still remained with some distant tribe, which accounts for twenty-three in all. Chevigny further states there were twenty when the *Sv. Nikolai* sailed, but does account for the Aleut rescued by Eayers, thirteen rescued by Brown, and seven who died, making a total of twenty-one. He writes of one more, the "young student Kotelnikov," known to be alive, but whereabouts unknown. Did Chevigny believe this Russian to be an Aleut, and the one whom Eayers rescued?

In Owens' *The Wreck of the* Sv. Nikolai a Quileute informant, Ben Hobucket, does not give the number of those rescued and those who died. In his "The Wreck of the St. Nicholas," (p. 31), C.L. Andrews, working from a translation of Tarakanov's *Narrative*, presumably from a different translation from that of Owens, states that Brown rescued thirteen at Neah Bay, and that seven died in captivity. He accounts for the Aleut taken by Eayers, and, for one Russian, Kotelnikov, who was not heard from at the time of the rescue. Andrews lists the total number of the party at twenty-two and the rescue in 1811 (p. 31). Other sources give the year of the rescue as 1810 excepting Harry M. Majors in his *Exploring Washington* (p. 63), who states that the party consisted of twenty-one Russians and Aleuts and the one Englishman, and dates the rescue at May 1811 when the thirteen of the party and the Englishman were freed.

In a letter to the authors, May 7, 1987, Owens writes that "Twenty-two people were stranded in the wreck of the *Sv. Nikolai*. Thirteen were ransomed and rescued by Captain T. Brown, master of the brig *Lydia*, in May of 1810. Seven had died during their captivity. One was sold apparently to some Columbia River (Chinook?) people and was never heard from again. And one had been purchased by Captain George W. Eayers, master of the ship *Mercury*, on the Columbia in 1809 according to Tarakanov."

drifted helplessly westward from Asia toward the Northwest Coast. In 1833 three Japanese survived the wreck of their junk near Tatoosh in territory of the Makahs, who then captured and enslaved them. Hudson's Bay Company clerk Archibald McDonald (MacDonald) ransomed and brought them to the Fort Vancouver school for native women, orphaned children (usually child slaves freed by the Company) and those of half-blood employees.[32]

During the 1820s the Reverend John West of the Red River Anglican Mission school adjacent to Bay Company headquarters at Fort Garry (present-day Winnepeg) sought Indian slaves for instruction. Noting many among the Chinooks, he believed they could be acquired without purchase for this purpose.[33] In similar vein Baron August von Schirnding, who in 1798 backed a plan to purchase, liberate and instruct African slaves so they could Christianize others of their own race, also wished to see a mission station established among natives of the Northwest Coast.[34] On the basis of George Simpson's journey to that coast, it would appear that, unlike West, the Governor-in-Chief had no wish to purchase its slaves in order to educate them. Instead, he devoted his energies to recruiting the sons of prominent chiefs to be educated at Red River. By contrast, Chief Factor McLoughlin was not above educating the lowly, which was one of several differences between him and Simpson.

At Fort Vancouver the freed Japanese would have observed the feeling of community engendered by McLoughlin. Under his watchful eye, slaves around the fort were generally spared the cruelties to which they were exposed when away from the post. The intermingling of

---

[32]Befriending the freed Japanese slaves, who also attended the Fort Vancouver school, Ranald McDonald, son of Archibald and Comcomly's daughter, Princess Sunday, learned of the slaves' account he sailed to Japan, feigning shipwreck to be admitted there, even before Commodore Matthew Perry entered it. See William S. Lewis and Naojiro Murakami, eds. *Ranald MacDonald: The Narrative of His Early Life on the Columbia...and of His Great Adventure to Japan.*

[33]John West, *The Substance of a Journal During a Residence at the Red River Colony, British North America,* 147.

[34]J. Orin Oliphant, "A Project For a Christian Mission on the Northwest Coast of America, 1798," p. 111.

races and peoples at the fort carried over to fur-trapping brigades. These consisted of natives, half-bloods and slaves and up to one hundred-fifty pack horses strung out for over two miles en route to points as distant as California's Sacramento Valley to exchange European goods for furs and other native products. The brigades kept sharp lookouts for hostile tribes, despite the Babel-like noises emanating from the train. With slave help, lodges were pitched at eventide and meals prepared. Slaves also cared for the horses, packing and repacking them along the way. They performed valuable service in other ways. In September 1830 Blackfeet attacked a brigade in which one of the slaves was killed while valiantly allowing two others to escape.[35]

On his own western journey Simpson was primarily concerned with trouble-shooting problems in his firm's operations. Not escaping his critical eye were native practices which posed a threat to those operations. He learned that Comcomly, on the death of his son, had killed a slave, rationalizing his action, when challenged, on the pretense that the slave was ill and would not recover. This prompted Simpson to observe that a Columbia River slave "was the most unfortunate Wretch in existence."[36] In keeping with his wish to streamline operations, Fort Vancouver was established. Chinook politics threatened the establishment of the fort. Removal of properties from Fort George up the Columbia to Vancouver was delayed after one of Comcomly's sons ordered a slave to kill a village chief near Fort George. Natives in council chose to either avenge or support the assassination.[37] More palaver than action enabled Company crews to make the upstream journey in seven canoes, three of which were manned by slaves.[38] Comcomly, whose slaves jumped at his command, was powerless to prevent the move.

[35]Robert H. Ruby and John A. Brown, *Indians of the Pacific Northwest: A History*, 54.

[36]Merk, *Fur Trade and Empire*, 101.

[37]E.E. Rich, ed., *The Letters of John McLoughlin from Fort Vancouver to the Governor and Committee, First Series, 1825-38*, p. 237.

[38]Nellie B. Pipes, ed., "The Journal of John Work, March 21-May 14, 1825," p. 143. At the time of the move from Fort George to Fort Vancouver roughly forty families at Fort George held eleven slaves. Robert C. Clark, "The Archives of the Hudson's Bay Company," 6.

He not only lost the principal fur trading post in his domain, but much control of furs brought there to sell since Fort George, his principal outlet, was now relegated to a sub-post.[39]

Like the blood-feud boiling among the natives at the time of the move, the Bay Company was similarly caught up in retaliation. In 1828 McLoughlin sought revenge on Clallam Indians for their January murder of Alexander McKenzie, four other Company men, and the enslavement of an Indian woman of the party as it was returning from the lower Fraser River. In better summer weather McLoughlin dispatched a fifty-man party which included Iroquois Indians, Owyhees (Hawaiian Islanders) and two Chinook slaves. They were dispatched not only to avenge the murders, but to rescue the women the Clallams had enslaved. McLoughlin reported to his superiors that his avengers killed eight Clallams, firing from the Company ship *Cadboro*. He also reported that, extending the attack, they killed others and destroyed a village and its properties including forty-six canoes. Governor Simpson reported that "the [Clallam] Village was attacked and reduced to ashes, all their property...destroyed, 10 or 12... killed and many wounded." The Bay Company party had wreaked its vengeance inflicting loss of life and property and rescuing the enslaved woman.[40]

The following year another Company ship, the *William and Ann*, carrying supplies from England to Fort Vancouver, failed to safely negotiate the treacherous Columbia River bar. Clatsops living near the site of the wrecked ship appropriated her cargo, justifying their action on grounds that ancient custom allowed them to claim whatever washed upon their shores. McLoughlin demanded that they return the goods.

[39]Ruby and Brown, *The Chinook Indians*, 178-79.

[40]Rich, *The Letters of John McLoughlin from Fort Vancouver*, 63; Frank Ermatinger, "Earliest Expeditions Against Puget Sound Indians," 29. Ermatinger states that twenty-five were killed. Dorothy O. Johansen states that the "Clallams lost possibly as many as 23 people." "McLoughlin and the Indians," 19; Simpson, *Simpson's 1828 Journey to the Columbia*, 76-78.

The Clatsops responded by offering to exchange two slaves for what they had taken. Preferring not to appease them by accepting the offer and thinking the episode involved murder on their part, McLoughlin dispatched a punitive expedition to chastise them for their actions. Several of the Clatsops were killed in the resulting conflict. Slaves were in the party, but what role they played in the retribution is not clear. The result was similar to the punishment meted out to Clallams, only in this instance it was an overreaction to an unfortunate incident involving basic cultural differences.[41]

In another incident involving Indian-type blood-feud payment, Company clerk Dr. William Fraser Tolmie, at Fort Nisqually at the southern end of Puget Sound, noted in his journal, May 28, 1833, that an elderly chief was enroute to visit him to deliberate on the propriety of accepting two slaves as payment from the Northern Indians who had murdered two of his relatives.[42]

Blood-feud retribution committed by slaves against white men concerned not only the latter, but Indian chiefs as well since they wished to keep on good terms with the Bay Company which supplied and purchased their goods. That relationship was strained when in August 1840 a Company employee, Kenneth McKay, was killed while salting salmon at Pillar Rock on the Columbia right bank above Fort George by a slave at the behest of his owner. With Comcomly's death the new Chinook Chief Chenamus, with several warriors, and accompanied by Fort George manager James Birnie, went to the murder scene. During their pursuit an innocent bondswomen was shot and killed. McKay's killer was also found and ordered hanged by McLoughlin.[43]

The event occurred four years after the United States government dispatched Naval Lieut. William A. Slacum to report on conditions in the Pacific Northwest, for whose ownership the United States and Britain were contesting.

---

[41]Rich, *The Letters of John McLoughlin from Fort Vancouver*, 71-73.
[42]Edmond S. Meany, ed., "Diary of Dr. W.F. Tolmie," 223.
[43]Ruby and Brown, *The Chinook Indians*, 204-05.

His fact-finding resulted in an indicting "Memorial" of Company management of regional affairs. The incident involving McKay's murder is evidence that the report was little heeded. Little escaped Slacum's critical eye, including the practice of slavery. In finger-pointing at McLoughlin and his company he conveniently overlooked the fact that slavery, practiced in America for over two hundred years, was still entrenched in the South. He was also apparently oblivious to the fact that slavery had been abolished in Britain in 1833, just three years earlier. It thus appears that he was less interested in Indian slave welfare than he was in demeaning Britain and the Hudson's Bay Company, which had a monopolistic hold on the country. His indictment of the Company nevertheless revealed some important facets of Indian slavery including the fact that

> The price of a slave varies from eight to fifteen blankets. Women are valued higher than men. If a slave dies within six months of the time of purchase, the seller returns one-half the purchase money. As long as the Hudson Bay Company permit their servants to hold slaves, the institution of slavery will be perpetuated, as the price, eight to fifteen blankets, is too tempting for an Indian to resist. Many instances have occurred where a man has sold his own child. The chief factor at Vancouver says the slaves are the property of the women with whom their workmen live, and do not belong to *men* in their employ, although I have known cases to the contrary. We shall see how this reasoning applies. These women, who are said to be the owners of the slaves, are frequently bought themselves by the men with whom they live, when they are mere children; of course they have no means to purchase, until their husbands *or their men* make the purchase from the proceeds of their labor; and *then* these women are considered the ostensible owners, which neither lessens the traffic, nor ameliorates the condition of the slave, whilst the Hudson Bay Company find it to their interest to encourage their servants to intermarry or live with the native women, as it attaches the men to the soil, and their offspring (half breeds) become in their turn useful hunters and workmen at the different depots of the company. The slaves are generally employed to cut wood, hunt and fish, for the families of the men employed by the Hudson Bay Company, and are ready for any extra work. Each man of the trapping parties has from two to three slaves, who assist to hunt, and

take care of the horses and camp; they thereby save the company the expense of employing at least double the number of men that would otherwise be required on these excursions.[44]

Slacum did not realize that had the Company taken a sudden hard line against Indian slavery it would have severely damaged its relations with native chiefs and, in turn, Company business. More than ever, the Indians came to depend on the Company which depended on them. In some cases the Company had cooperated with Indians by establishing as their chiefs persons with whom it could do business.

To Slacum's charges that the British were perpetuating slavery as a matter of fur trade economy, Company officials at Fort Vancouver replied that difficulties of emancipation were insurmountable.[45] Slacum and others critical of Company policies conveniently overlooked the fact that Indian slavery was well established before the firm entered the region. They also overlooked the fact that Company officials were mercantilists, not abolitionists. A mere glance at the problems attending the 1863 decree "emancipating" American Negro slaves attests to the fact that edict and fulfillment were two different things.

In correspondence to the London-based Governor & Committee prior to his journey to England, McLoughlin had not alluded to slavery, apparently grouping slaves under the designation "servants," or those working for the Company. On returning to Vancouver with a seemingly stronger anti-slavery posture, he now openly cited several instances where emancipated slaves would not return to their former villages.[46] Rightly so since in most tribes escaped or liberated slaves were looked down upon by their own people, stigmatized as "once a slave always a slave."[47] In a memorandum to the Governor & Committee he reported a plan to ameliorate the slave situation among his personnel: the Company would

[44]Slacum, *Memorial,* 10.
[45]Merk, *Fur Trade and Empire,* 352-53.
[46]Ibid., 354.
[47]Gibbs, *Tribes of Western Washington and Northwestern Oregon* 1, Pt. 2, p. 188.

not free its slaves, but would send them as presents to their relatives. This, however, only meant that they could be more poorly treated by their own people than by their Fort Vancouver owners.[48]

Many slaves whose welfare concerned Lieut. Slacum belonged to French-Canadian retirees of the Company settling in the Willamette and other valleys such as the Cowlitz and Walla Walla. Because of their prominence in the Willamette valley, the area around present-day Salem, Oregon was known to white settlers as French Prairie. Among early French-Canadian Astorian trapper-traders settling there were Joseph Gervais, Etienne Lucier and Louis La Bonte, and the Nor'Wester Pierre Bellique. These were known as the "Big Four" on the Prairie.[49] By 1833 eight families also lived on fertile lands extending southerly above Willamette Falls. Some settlers in the area married slaves who, in turn, owned slaves. Since fur companies encouraged their men to marry native women to facilitate the trade, this practice understandably did not suddenly end when they terminated their services with the companies.[50] These firms, however, had frowned on non-retired employees who married Indian women and abandoned the gathering of furs.

One French-Canadian in 1841 boasted that he would not bend his back hoeing while he had so many women to do his work. Most of those of whom he spoke were purchased from Willamette Valley Indians.[51] In the early 1840s, whites in the valley who at times raised their voices against such enslavement, did so futilely since the Oregon Provisional Government took no strong action against it. In fact, some early American settlers in the valley did not oppose enslavement of Indians. Like their French-Canadian neighbors they bought and sold slaves.[52] Several French-Canadians, however,

[48]Merk, *Fur Trade and Empire*, 355.
[49]Oswald West, "Oregon's First White Settlers on French Prairie," 200.
[50]Ruby and Brown, *Indians of the Pacific Northwest*, 58.
[51]J.A. Hussey, *Champoeg: Place of Transition*, 117.
[52]Robert Carlton Clark, *History of the Willamette Valley Oregon* 1, p. 57.

emancipated their slaves. One who did so was Baptiste McKay, who had in his possession a small boy captured from the Umpqua region of southwestern Oregon. When the lad reached his eighteenth year in the mid-1820s, McKay gave him to the visiting English botanist, David Douglas.[53]

When Roman Catholic Antoine Langlois of the Cowlitz Mission north of the Columbia on its Cowlitz River tributary left Quebec for the Pacific Northwest he had not anticipated the prevalence of slavery in the region. "Who would have thought that slavery would be here in full vigor," he asked, observing that "they traffic in slaves as if they were low animals... They do not regard them more than dogs (that is the name ordinarily given them)."[54] Others coming to the Pacific Northwest like Langlois were surprised to find slavery so widely practiced. One of these was Achilles De Harley. On the basis of observations during his travels there in 1849 he reported in a letter to Horace Greeley's *New York Tribune,* January 11, 1850 that

> You will probably be surprised that slavery so generally prevails among these Indians. This odious and most wicked system of oppression exists among all the tribes in every portion of Oregon. I have been among the Indians as a traveler or upon business, either public or private, in most sections of this territory, and my personal observation confirms the statement which I have made respecting a system the same in kind with that by which the unhappy African race are down-trodden in our Southern States.

As Langlois and De Harley were writing, there were signs of a weakening master-slave relationship in tribes traditionally exerting a strong control over slaves and freemen alike. The eventual breakdown of tribal culture worked to the advantage of slaves, especially those among tribes such as the Chinooks where servitude had been deeply entrenched. A traveler to the region in 1839, Richard Brinsley Hinds, aboard H.M.S. *Sulphur,* noted this trend, citing slaves in the

---

[53]David Douglas, "Sketch of a Journey to Northwestern Parts of the continent of North America during the Years 1824-'25-'26-'27," p. 83.
[54]*Notices & Voyages,* 149.

vicinity of Fort George who had acquired wealth, power and property. Some of that property was in the form of slaves.[55] By mid-19th century, freed of tribal restraint, several former slaves around Willamette Falls and adjacent Oregon City became owners of land and slaves alike.[56]

French-Canadians remaining in the fertile Willamette Valley generally avoided taking less fertile prairie lands north of Fort Vancouver. In that region Fort Nisqually trader Dr. Tolmie in essence ransomed a slave boy whom he had purchased to do farm work and break horses, paying him for his labor.[57] Such transactions were familiar to Tolmie, who was stationed at the southern end of Puget Sound in a strong slavery zone. From the fort a slave-owning Company employee, Simon Plomondon, left for Fort Vancouver, October 28, 1843, with other slave owners, J.B. Perrault and wife. Tolmie had previously freed the slave accompanying them but perhaps to retain peaceful relations with his native clients, succumbed to the Perraults and let him go with them.[58]

Although in decline, slavery in the region made Fort Vancouver and its managers targets for critics who believed their company either fostered the practice or did too little to eliminate it. In the face of negative representations by the missionaries, Company officials, acknowledging in 1837 that many of its employees retained slaves, assured critics that Company policy mandated that slaves remaining in the employ of their masters after emancipation enter into written contracts of fixed wages for their services as Company employees.[59] In McLoughlin's absence from Fort Vancouver Chief Factor James Douglas, trying to allay concerns of the Governor and Committee, expressed in an October 18, 1838, letter to them his willingness to suppress the slave traf-

---

[55]Richard Brinsley Hinds. "Journal, 1838-1842. Ms. 1524.

[56]Joel Palmer to Governor John W. Davis, O.T., January 23, 1854. *Records of the Oregon Superintendency of Indian Affairs, 1848-1872. Letter Book C:10.*

[57] Meeker Family, "Notebooks" 2, pp. 53, 54.

[58]Bagley, "Journal of Occurrences at Nisqually House, 1833-1835," p. 147.

[59]Merk, *Fur Trade and Empire,* 352.

fic. In the letter he assured that he was taking steps to comply with a new anti-slavery policy, but was meeting all sorts of opposition to end the practice. He did assure them that he had "denounced slavery as a state contrary to law, tendering to all unfortunate persons held as slaves by British subjects the fullest protection in the enjoyment of their natural rights."[60] He was surely aware that his superiors thousands of miles away did not realize the difficulties attending the solution to a problem long ingrained in native culture. Nevertheless, he tried to put his words into action on at least one occasion by seizing a runaway slave boy whom his pursuers had overtaken, and put him to work for the Company as a free laborer.

Douglas' London superior also requested him to see that the term " 'Slave' must on no consideration or account be applied to any inmate or resident of any of the Company's Establishments."[61] In the previous decade Governor Simpson, aware that "freemen" in Company employ were called "slaves," clarified the distinction between slaves and freemen, by stating that the latter had left Company service. "There are," he wrote, no

"slaves"—slaves in any sense—in the country, and there never were, nor, in fact, could be; but some distinctive appellation was necessary to distinguish those in the country, in the service of the Company, from those who were not, and hence the name. No offence was meant in this application, and as to those to whom it was applied, it bore the import of honourable service faithfully done and finished.[62]

Much closer to the problem than the visiting Simpson, Douglas observed that the "state of feeling among the natives of this river precludes every prospect of the immediate extinction of slavery, unless we resort to the very objectionable plan of a forcible emancipation." He also assured his

---

[60]Ibid., 353.

[61]Ibid.

[62]George Simpson, *Peace River. A Canoe Voyage from Hudson's Bay to Pacific, By the Late Sir George Simpson...in 1828*, p. 54.

superiors that he had tried to discourage the practice of exerting a moral influence alone, but did not wish to provoke excitement or animosity on the part of the Company were force used to enforce the policy.[63] He cited as one reason for his reluctance to release slaves his wish to spare the Company the cost of providing for their support. He also explained that it was apparent that slaves, as yet unfreed, were destitute, friendless, and ignorant of how to subsist independently, having no recourse other than to remain with their masters.[64] On October 18, 1836, he had written the Governor and Committee that "the plan I now follow, of considering every person without distinction, residing on our premises as free British subjects, who may at any time under the Company's protection, assert the exercise of their absolute and legal rights, will greatly mitigate the evils of slavery by operating as a security against abuse, and making affection the only bond that supports the immoral system."[65]

While Douglas and McLoughlin believed they were making progress in solving the slave problem, the Anglican Reverend Herbert Beaver (and wife) arrived at Fort Vancouver from England in 1836 to investigate rumors that the Company was mistreating natives under its control. He observed that not only did the Company's personnel in areas as the Willamette and Cowlitz valleys hold slaves, but so did those at the fort itself. On November 15, 1836, he wrote to Benjamin Harrison, a member of the Governor and Committee and the Clapham group, a prominent British evangelical body which became prominent in the aftermath of the Napoleonic wars. In his letter Beaver stated that he had

> seen more real slavery in the short time I have been here, than in the eight years and a half I was in the West Indies. There are also Indians, but I cannot say correctly the number, I think about forty, held in actual bondage, having been purchased by persons of all classes in the Establishment [Fort Vancouver]. It is true that discipline is

---

[63]Merk, *Fur Trade and Empire*, 353-54.
[64]Ibid.
[65]Ibid.

maintained, but it is by the use of the lash and the cutlass, supported by the presence of the pistol.[66]

Had Beaver not been so eager to find trouble, he would have
discovered instances of Company fair treatment of Indians
such as the slave lad whom Company people rescued and
hospitalized after his master had thrown him into the river to
drown. Beaver also might have discovered the many
instances of Indian mistreatment of slaves. Unlike
McLoughlin, he was unfamiliar with the facts of frontier life,
and he did not understand that neither Indian mores nor
Company management could be changed quickly and in the
manner he wished. What appeared to him as Indian involun-
tary servitude was more voluntary than met his eye, for its
subjects preferred taking their chances at Fort Vancouver
than in their former villages.

At least by the time of his fifth report to the Governor and
Committee, Beaver had divined that the crux of the slavery
problem lay with Indian women who were important principles in native servitude. Beaver wrote that

> it is a vain excuse to say, that they [the slaves] belong to the Indian
> women, who are living with their Masters, and to whom the cus-
> tom of the country concedes the right of retaining them in slavery.
> That they should not be so retained by the Company and their ser-
> vants, admits of no question; but I maintain further, that not even
> women, so living, ought to be allowed so to retain them; nor should
> they be suffered to reside in any of your houses, over which, at least,
> as belonging to yourselves, you can exercise whatever control you
> please. Your men should be strictly forbidden to make use of their
> services in any way; and they should by every practical method, be
> kept away from your establishment and its environs. Nor am I
> without some idea, that the prevention of this evil would work the
> partial cure of another; I believe, that not a few of the women who
> have been accustomed to their services, would, when deprived of
> these, take their departure from them.[67]

One can only speculate how the Governor and Committee
would have viewed the problem had they journeyed to the

---

[66]Thomas E. Jessett, *Reports and Letters of Herbert Beaver 1836-1838*, p. 20.
[67]Ibid., 132-33.

Pacific Northwest to examine it for themselves. Hopefully, they would have better understood the difficulties their firm faced not only in profit-making, but in managing its Indian clientele and its own personnel as well. Among other things, they would have learned that their firm was not responsible for slave-owning ex-Company men;[68] nor that much control could have been exerted over freemen like Iroquoy George, who in the early 1820s, apparently with slave help, had hunted sea otter for the Company along the coast near Grays Harbor.[69]

Other churchmen-missionaries along the lower Columbia became involved in the Indian slavery problem about which they had been ignorant before coming into the region. The Methodist missionaries who arrived in May 1840 were typical. On board the *Lausanne,* which inched across the treacherous Columbia River bar, was the Reverend Gustavus Hines who described what was for him and his fellow missionaries their first evidence of Pacific Northwestern Indian slavery:

> Towards evening a number of Indians of the Chenook tribe came on board, among whom were some of the *nobility,* one of the principal chiefs, whose name was Chenamus, and his wife, whom they called the queen [whom white men called Sally], being of the number. Most of them were very small in size, and very poorly clad, some of them not having sufficient clothing to cover their nakedness...Soon they were reinforced by the arrival of a band of Indians from the south side of the river, called the Clatsops, who were very savage in their appearance, some of them being painted in the most hideous manner... Many of them continued on board during the night, and though it was very cold, some slept in their open canoes which lay along side the vessel, with nothing around them. Their appearance, as they lay shivering in the cold, was truly deplorable. These, we learned, were slaves, and were not allowed by their masters to come on the deck.[70]

The Reverend Jason Lee and his nephew Daniel, who

---

[68]Their service with the Company ended, many former employees, rather than retiring north of the Columbia River, settled on farms in the more fertile Willamette Valley even before the Anglo-American boundary settlement of 1846.

[69]T.C. Elliott, "Journal of John Work, November and December, 1824," p. 205.

[70]Gustavus Hines, *Wild Life in Oregon,* 88.

established their Methodist mission in the Willamette Valley in 1834, were soon made aware of Indian slavery. According to mission historian John M. Canse, the establishment had set a precedent against slavery. At that time the Methodists were strict abolitionists. When a nearby settler and former Company trapper Louis Shangarate died leaving three orphaned children and several Indian slaves, Jason Lee yielded to McLoughlin to become their guardian. Emancipating them, Lee received them into the mission.[71] Canse stated that when such servile ones came on the mission farm they were freed, "for we allow no slaves here."[72] His statement is confirmed in official mission records under entry of "Sabbath 18th Oct. 1835—" stating that "They [the Indian children] pass our threshold and their shackels [sic] fall."[73] A traveler from the States, Peter Burnett, however, found little difference in the servile labor which the Indians performed at the mission from that which they performed for the Hudson's Bay Company, writing that "if there is anything which smacks of slavery in the one case, it necessarily follows in the other."[74]

The Methodists found stony ground on which to spread the seed of the Gospel. No place was this more true than at their outstation among the Clatsop Indians, the plight of whose slaves caught the eye of the Reverend Hines. Their chief promised the Reverend Joseph Frost to have his people attend his services, but when the "Sabbath" came, they scattered, leaving Frost to preach to him and his slaves. At the mission in 1840 an Indian told Solomon Smith and Celiast that they were angry at the King George people, the British, for refusing to let them drink rum, and trying to make them liberate all their slaves. Then, they asked, "who would get

---

[71]John M. Canse, *Pilgrim and Pioneer Dawn in the Northwest*, 127. The Reverend Jason Lee assented to the taking in of slaves, but stated that "in that moment the enslaved must be free…and in the mission equal with those they once served." Lee and Frost, *Ten Years in Oregon*, 133.

[72]Canse, *Pilgrim and Pioneer Dawn*, 123.

[73]Charles Henry Carey, "The Mission Record Book of the Methodist Episcopal Church, Willamette Station, Oregon Territory, North America, Commenced 1834," p. 239.

[74]George Wilkes, *The History of Oregon, Geographical and Political*, 102.

wood and water and catch salmon?"[75] Since Frost's congregation was composed of the chief and his slaves, perhaps Frost did not wish to jeopardize their continuing attendance by condemning him for having slaves.

It must be kept in mind that in the 1830s and 1840s accounts of Pacific Northwestern Indian slavery as recorded by Hudson's Bay Company personnel, as well as that by Methodists, Roman Catholics and other white observers, reflected bias engendered by the great debate on black slavery among Atlantic nations. Many of these observers in the Pacific Northwest wrote for like-minded audiences, especially in eastern America and in Britain. Thus it could be assumed that personnel of these various groups and individuals in the Pacific Northwest exaggerated what they saw in Indian slavery. Possibly included in this over-assessment was the Roman Catholic Reverend Modeste Demers, who observed Indians across the Columbia from the Methodist Clatsop mission. He wrote:

> Slavery and the treatment of slaves exist in all their hideousness among the tribes near the sea. The pitiful state, the suffering of the slaves of both sexes cannot be imagined. They are treated more harshly than dogs, their companions in servitude; for a native master will see his slave perish of hunger without condescending to help him, while he will share his food with his dog. These unfortunates are condemned to the hardest tasks; but what is more deplorable still is the condition of the women enslaved to the brutality of these monsters. One of these unfortunate creatures escaped this winter from the lodge of her master, who wanted to make her the instrument of a criminal traffic. The latter pursued her, seized her, and dragged her home by the hair; there, he choked her, whipped her cruelly, and slit the soles of her feet with a knife. Told of these horrors, Mr. [Dr.] McLoughlin demanded the poor slave; he had her placed in the hospital [at Fort Vancouver], where she could receive suitable treatment.[76]

In a March 1, 1839, letter to his Superior, Demers confirmed

---

[75]Jason Lee, "Journal of Jason Lee, Written at Mission House, Willamette, March 15, 1841." Typescript copy of ms.

[76]*Notices & Voyages*, 187-88.

that Chinooks were involved in the "shameful traffic" in female slaves whom they hired "at a price to the first who asks them."[77]

Catholic and Protestant missionaries alike believed slavery was linked to other Indian malpractices such as gambling and consumption of liquor. No one understood the pernicious effect of liquor on Indians more than did McLoughlin, who faced a problem worsening since the first decade of the century. At that time Ross Cox had observed that "all the Indians on the Columbia entertain a strong aversion to ardent spirits, which they regard as poison…[alleging] that slaves only drink to excess; and that drunkenness is degrading to free men."[78]

The first liquor which supposedly reached natives at The Cascades of the Columbia was a barrel from Vancouver for which they traded a slave girl, causing drunkenness of several chiefs.[79] In 1824 Company trader John Work recorded the practice of permitting the men to engage in drunken brawling *regales*. At Fort Simpson in the North he reported in 1835 that since Americans were fighting trade wars with the British, with liquor as their ammunition, Company officials were being forced to fight with the same weapons. On March 28, 1835, he reported that the scarcity of beaver had forced the Company to raise its price of a gallon "Indian" liquor per slave.[80]

The American finger of guilt pointed at McLoughlin as being responsible for the liquor problem on the Columbia. In fact, American traders on the river had no compunction about attempting to break the Company monopoly with liquor or by other means. McLoughlin tried to remedy the liquor situation by ordering tight regulations on dispensing it

[77] *Catholic Sentinel,* March 28, 1878.

[78] Cox, *Adventures* 1, p. 321.

[79] Lucullus V. McWhorter, "The Chiefs of Some of the Columbia River Tribes," 15. Ms. 1535, Item 6.

[80] Henry Drummond Dee, "The Journal of John Work, January to October, 1935," p. 30.

from Company stock, and in the 1830s cooperated with Jason Lee in a temperance movement.[81] His efforts came too late for such anglophobic Americans as Ephraim W. Tucker, who wrote in 1844 that rum introduced by the Company was the "besom of destruction," forcing Indians into enslavement by British subjects.[82] On the other hand another American, Robert Greenhow, a geographer in the region in 1844, stated that the Company seemed to have reconciled policy with humanity in prohibiting the supply of ardent spirits to the natives and rigidly enforcing the policy.[83]

Liquor and slavery continued to flourish along the Columbia despite McLoughlin's attempts to prevent the former and retard the latter. On June 17, 1847, one whom the *Oregon Spectator* reported as Ramsay took his daughter and two other girls to the American ship *Brutus,* a floating grog-ship as treacherous as her namesake. When trouble ensued, Ramsay was threatened with death. He sought to escape by offering his daughter as a slave to his pursuers. When the daughter refused to submit to this proposition the pursuers shot and killed her father.[84] Americans continued blaming Indian attrition on the British for selling liquor in exchange for furs, but as the preceding incident would tend to confirm, their accusations were like the American pot calling the British kettle black.

One doing his best to blacken the American kettle was Company clerk John Dunn at Fort George during the 1830s. The Americans, he claimed, "consider that every artifice is legitimate in trade..." By contrast, he claimed his company

---

[81]The temperance society which Lee organized with McLoughlin's financial aid offered reimbursement to cattleman-entrepreneur Ewing Young for expenses already incurred should he abandon his still. Young agreed to do so. Johansen and Gates, *Empire of the Columbia,* 179.

[82]Ephraim W. Tucker, *History of Oregon, Containing a Condensed Account of the Most Important Voyages and Discoveries,* 72.

[83]Robert Greenhow, *The History of Oregon and California,* 397.

[84]*Oregon Spectator,* July 22, 1847, p. 4. In the *Spectator* the father appears as Old Ramsay, who is probably George Ramsay. The initial Old Ramsay is thought to be an Englishman, and father of George Ramsay, escaping ship near mid-18th century. See Ruby and Brown, *The Chinook Indians,* 29.

George Ramsay, or Lamazu, a ransomed slave, was reported by Lieutenant Charles Wilkes as having one
eye and a flattened head in 1841.
Despite his physical handicap, he
piloted ships entering the Columbia
River in the early 1800s. He was shot
and killed after an evening's
debauchery aboard a "floating grog-
ship" to which he took his daughter
and two other girls. *Sketch from* The
Narrative of the United States
Exploring Expedition...

RAMSEY.

had abolished the "barbarous superstition" of killing slaves on
the deaths of rich men wanting them to serve these overlords
in the other world.[85] He also claimed to have personally
stopped practices such as stabbing human flesh in curing ceremonials.[86]

Company officials in the field were not as naive as Dunn,
for they were aware that slaves still assassinated for masters
and, that Company employees could become targets of these
killers. Such trouble could easily erupt at native marketplaces
where goods were exchanged. There was also the danger that
liberated slaves might not easily shed their murderings.
Company officials sought to minimize trouble by seeking to
avoid coalitions of various tribes and by remaining as neutral
as possible in intertribal squabbles. They also gave presents
to chiefs to gain their support.[87]

The policy of non-interference with native customs had its

[85]Dunn, *History of the Oregon Territory,* 73, 120.
[86]Ibid., 128.
[87]A good example of fur trader diplomacy occurred during Nor'Wester trading days
when Shoshoneans scarcely three miles from Fort Nez Perce killed a man, four women and
five children and then carried off as slaves two young women and a man. The Wallawalla
Chief Tumatapum demonstrated before the fort carrying bodies of the dead and blaming
white persons for supplying the attackers guns and ammunition. In defense of his company,
Alexander Ross examined the bodies to discover the victims had died from arrows, not bullets, thus clearing his firm of any wrongdoing, and thus preventing retaliation from its
native clientele. Ross, *The Fur Hunters of the Far West,* 158.

limits in preventing deleterious effect on the trade. To prevent
Nisquallys from binding favorite slaves to bodies of dead masters and tying them to high poles Company officials agreed to
protect the tribe from aggressive Puget Sound Indians.[88]
They felt that much of the Indians' time and energy involved
in slavery should have been directed toward the fur trade. To
discourage such bondage they presented gifts to chiefs who
liberated their slaves.[89] Their motives for doing so were not
strictly humanitarian, for they knew that such gestures would
tend to minimize troubles in the trade. This did not mean that
Company officials followed an appeasement policy, for, as
noted, when it felt its personnel and property endangered or
damaged, its Chief Factor McLoughlin ordered retaliation.
Moreover, its posts did not go unprotected.

Permission of Company officials for their employees to
marry free and slave women brought little criticism from
these women. They were only too happy to marry Company
men if for no other reason than to free themselves from their
previous servitude, giving them lives of better quality. The
Company policy of live and let live was evident at Fort Vancouver. Mechanics and laborers occupied substantial log cab-
ins outside the fort where two or three families beneath
single roofs in native manner had from two to five slaves to
support them by hunting and fishing.[90] Compared with their
former enslavement this type of family life would have
seemed to these workmen and their slaves the height of
domestic tranquility.

The Company way of life for these people began to come
apart after the Anglo-American boundary settlement at the
49th parallel in 1846. That year the Britisher M.A. Nattali
fired a parting shot at Americans by stating that the abolition

---

[88]"Old Fort Nisqually," 5.
[89]Gift-giving was a form of "bribery" to induce owners to free their slaves. The latter were known to commit murder on orders of these owners. White persons were fearful of being targets of their assassinations and were also known to have kept tribesmen at enmity so as to consume their time and emotions. Roderick Finlayson, "The History of Vancouver Island and the Northwest Coast." Ms. P-C 15.
[90]Slacum, *Memorial,* 6.

of slavery was "the greatest test of the progressive advancement of civilization." This was an obvious indictment of the
uncivility of Americans still practicing it. He concluded that

> if anything could reconcile us to the prospect of war with the Unit-
> ed States to determine the disputed possession of this territory, it
> would only be hopeful consideration, that this mighty empire
> would, when once armed and in the field, and on the waves, and
> arrayed with the awful attributes of an avenging Nemesis, never
> consent to withdraw her overwhelming energies until, as a condi-
> tion for her acceptance of the submissively-tendered palm and
> olive, the total abrogation and abolition of slavery in the States,
> where the lustre of the starred standard is dimmed by its red
> stripes.[91]

Natalli's sword-rattling words were laid to rest when fur sales
fell off in the European marketplace where the well-known
beaver hat went out of style, weakening the Company position in the region as had the boundary settlement.

Important changes also occurred in the Indian community
due to such catastrophes as the intermittent fever which
broke out in 1830, further disrupting fur gathering and missionary activity. One victim of its ravages was the slave-holding Comcomly, whose head was carted off to England for
phrenological studies.[92] When his granddaughter succumbed the year prior to the onset of the fever, her mother
killed two slaves to attend her to the spirit world.[93] Nowhere
did the fever strike harder than in Casino's homelands. No
longer could he muster numerous slaves and warriors to do
his bidding as before the plague. Possibly he treated his
remaining slaves more humanely to placate Company officials so he could remain in their good graces. In the latter
days of the trade he was hardly noticed eating free meals in
the Fort Vancouver dining hall. His glory days were over.

American governmental involvement in Pacific Northwestern white and Indian affairs was slowed not only by the

---

[91]Nattali, *The Oregon Territory*, 52.

[92]For an account of "The Saga of the Skull," see Ruby and Brown, *The Chinook Indians*, 195-96.

[93]Samuel Parker, *Journal of an Exploring Tour Beyond the Rocky Mountains*, 251.

tardily established international boundary, but by its involvement in the Mexican War which broke out in 1845. With the end of the war and establishment of the Oregon Territory in 1848, government officials became more deeply involved in area Indian affairs. A case in point had its beginnings on southern Puget Sound on May 1, 1849, when a number of Coast Salish Snoqualmie, Snohomish and Skykomish Indians descended on Fort Nisqually where the Company operated its Puget Sound Agricultural Company subsidiary and fur post. Under Chief Patkanin the Indians had come to avenge beatings which a Nisqually, Lachalet, had administered to his Snoqualmie wife. Some fur officials believed the Indians had come to fight the Nisquallys to enslave them, intending to start a fracas on pretense of punishing Lachalet. Patkanin was barely admitted to the fort grounds when his brother Kussas readied an assault on the post. A gunshot which wounded a fort guard precipitated a melee in which an American, Leander Wallace, and a Skykomish shaman were killed. Two Snoqualmies were wounded and Patkanin slipped away.

Newly appointed United States subagent for Oregon Territory J. Quinn Thornton visited the troubled area. On July 7 he notified Oregon Territorial Governor Joseph Lane that he was authorizing eighty blankets as a reward for delivering the offenders to Capt. Bennett Hill within three weeks. This ran counter to plans of Lane who had authorized no reward, but had planned to dispatch troops to the Sound in a show of force to bring about the surrender of the guilty. Lane believed that offering rewards to the Indians would induce them to murder other Americans, then await offers of larger rewards for apprehending the murderers after which they would deliver up some of their slaves so as to receive "ten times the amount that they would otherwise get for them."[94] At the same time Lane reasoned that such governmental rewards would cause the Indians to underrate American military

---

[94]Evans, *History of the Pacific Northwest: Oregon and Washington* 1, p. 308.

power. The episode had at least one positive result; it gave Thornton a strong platform from which to urge Indians from the Columbia to the Fraser River to abolish slavery. In his words "some of them consented to do so."[95] Subsequent events would prove that Patkanin at least had no idea of doing so. Six of those deemed guilty in Wallace's murder were brought before a judge at nearby Fort Steilacoom where a jury found two of them, Kussas and Quallahwout, guilty of murder. In October they were hanged, the first such "legal" hanging on Puget Sound. Four were exonerated, including Sterhawai, an innocent slave whom they hoped to substitute for the guilty in keeping with their traditional practice.[96]

Oregon Superintendent of Indian Affairs Anson Dart, who had effected treaties with southwestern Oregon tribes in the 1850s, continued treaty-making in early August 1851 with those in portions of northern Oregon along the Columbia River at places such as Tansey Point (near present-day Astoria, Oregon). Before the Indians would consent to treaty-making they demanded that George Washington Hall, a surveyor and free-wheeling frontiersman, be removed from their country. They objected to his presence because, in their thinking, his marriage to an Indian slave had made him a person of low estate since only slaves, who were non-persons, or property, married slaves. They were also angry that Hall had confiscated good lands in the middle of the main Chinook village near what would later become the town of Chinook, Washington. Consequently, they refused to sign any treaty with Dart until it was stipulated that Hall be removed from the area. Since the treaty remained unratified, he stayed on, but died a pauper.

---

[95]Owen Thornton, Second Subagent, Oregon Terr. to Lane, September 6, 1849. *Records of the Oregon Superintendency of Indian Affairs, Letter Book A:10.*

[96]Ruby and Brown, *Indians of the Pacific Northwest,* 123. In a letter to Makah agent, Henry A. Webster, March 31, 1863, James Swan stated that the Makahs said they would retaliate against white men by sending their slaves to kill the whites for bringing sickness among them should any of their people die and then, should white men come to retaliate against them, they would set their slaves to killing them and then deliver up these slaves, thus freeing themselves. *Records of the Washington Superintendency of Indian Affairs, 1853-1874, No. 5, Roll 14.*

None of the Oregon treaties contained provisions banning slavery. The severe decline in Indian numbers at that time may have accounted for that absence and a general failure on the part of the government to take action against it. The decline of the Chinooks was noted by Dart, who wrote that "as late as the year 1820 this point [the Chinook country] was the rendezvous of the most powerful Nation upon the Pacific Coast; now wasted to a few over three hundred souls."[97]

Down in the Rogue River country of southwestern Oregon Indian-white relations, smoldering since the 1840s, erupted in war in the early 1850s. In that conflict a white man, Mr. Bozaet, removed a bullet from an Indian lad. His motives were not entirely humanitarian since he planned to sell this youth when he returned to Missouri, then a slave state under terms of the Missouri Compromise of 1820. This was unlike the situation in the Oregon Territory for which the president on August 14, 1848, signed a bill excluding Negro, but not, Indian slavery. Another Missourian and one-time special Indian agent in Washington Territory, Sidney S. Ford, traded a pony for a Chehalis Indian slave (whose gender was not revealed in a newspaper account of the transaction) whose master had died. Saving the slave from possible death at the demise of this master, Ford held his human possession for two or three years before releasing him.[98]

Governor Lane so impressed Rogue River Chief Apserkahar, in the southern Oregon theater of conflict, that he presented Lane a Modoc slave boy. As chief, Apserkahar sought Lane's permission to assume his (Lane's) first name.[99] It was more difficult for Lane to present to the Indians those things for which they had greater need. His gratuities were thus confined to sympathetic words for these peoples held in virtual bondage to an alien culture. In his words the white man's

---

[97]C.F. Coan, "The First Stage of the Federal Indian Policy in the Pacific Northwest, 1849-1852," pp. 69, 70, 76.

[98]The Missourians' involvement in slavery is found in T.W. Davenport, "Slavery Question in Oregon," 258, and in *The Nugget*, November 14, 1885, p. 3.

[99]Ruby and Brown, *Indians of the Pacific Northwest*, 109.

"arts of civilization" had doomed them to "poverty want and crime." His statement that they would be better served by removing to "a district remote from settlement" offered them little consolation.[100]

One such place removed from settlement, but where Indians might have suffered enslavement, was along a north-south trading complex—the wild stretch of coast between the mouth of the Columbia River and northward to where the Strait of Juan de Fuca meets the Pacific.

---

[100]Johansen and Gates, *Empire of the Columbia*, 251.

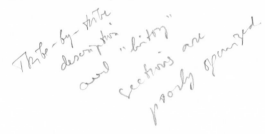

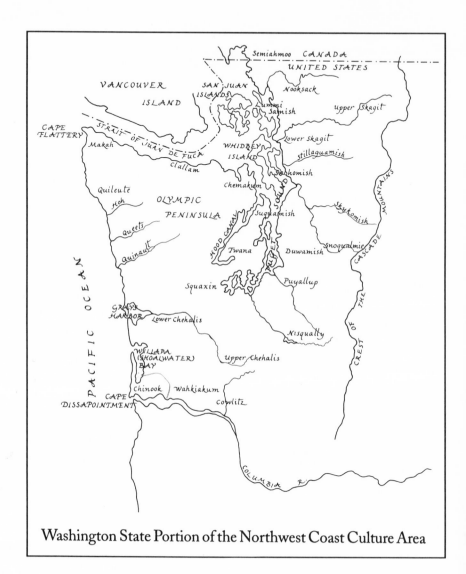

Washington State Portion of the Northwest Coast Culture Area

4

Coast Salish-Chinook:
Disappointment to Flattery

An extensive slave traffic developed between Chinooks and natives to their north. A main overland route extended between Puget Sound and down the Cowlitz River corridor where Interstate Highway 5 runs today. Not to be overlooked was the coastal route along the Washington shore, where tribes relayed slaves in trade from one tribe to another, and these human cargoes were moved along with Euro-American wares between the Strait of Juan de Fuca and the Columbia River.

Between capes Disappointment and Flattery on the coast of Washington lived tribes of differing linguistic families. The diversity of their languages did not prevent slaveholding and slave-trading among them. As elsewhere along Pacific Northwestern coasts societies in this region evidenced three basic classes: aristocrats, commoners and slaves—a spectrum based on wealth at one extreme and on purchase or capture of the other.[1] Despite their diversity the combined classes formed autonomous local cell-like village units whose nuclear head men dominated them by their prestige, personality and property. The social unit between the capes, although less strong than that of the Northern Indians, was marked by strong village autonomy similar to natives of Puget Sound to the east. The lands and waters provided subsistence with only modest labor on their part. The abundance and availability of natural resources contributed to the stratification of their society, enabling upper class persons to accumulate slaves and other properties. Governor Simpson had these and the Northern Indians in mind when he observed

---

[1] Gunther, "The Indian Background of Washington History," 198.

that "Slaves form the principal article of traffick on the whole
of this Coast and constitute the greater part of their Riches…"[2] By contrast, climate and topography were more beneficent to these coastal groups than to dwellers of the Plateau.
The latter had to travel widely to secure subsistence, and
their lessened leisure helped force on them a less structured
society. Their slave-holding proved as much hindrance as
help.

Some villages between the capes, like others of the coast,
were homogeneous and geographically compact. Status in
their ranking system was more social than strictly political.
The word "chief" conjures up images of strong inter-tribal
leaders, when in fact these chiefs stood mostly at the head of
village groups. In his *The Oregon Territory* (1846), Nattali
wrote that "He also who exceeds his neighbors in the number
of his wives, male children, and slaves, is elected chief of the
village."[3] The chieftaincy was not solely a masculine position,
for females of strong will and character also composed chiefly
ranks. Many of them were slaveholders. In the 1850s George
Gibbs observed that Pacific Northwestern Indian women
assented and dissented in tribal deliberations.[4] After Chinook chief Chenamus died, his widow, Sally, enjoyed great
authority among Indians as well as immunity from whites.
Gibbs observed one whom he called "The queen, an old lady
of the Tsihalis [Chehalis] who patronized Lieutenant
Wilkes's party in 1841, yet rules her neighborhood with
undisputed sway…"[5]

Edward Curtis, who observed the Indians in the twentieth
century, found those between the capes "vindictive, bloodthirsty, cruel and avaricious," withal "neither brave nor especially crafty," but paradoxically generally treating their
war-captured slaves in a kindly manner. Despite this assess-

---

[2]Merk, *Fur Trade and Empire*, 101.   [3]Nattali, *The Oregon Territory*, 51.
[4]Gibbs, *Tribes of Western Washington and Northwestern Oregon* 1, Pt. 2, p. 185.
[5]Ibid.

ment, the slaves suffered punishment and subjection to ridicule of free persons who sheared slave heads to symbolize their non-person status. James Swan, a white settler among these peoples near mid-19th century, corroborated Curtis' observations, writing that for the most part that slaves there were "well treated, and, but for the fact that they can be bought and sold, appear to be on terms of equality with their owners, although there are instances where they have received rather harsh usage."[6]

The slave trade paralleled trade in other sought-after items, such as canoes manufactured in the north. They were moved south along the open coast of Washington State and traded for slaves which were moved north. The reverse flow of slaves, from north to south, came with contact, and when there developed a market for slaves of northern origin in the southern area under consideration. The primary bilateral movement of slaves following contact was the Puget Sound-Cowlitz-Columbia trough with its extension south to tie up with the Willamette slave route. Today Interstate 5 traverses this route, which is also a railway corridor. This route shortened the distance from The Dalles to the north.

Besides acquiring slaves by trading, Quinaults, and Quileutes also between the capes, obtained slaves by the twin tactics of surprise and ambush. These forays were conducted in large war canoes which came to them through intertribal trade from their mostly Nootkan place of manufacture. Their short forays often resulted in violent confrontations after which their superb ocean-going craft transported captor and captive alike to the victors' villages. Tribes between the capes sometimes collected human heads on raids. These were for ostentatious displays of vanity and vengeance, but not used to the extent of that of natives of the Strait of Juan de Fuca (including the Makahs whose lands bordered both ocean and strait), Puget Sound and northward along the west shores of

---

[6]Curtis, *The North American Indian* 9, p. 158; Swan, *The Indians of Cape Flattery*, 10.

Vancouver Island and the British Columbia mainland. Live human booty served captor-owners both economically and socially as reported by Royal Engineers Lieutenants H.J. Warre and M. Vavasour on their "secret mission" to the Oregon country in 1845. They observed that "...he who possesses the most slaves...is considered the greatest chief."[7]

Although slavery flourished among natives prior to white contact, it was more intense during the first four post-white contact decades of the 19th century. Tribal economies changed during that period as white merchants appeared along the coast in increasing numbers, especially in the forepart of the century. Initially their Euro-American goods created insatiable native appetites for trinkets, but later on, for items of personal adornment, foods, clothing, weapons and metals exchanged for furs. In pre-contact times standard items which natives exchanged included slaves, but the increase in imported goods enabled them to purchase even more slaves than previously.

Slavery slackened after the mid-19th century treaties with the United States. Agents kept watchful eyes on the tribes, considerably denting the practice. Slavery also fell off as white settlement increased. Changing trade patterns enabled poor commoners to join the ranks of the nouveau riches. As these new wealthy rose to prominence, former wealthy families went into decline since their means of accumulating wealth declined, making their commerce in slaves unprofitable, impractical and outmoded. Furthermore, rituals of secret societies such as the Black Face Society of the Quinaults were coming under government surveillance and censure. This society's ritual involved initiates who, after freeing themselves from self-imposed starvation, tore dogs apart and ate them in orgiastic frenzy. Ridicule of the initiates was not allowed. The Reverend Myron Eells related how on one occasion two slaves of the Twanas east of the capes on Hood Canal, an appendage of the Strait of Juan de Fuca, were torn

---

[7]R.M. Martin, *The Hudson's Bay Territories and Vancouver's Island*, 83.

to pieces and "eaten" by black face performers for laughing at one of their ceremonials.[8]

Throughout time war captives have been enslaved and performed gainful work for their captors. Slaves of indigenous Northwest (Pacific) Coastal natives were more likely fixtures for the wealthy, rather than mere workers, serving to validate and substantiate their masters' wealth in wasteful and extravagant displays. Anthropologist Joseph Jorgensen states that Indian slaves worked like others, meaning that by doing their part they existed without special effort to produce income for their masters, often assisting or providing comfort for them and their households.[9] Wrote Jorgensen: "Whereas slaves usually worked like everyone else, in some societies they were more ornamental than productive. The burdensome slave was a testimony to the owners' wealth and enhanced his prestige."[10] The exception were female slaves put to work by masters to prostitute for income. Increasingly this may have been done for subsistence and survival, since traditional methods of obtaining a livelihood were being taken from the natives with the increasing presence of whites. Free women were likewise caught in this need to submit to prostitution with the changing economy.

Prior to white settlement on Vancouver Island, male slaves, rarely acquired from raidings, were preferred, but after white settlement women were preferred because of their use in and income from prostitution. Such preference was reflected in higher prices for female slaves. Increasing presence of whites promoted this use of women slaves. At more remote areas such as northern Vancouver Island, distant from white populations, thirty blankets purchased a female slave. But at the same time, sixty blankets were required for the same purchase at more populous places such as Victoria on the southern end of the island.[11] As for slaves at either end of

---

[8]George Pierre Castille, *The Indians of Puget Sound: The Notebooks of Myron Eells*, 404.
[9]Joseph G. Jorgensen, *Western Indians*, 247.
[10]Ibid.
[11]Gilbert Malcolm Sproat, *Scenes and Studies of Savage Life*, 92.

the cape complex, there were reports of their being used for heavy and difficult tasks only among one group, the Chinooks.[12] Among Makahs, James Swan reported slaves at Cape Flattery as having performed the same tasks as others, making rugs and baskets and cleaning fish. Averkieva pointed out that such rug and basket-making among Makahs was an exception, since these crafts were performed by free women, just as whaling was performed by free men.[13] Peter Farb states that slaves' work had been no more than menial.[14]

In performing some of their tasks, slaves prevented death or injury to masters. One way they rendered this kind of service was to function like cupbearers of ancient kings, sampling foods for their edibility and possible poisoning. Poisoning food was a not uncommon way of disposing of rivals in that highly competitive coastal country. Slaves also went before masters when traveling, like hunting dogs sniffing out potential trouble. When first visited by unfamiliar vessels, tribes holding slaves sent them to ascertain the friendliness or hostility of the visitors. For example, when a strange ship appeared in Neah Bay at the confluence of the Strait of Juan de Fuca and the Pacific Ocean, an elderly slave of a Makah chief was forced to approach the ship to test the disposition of her crew. The alternative to this perilous assignment was death. When the slave returned with previously unseen objects given him by the mariners, he was offered his freedom for a knife. He refused to make the exchange preferring slavery to parting with his treasure. Nevertheless, the knife found its way into the hands of the chief who would not part with it.[15] In those northerly quarters were slaves not to return from dangerous missions their masters would have grieved but little for their loss, despite the

[12]Michael Silverstein, "Chinookans of the Lower Columbia," In Wayne Suttles, ed., *Handbook of North American Indians Northwest Coast* 7, p. 542.

[13]Swan, *The Indians of Cape Flattery*, 11; Averkieva, *Slavery Among the Indians of North America*, 67.

[14]Farb, *Man's Rise to Civilization as Shown by the Indians of North America*, 141.

[15]Samuel Hancock, "Journal Whidbey Island, W.T. February 17, 1860." Typescript copy of ms.

fact that these servile ones might have saved their masters lives.[16] In the manner of those who would have killed for the likes of Comcomly and Casino, others of this slave class between the capes were important protectors in that area where intrigue and murder were common. Masters on raids often depended on slaves to guide them through various waterways with which the slaves were familiar, leading finally to former homes of these servile ones.

As whaling among Makahs and Quileutes was the work of professional freemen using special spiritual gifts, so were house and canoe-building the province of those with special spirit powers. Slaves were used only in supporting tasks such as cutting and hauling trees, tasks which required no special spirit powers. Slaves also carried trophies of the hunt, but were usually not taken along on whaling expeditions where spirit powers were called upon to assure success in that dangerous venture. There were exceptions, such as the slave of Hoh ancestry who became so successful at whaling and sea otter hunting among Quinaults that he became known as "slave chief."[17]

Spirit powers which helped Quinaults and their neighbors in hunting, in house building and other subsistence tasks qualified them to provide for not only the living, but for the dead. The Quinault practice of laying bodies out for viewing appears to have been unique among area tribes. At white contact their custom was to place corpses in large covered canoes atop posts and poles. When prominent leaders or their children died, one or more slaves were killed and placed in canoes with them. There were instances of live slave burials amongst them.[18] Non-slaves, on the other hand, were respected in death and even bones from their rotting flesh, in

[16]Slaves were sent by their owners to kill even those who were only obnoxious to the owners. Poisoning was a common method of homicide. Elizabeth Colson, *The Makah Indians: A Study of an American Society*, 226-27. Later on, Indians were able to purchase poisons from white men's stores.

[17]Ronald L. Olson, *The Quinault Indians and Adze, Canoe, and House Types of the Northwest Coast*, 95.

[18]Curtis, *The North American Indian* 9, p. 87.

about two years, were interred in village cemeteries. After 1880 bodies were interred in death houses, as were those of free Twanas to the east across the Olympic Mountains. Slaves had no part in funerary transactions involving non-slaves. Only slaves handled dead slave bodies, which were cast out without benefit of burial.

The Quinaults believed that souls of deceased slaves went to the land of the dead to serve their masters, just as they had on earth. Slaves did have the dubious privilege of dispatching enemies to the hereafter on orders of their lord lieges. Were slaves themselves killed, their murderers paid owners equivalent sums in money or slaves. Were freemen murdered, the payment of the blood-feud price could be as many as three slaves.[19] When masters died, their surviving sons received their divided properties, although many worldly goods were burned up on their deaths. Only before masters died could they bequeath spiritual "properties" such as songs and guardian spirits.

Indians between the capes were shrewd negotiators, paying more for slaves with talent and ability than for those lacking such qualities. The Quinault system of bondage was less rigid than that of some tribes, for their slaves could purchase freedom with accumulated properties, usually furs.[20] Slaves accumulated from nearby tribes could be ransomed by relatives for up to three times their purchase price.[21] Unlike slaves of other tribes, Quinault slaves were acquired from nearby peoples to which they could more easily escape than those taken at greater distances. This might help explain the certain liberalities which were extended to them, such as permission to keep gambling winnings, join potlatches although receiving no gifts, and marry other slaves within the tribe.[22] This departure from orthodoxy was mitigated in other ways; offspring of slave mothers married to free males could not

[19]Olson, *The Quinault Indians*, 116.
[20]Underhill, *Indians of the Pacific Northwest*, 161.
[21]Olson, *The Quinault Indians*, 97.
[22]Ibid., 128.

have the aristocratic badge of flattened heads, a restriction also placed on children of ne'er-do-well freemen. In the heyday of Quinault slavery wealthy males possessed as many as twelve slaves. One Quinault was reported as having owned thirty slaves, but in 1910 only two slaves remained among the tribe.[23]

Slaves were involved in intertribal affairs between the capes as they were among other tribes. Their status appeared to have improved as their place in storytelling moved from the real to the mythical world. The following legend involving not only intrigue, but murder, reveals their role in love affairs. Although most native legendry was mythical, the following abbreviated account may have been based on more truth than fiction: A worthless young fellow fell in love with the daughter of a Quinault chief, whose female slave told him of the girl's intent to elope with the fellow. The chief's slave persuaded her not to go with him, but the suitor continued to haunt the village. In the spring a Makah chief took her away, giving her parents four ocean canoes, five slaves and a quantity of dentalia. In return, her father gave considerable property including three slaves who were to be her servants. When she returned home to prepare for the birth of a child, her former suitor returned. In a fight she persuaded her mother to return with her to Neah Bay. Along the way the suitor "shot" his "power" into her which resulted in her death after delivering a stillborn child. The suitor fled southward to Grays Harbor to which place the chieftain father sent two slaves to kill him. They stabbed him in the abdomen, but he rose up because of his great "power." One of the slaves then stabbed him in the back and the two returned to the chieftain father to tell him what they had done.[24]

The Quileutes, occupying an intermediary position between Quinaults and Makahs, logically traded with both, but in typical Pacific Northwestern Indian fashion, also con-

[23]Ibid., 98, 131.
[24]Olson, *The Quinault Indians*, 110.

tested with them. From Makahs the Quileutes took prisoners which they then traded to Hohs to their immediate south. The Hohs, in turn, traded them to the Queets, Quinault, Humptulip and Hoquiam Indians. These, in turn, traded them to Chinooks for trans-shipping to more southerly and inland tribes.[25] Fighting in canoes, the Quileutes gained prestige by capturing slaves, a measure of their wealth as well as of their fighting abilities. According to one Quileute source, they most frequently warred against Makahs. A late 19th century Quileute informant told how in early times his ancestors, then occupying James Island off the coast, drove off Makahs with guns and bows, sweeping down on them in a fifty-three-canoe flotilla. Before retreating, however, the Makahs severed the heads of wounded Quileutes to take home as trophies.[26] Also in the "long ago," Quileutes reportedly killed or captured entire Clallam villages when apparently seeking revenge more than captives.[27] They also canoed north to Vancouver Island to fight its natives, and south to Grays Harbor for the same purpose.[28] Long after such warrings ceased, subtle conflict, fueled by a lingering upper class mentality, stigmatized descendants of slaves captured in such engagements.[29]

Like their neighbors, the Quileutes owed much of their transportability to Nootkas, the prime canoe makers of the coast. They sometimes acquired Haida craft, some sixty-feet-long and six and a half-feet-wide, to accommodate up to a hundred persons. Exteriors of better canoes were carved and painted and gunwales inlaid with otter teeth.[30] In Nootkan canoes the Makahs carried slaves, dried halibut pieces and eulachon oil from Tsimshians at Nass River. Further south in Canada, the Makahs, from raiding Comox and

[25]Curtis, *The North American Indian* 9, p. 75.
[26]George A. Pettitt, *The Quileute of La Push, 1775-1945*, p. 14; Willie Wilder to Mrs. H.S. Pullen, December 19, 1896. A. Wesley Smith Papers. *Neah Bay Indian Agency, 1876-1909*, Mf1.
[27]Albert B. Reagan, "Traditions of the Hoh and Quillayute Indians," 181-82.
[28]Pettitt, *The Quileute of La Push, 1775-1945*, p. 14.
[29]Ibid., 84.
[30]Bancroft, *Wild Tribes*, 166.

Nitinaht Nootkas, carried off slaves which they sold to tribes along the coast to their south.[31] Since Makahs lived along both ocean and strait, their slavery is further discussed in a subsequent chapter.

In an attack on Vancouver Island the Quileutes were said to have killed half a Nootkan village, preventing the other half from escaping by taking them captive and appropriating their canoes.[32] As late at 1866, American soldiers, dispatched to apprehend a Quileute for murder, arrested tribal members for trafficking in slaves.[33] Formerly their raidings had taken them to Chinook and Clatsop villages under guidance of slaves of Chinook origin who knew the way through the bars and shoals of Willapa Bay and the Columbia River.[34] On one such raid they were guided by a slave who led them against his former village at the mouth of the Columbia River. There he mingled undetected among his former people, returning at night to the waiting Quileutes with intelligence of the village. Thus informed, they brought their canoes ashore and sneaked upon their human quarry, clubbing many to death. The raid was pyrrhic, since once aroused the Chinooks killed many of their attackers.[35]

On a raid against Quileutes their Satsop neighbors to their south were repulsed, losing a warrior to an arrow in the windpipe. The Quileutes fought them all the way down to Grays Harbor where the Satsops were reinforced by their Chinook allies. The Quileutes lost some of their warriors when their canoes stuck in mud flats, but would have lost more had the tide not come in to refloat their craft. Both sides suffered losses since no trees or brush covered their tidal battlefield. The Quileutes managed to return home to display the heads of several victims who suffered death rather than capture as slaves.[36] On another occasion the Satsops canoed down the Chehalis River where they attacked Lower Chehalis vil-

---

[31]Scouler, "Dr. John Scouler's Journal of a Voyage to N.W. America," Pt. 2, p. 195.
[32]Reagan, "Traditions of the Hoh and Quillayute Indians," 181.
[33]Ruby and Brown, *A Guide to the Indian Tribes of the Pacific Northwest*, 172.
[34]Ruby and Brown, *The Chinook Indians*, 136.
[35]Reagan, "Traditions of the Hoh and Quillayute Indians," 183.
[36]Harry Hobucket, "Quillayute Indian Tradition," 53.

lagers, putting adrift their infants in cradleboards and killing the elderly, taking children and young women as slaves. A year later the Chehalis and tribes allied to them retaliated by having one of their own who had been enslaved by the Satsops, with help from other Satsop slaves, slash the Satsops, bowstrings, thus allowing the Chehalis and their allied attackers to move in for a greater slaughter. In the attack they thrust stakes into bodies of enemy children and then set them afire. Before the attack was over many young Satsop women were captured and enslaved.[37]

The Queets Indians to the south of the Quileutes were said to have invaded the Quinaults. The Quinaults pursued them to their home villages, burning houses before returning to their own villages with captured slaves and head trophies which they lofted to pole tops for all to see.[38] On one occasion an "outlaw" band of Quinaults went berrypicking in the Olympic Mountains, an unlikely place to capture slaves. There they stumbled onto some Skokomish (Twana) Indians entering the mountains from the east. Since the Skokomish men were off hunting, the Quinaults captured their women and set out for home with them. Along the way the captives tore bits of clothing to mark the route of their captivity. Their men later discovered and followed these clues. Then, in an ensuing nighttime skirmish, the Quinaults attacked and killed these pursuers. Returning to their camp they mutilated their victims, placing their heads atop poles after having strung enemy intestines along the way. Along that route they named various places where they dismembered their victims.[39]

Despite such encounters one anthropologist suggests that most Quinaults, being peacefully disposed, did not raid for slaves, and attributes their posture to lack of tribal solidarity due to the scattered location of their villages.[40] They did

[37]Curtis, *The North American Indian* 9, p. 8.
[38]Ibid., 11.
[39]Olson, *The Quinault Indians*, 119.
[40]Ibid., 11.

trade items as varied as slaves and bear grass to the south. One time during the fur trade era they stopped two nights along the way south, arriving the third day in Clatsop country inside the Columbia bar at Youngs Bay, on the left bank of the river.[41] This was a rendezvous for northern traders because of its nearness to trading posts of Astorians, Nor'Westers and men of the Hudson's Bay Company.

Fur posts established along the Pacific Coast by Americans, British and Russians were sources of items of foreign manufacture much desired by natives. These wares found their way into the trading system increasing its intensity, especially of slaves which became the prime commodity of trade. There developed direct links of Indians in the North with those in the South through intermediaries which created a flourishing business for natives until its demise began at mid-19th century.

---

[41]Curtis, *The North American Indian* 9, p. 11.

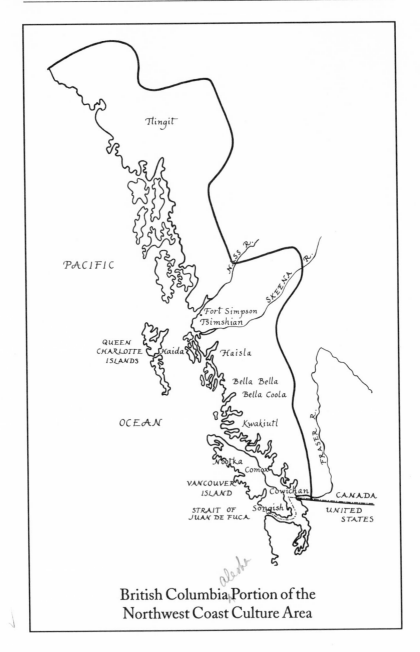

Tlingit

PACIFIC

NASS R.

SKEENA R.

Fort Simpson
Tsimshian

QUEEN
CHARLOTTE
ISLANDS

Haida

Haisla

Bella Bella
Bella Coola

FRASER R.

OCEAN

Kwakiutl

Nootka
Comox

VANCOUVER
ISLAND

Cowichan

CANADA

STRAIT OF
JUAN DE FUCA

Songish

UNITED
STATES

British Columbia Portion of the
Northwest Coast Culture Area

5

The Northern Slave Cluster and Wakashan Speakers

This slave cluster was located in the northernmost zone of the Northwest Coast cultural area. Here four linguistic families lived in economic abundance, and their surplus products available for trade made them wealthy. Such affluence helped separate people into aristocratic and poorer classes. These tribesmen raided those to their south for captives in which milieu slavery developed. The dehumanization of the captives reduced them to chattel within an elaborate institutional structure. The most extreme form of wealth display was the destruction of property, by which a rich man could destroy his own accumulation. The killing of slaves was the ultimate in this behavior. That cannibalism occurred among these speakers has been viewed with some reticence by certain scholars, despite many reports of it. Slaves, the object of this practice, became a commodity of great value extending even further southward in which more distant tribes were tapped.

Anthropologist Philip Drucker describes peoples of the Northern cultural zone of the Pacific Northwest Coast as occupying an "anomalous position in the broad over all pattern of native American civilizations," since it was "an area of advanced cultures with highly elaborate technologies and intricate social and ceremonial systems..."[1] Its native peoples: Tlingits, Haidas, Tsimshians, and Haislas (formerly, the Northern Kwakiutls) were composed of matrilinear family clans which believed they descended in common from a legendary or mythological ancestry of ranked nobility which

---

[1]Drucker, "Sources of Northwest Coast Culture," 59-60.

adhered to strict social behavior. Their culture of abundance produced wealth for this elitist group prior to the indigenous inception of slavery among them. As noted, this inception and times thereof are shrouded in mystery despite Averkieva's assessment that slavery existed among them from the 9th to the 10th centuries.

The Wakashan zone to the south was composed of bilateral kinship families, like others of the Northwest Coast culture area except Athapaskan speakers of patrilineal descent to the south along the Oregon coast. Except for the Salish Bella Coolas, tribes of the Wakashan zone spoke the Wakashan language. Originally these speakers provided a pool from which Northern raiders acquired captives to enslave. Kwakiutls of the Wakashan zone originated such complex ceremonials as the Winter and Cannibal dances and the wealth-exhibiting potlatch, ceremonials which were borrowed by the Northern Indians. In time, Wakashans borrowed elements of the Northern Indians' clan and ranking systems.

In the northern non-agrarian society, whose wealth came primarily from sea and forest, slaves were sustained by the same life-giving elements of their masters. Being primarily non-producers, the cost of slave maintenance outweighed the value of their contributions.[2] It stands to reason that with ongoing raidings, at some point they would have become surplus, causing their masters to give them away at potlatches or in some cases destroy them, or keep them to amuse masters and families. Whether in destroying or in such largess, the masters were consequently able to demonstrate their lofty positions.

In time, the prosperity of extravagance which was nourished by the acquisition of slaves from Wakashans and later from Coast Salish peoples, caused the owners to seek captives by trade from other native groups rather than by raids. This in turn caused a demand for slaves, creating the tribal

[2]Averkieva, *Slavery Among the Indians of North America*, 36; Wayne Suttles and Aldona Jonaitis, "History of Research in Ethnology." In Wayne Suttles, ed., *Handbook of North American Indians Northwest Coast* 7, p. 87.

relay of human chattel from south to north. Should future archaeologists confirm this development, then it may be supposed that slavery originated or most likely occurred following the introduction of gift giving potlatches among the Northern tribes. It is believed that slavery originated in a war captive economy and a corresponding rise in accumulation of private property.[3] This being the case, then an abundance of non-productive war captives in Northern native society would have been an economic burden for their masters. What resulted was a method of disposing of slaves, enhancing the owners' prestige and reputation. In time the demand for slaves to support these displays of wealth outdistanced what the Northern tribes could acquire on their own. Thus, these owners began trading with tribes to the south for captives.

Eventually this trade in human flesh and blood expanded as far south as the lower Columbia River, thus creating the south-north flow to satisfy demands of the Northerners. When trade intensified with the introduction of Euro-American products, tribes between the Northerners and those of the Columbia River began practicing slavery as well as trading in human products in what became a bilateral movement of slaves. The southern extent of Northerner raiding was the southern reaches of Puget Sound. Wakashans raided across the Strait of Juan de Fuca and occasionally along northwestern shores of Washington.

Northern Indians acquired slaves in a milieu of violence. Traversing sheltered sea passages in superbly crafted canoes, they moved swiftly to villages targeted for raiding. Meticulous preparation for such raids was found in the area. Among the Queen Charlotte Islands Haidas, writes John R. Swanton, the wife of each warrior "made two belts out of whale sinew,—first one for her husband, then one for herself." On the back of each belt was worked a human figure representing the spirit of slaves whom the warrior was supposed to

---

[3] Igor Kopytoff, "Slavery," 209.

capture. Following such raids the belts were removed. Before raids, wives slept in one house, their heads in the direction their husbands had taken. Wives also made mock raids simulating the taking of slaves, using their own children to guarantee success for their husbands. Failure brought disgrace among these male raiders.[4]

Even further north of the Haidas were the Tlingits who raided southerly places for heads of male captives, and women and children doomed to enslavement. Typical of the violence attending such excursions and incursions were males who drank the blood of severed male heads. Female captives not enslaved were killed, but not beheaded.[5]

Described by pioneer Charles Prosch as "physically superior" to natives as far south as Puget Sound, these Northern Indians swept down ocean, strait and sound in canoes carrying from twenty to forty "savages," traveling faster than steamers into waters where such white men's craft could not go. They continued raiding in Puget Sound even after early white settlement. Several settlers' parties, disappearing without a trace in small boats on the Sound, were believed to have met their fate at the hands of the marauders.[6]

Among the objects of Northern raiders were Nootkas, who might have conducted retaliatory raids more frequently but feared to do so thinking they might be enslaved by the Northerners. Trader John Meares, who visited the Nootkas in 1788, wrote that they "...must live in constant expectation of an enemy, and never relax from that continual preparation against these hostilities and incursions which doom the captives to slavery or death." Such fears still had not abated four decades later with the advent of fur posts in the north when tribes such as Tsimshians, middlemen in the north-south slave trade, sought to exchange slaves for furs to sell at fur posts, prompting their continued raids against Nootkas. Fear

[4]John R. Swanton, *Contributions to the Ethnology of the Haida*, Memoirs of the American Museum of Natural History 8, pt. 1, p. 55.

[5]Homer G. Barnett, *The Coast Salish of British Columbia*, 268-69.

[6]Charles Prosch, *Reminiscences of Washington Territory Scenes, Incidents and Reflections of the Pioneer Period on Puget Sound*, 39.

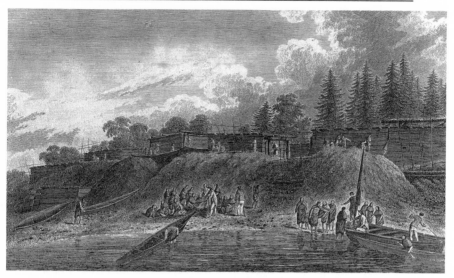

Nootka Sound, on the northwestern coast of Vancouver Island, was an important outfitting place for British, Spanish and American mariners. It was the
home of the Nootkas and their notorious slave owner Chief Maquinna.
Courtesy Provincial Archives of British Columbia. Neg. #Pdp 237.

of capture and enslavement haunted Nootkan groups until
the latter part of the 19th century. Northern tribesmen were
known to have enslaved peoples of their own Northern zone.
These people may have been subjected to a north-south slave
trade occasioned, as Bernard J. Siegel has pointed out, by the
presence of a strong clan system among such tribes as
Tsimshians whose prominent men would not keep clansmen
as slaves.[7]

Natives in the vicinity of Vancouver Island and the British
Columbia mainland did not escape retaliatory raids by tribes
to their south or those from the north. On one occasion Clallams canoed north across the Strait of Juan de Fuca to

[7]Meares, *An Introductory Narrative,* 267; Augustin Joseph Brabrant, *Vancouver Island
and Its Mission, 1874-1900,* p. 12; Sumner, *Folkways,* 270; Bernard J. Siegel, "Some
Methodological Considerations for a Comparative Study of Slavery," 366.

slaughter thirty Cowichans (of southwestern Vancouver Island), after which they carried home their victims' heads and an equal number of women and children to enslave.[8] In their new homes these thralls would have been exposed to the gruesome sight of their tribesmen's heads attached to poles in Clallam villages. The few adult male slaves found in villages of slave-raiding tribes were primarily captured children grown to manhood and thus less likely to escape. Full-grown males were seldom captured because of the difficulty of controlling them.

With few superiors in the practice of decapitations, Kwakiutls went slave-raiding well prepared with cedar withes which they called "slave ropes." With these they secured their victims' jaws. Kwakiutls were especially adept at encircling heads with single knife strokes without twisting them in the process. Cutting too closely to skulls left small patches of hair in contrast to slashes of less experienced head severers who cut too low on necks making heads difficult to detach. Paddling homeward displaying head trophies, they composed songs boasting of their deeds or reviling their foes. In their home villages they displayed their prizes in prominent places. Curtis states that Kwakiutls were unsuccessful on one raid, having taken no heads, but capturing a slave woman whom they killed and decapitated so as to have a head to exhibit.[9]

Averkieva speculates that the Kwakiutl term for "slave" indicates that tribe's military character with head cuttings and boastings. She writes that "whereas in the distant past an enemy taken prisoner had his head cut off because, as yet, there was no place in society for a slave, he later began to be inducted into Kwakiutl slavery..."[10] Once enslaved, these thralls served masters as symbols of wealth and objects of ostentatious display of power, since slave-killing gave owners much recognition among their peers. An oft-told story

[8]Curtis, *The North American Indian* 9, p. 22.
[9]Ibid., 10, pp. 100-101, 118.
[10]Averkieva, *Slavery Among the Indians of North America,* 80.

involved Kwakiutls who were said to have laid slave bodies out on a beach like so many goods at a marketplace to be used as "rollers" for canoes of visiting chiefs in order to impress them.[11]

White mariner-traders along the British Columbia coast in the latter 18th and 19th centuries had ample opportunity to observe slavery among its natives. We are indebted to close observers, especially Hudson's Bay Company personnel at Fort Simpson (1831 and 1834, the latter date indicating the removal of the initial fort from twenty miles inland of the mouth of Nass River to the northern end of the Tsimpsean Peninsula), Fort McLoughlin (1833) and Fort Taku (1840). In this vicinity lived Tsimshians, Tlingits, Haidas and Kwakiutls. Governor Simpson, for whom one of the posts was named, stated in an 1829 dispatch that the Northern Indians repeatedly took ships, killing and enslaving their crews. He noted that even the natives' improved relations with American traders, from whom they had obtained arms and ammunition, had not prevented these Americans from taking utmost precautions when dealing with them. In 1835 the Hudson's Bay Company trader, John Work, noted that Tsimshians from the Skeena River had brought skins to Fort Simpson to trade for liquor and other items, having procured at least some of their pelts from Tlingits at the Tongass in exchange for slaves. He also observed a Tsimshian canoe en route to the Tongass River carrying mostly slave children. These he described as being in a "wretched" state to be traded for skins. The incident provides a visible evidence of the nefarious link between liquor and slavery, especially since its passengers were in a drunken state.[12]

From Fort Simpson journals Donald Mitchell has reconstructed the malevolent link between the fur trade and slavery. These journals reveal that in late summer 1837 the Bay

---

[11]Drucker, *Indians of the Northwest Coast*, 123.

[12]Simpson, *Simpson's 1828 Journey to the Columbia*, 79; Dee, "The Journal of John Work, January to October, 1835," pp. 65, 69. Work wrote that Americans sold liquor cheaply to the Indians for furs. *Ibid.*

Company acquired an unusually short supply of furs from Kwakiutls at Nahwitti. They also reveal that the Nootkas were continuing to stand guard, afraid to hunt lest their villages be plundered and their people enslaved. The fort journal (August 11, 1837) records that Tsimshians from islands south of the Skeena River estuary had raided the Nootkas, killing their males and carrying off twenty women including a chief's wife, all of whom they enslaved. Five days later, Stikine Tlingits were observed leaving the fort to purchase the Nootka women from the Tsimshians. The wife of a Nootka chief begged in vain with fort personnel to rescue her. Two months later (October 18) Chief Sebassa (Sabassa, Shebases, Chebbaskah Tsibasa and the like), head of the Kitkatla group of Tsimshians appeared at the post with furs to sell. Sebassa was a ruthless leader who with his henchmen, known as the Sebassa men, were particularly feared by others in that area. In some respects he was like the Chinook Comcomly. Both men held powerful positions in the slave trade— Comcomly near the mouth of the Columbia and Sebassa, near the Nass River. Records of the Bay Company's Fort Simpson located near the latter stream describe him as an oppressor of natives of that area, and a "Tyrant" trading in furs and slaves, taking the latter "by stealth." Unable to cope with him, the records describe persons as being "under the necessity of submitting passively to his tyranny...," since many of them were slain by him and their women and children taken captive. According to John Work Tsimshians had acquired some furs from Stikine Tlingits which pelts they exchanged for slaves. Under Sebassa these Tsimshians completed a vicious cycle in which furs thus exchanged for slaves earned their overlord much wealth in goods, climaxed in potlatching which gave him prestige and status.

In 1837 one Hudson's Bay Company trader came across the daughter of a chief who had been enslaved and traded north to the trading center at Stikine River. There she was being taught to unload boxes from a canoe. According to the observer she "obviously was unaccustomed to such labour and still inept." In this respect she epitomized the plight of natives of high class who once had slaves to do their work but were performing such work themselves.[13]

Especially critical of Indian slavery among natives near Fort Taku, the Company's northernmost and shortest-lived post, was James Douglas, who on July 14, 1840, wrote:

> Slaves being through this national perversion of sentiment the most saleable commodity here, the native pedlars come from as far south as Kygarnie [on the southern end of Prince of Wales Island] with their human assortments and readily obtain from 18 to 20 skins a head for them. The greater number of these slaves are captives made in war and many predatory excursions are undertaken— not to avenge international aggression—but simply with a sordid view to the profits that may arise from the sale of captives taken.[14]

During his stay in the Taku area from June 24 to August 24, 1840, Douglas noted that the shrewd natives resisted Company attempts to raise the tariff by diverting their pelts from its fur market to their own slave market.[15] This made it all the more difficult for Company traders to comply with wishes of their London superiors to discourage slavery on humanitarian grounds. This may also have been one reason that Company men paid chiefs to free slaves from masters who might hire them to shoot and kill Company people. Ironically, the acquisition of Company goods helped provide chiefs additional wealth with which to purchase not only slaves, but liquor, guns and ammunition, all volatile ingredients in the trade. Equally ironic was the fact that although the Company tried to stop warfare and slavery, the raiding for, and trading

---

[13]Donald H. Mitchell, "Sebassa's Men," 82, 83; Mitchell, "Predatory Warfare, Social Status," 41; Kirk, *Tradition and Change on the Northwest Coast*, 44.

[14]Herman A. Leader, "Douglas Expeditions, 1840-41," p. 160.

[15]James Douglas wrote: "The Natives in this quarter hold a great many Slaves and set so high a value on them that they in a manner constitute the measure of wealth and rank in the Tribe. In consequence of this state of things, every attempt made on our part to raise the Tariff was unvariably resisted, and the Furs devoted by their owners to the purchase of slaves. This is an evil from which there is no present way to escape, as the detestable traffic in human beings, with its fearful train of guilt and wretchedness, will exist in unmitigated force as long as it proves a tempting source of profit to those engaged in it, and no means short of total revolution in the moral and social state of those Tribes will lead them to withhold the temptation." Ibid., 367.

of, slaves helped maintain the flow to Europe (and in the case of American traders, to eastern America) of furs which helped keep the firm in business.

Among those recording the evils of slavery was Robert Haswell, first mate of Captain John Kendrick's ship *Columbia* on her first voyage to the Pacific Coast (1787). He wrote that upon the capture of the first Nootkan whale of the season a slave was killed and his corpse laid alongside the whale's head which was adorned with eagle feathers.[16]

By the 1840s such incidents in that northern country had not abated. Traveling along its coasts at that time, Paul Kane reported a chief who sacrificed five slaves beneath a "colossal idol of wood" and then boasted of the killing. Kane also told of a girl of the chief's own household since infancy who was stabbed four times before ceasing her appeals for mercy. Kane wrote, "The only distinction made in her favour was that she was buried instead of being, like her miserable companions, thrown out on the beach." A similar example of such perfidy on the part of a chief was narrated by Commander R.C. Mayne. Traveling four years in British Columbia and Vancouver Island in the 1850s he wrote of a female slave murdered and her body thrown into the water. He learned of the incident from the Reverend William Duncan who ministered to Tsimshians from his Metlakatla Mission. Duncan theorized that the slave woman had been killed to remove disgrace from their chief's own daughter who suffered for some time from a ball wound in the arm.[17]

On the basis of reports coming to him, the Reverend Samuel Parker of the American Board of Commissioners for Foreign Missions wrote that Haidas did not "treat their slaves with as much kindness as the Indians in the lower

---

[16] Erna Gunther, *Indian Life on the Northwest Coast of America*, 60. Leland Donald writes that on some occasions the Nootkas killed a slave when a whale was killed, but does not specify that it was the first whale of the season. "Was Nuu-chah-nulth-aht (Nootka) Society Based on Slave Labor?" 114.

[17] Kane, "Incidents of Travel on the North-West Coast," 276; Richard Charles Mayne, *Four Years in British Columbia and Vancouver Island*, 285.

country of the Oregon Territory treat theirs." When they killed their slaves, he explained, "the loss of property is the only thing they regard."[18] Paradoxically, some slaves in southern Oregon came from tribes in the north, while those tribes to the north held slaves from Oregon. Of Haida slaves Bancroft wrote that they were without property and rights and consequently of no value to their owners except as property and thus, treated with extreme cruelty.[19] In similar vein Parker (in secondhand fashion) cited masters when driven to anger, rather than dueling rivals with guns and knives, dared them to kill more slaves than they, the challengers, in what were esentially contests of prestige and power. "The one who yields in this mode of combat ceases to be a gentleman," wrote Parker, concluding that the point of honor "with these barbarious gentry is fixed higher than in our Christian country, for here the life of *one* satisfies the powerful principle, but there, blood must flow profusely to quench the noble fire of highminded revenge."[20]

Unlike other tribes of the Northern zone, Queen Charlotte Island Haidas buried slaves under posts of newly constructed houses as part of potlatch celebrations unlike mainland Indians who were said to have done so when ceremoniously installing house posts.[21]

Among Haidas three slaves per family was said to be a large number. Some households were said to have none. By contrast, a third of the Tlingit population of the coast from 55° to 60° north latitude was said to be slaves, an overestimation in the opinion of some scholars. Like the powerful wealthy of other Northern Indians the Tlingits preferred head-deformed slaves from the Pacific Coast including those from tribes as far south as the Snohomish and Duwamish Indians of Puget Sound, whom these Tlingits captured on raids

---

[18]Parker, *Journal of an Exploring Tour Beyond the Rocky Mountains*, 267.

[19]Bancroft, *Wild Tribes*, 168.

[20]Parker, *Journal of an Exploring Tour Beyond the Rocky Mountains*, 268.

[21]Hodge, *Handbook of American Indians North of Mexico* 2, p. 598; George Peter Murdock, *Culture and Society*, 269.

into that area.[22] As recorded by a Hudson's Bay Company trader, a Tlingit chief in 1840 made a speech in his presence to prove that chief's importance and wealth, punctuating his words by shooting one of his slaves. Not to be outdone, another chief shot two slaves. Before the confrontation ended, ten more lay dead. Since free persons did not handle slaves, it fell to Hudson's Bay Company men to bury them.[23] Tlingits along the Chilkat River were said to have killed up to fifteen slaves upon death of their master. Family councils selected their victims, usually the infirm and the elderly. "Unconscious of their impending doom," wrote the Company trader, "they would be struck down behind with a huge stone hammer."[24]

Although slave-killing accounts appeared in the literature, there are few descriptions of how victims were murdered, except of those buried live beneath house posts and of those dying from occasional stranglings or, as noted, struck down with a stone hammer. Averkieva reported there was a special knife for killing slaves, its owner's totem depicted on the handle. The widely-adopted term, "slave killers," applies to a native weapon for which there are no witnesses of its being used in the killing of slaves. Albert Parker Niblack, a U.S. naval officer, was sent in 1882 to study artifacts in the U.S. National Museum. In the summers of 1885, '86 and '87 he was sent to southeastern Alaska to investigate native culture. As to the so-called slave killers, he wrote: "These are ceremonial implements formerly used by the Chiefs in dispatching the slaves selected as victims of sacrifice on occasions of building a house, or on the death of a Chief or other important personages."

Two types of weapons have been described as slave killers,

---

[22]Ibid., 285; A. Costello, *The Siwash: Their Life Legends and Tales of Puget Sound and Pacific Northwest*, 86.

[23]Hubert Howe Bancroft, *The Works of Hubert Howe Bancroft* 28, *History of the Northwest Coast* 2, p. 649. However, anthropologist Johan Adrian Jacobsen, as late as the early 1880s, observed that the many slaves among Tlingits seemed to have had as much freedom as their masters. Johan Adrian Jacobsen, *Alaskan Voyage 1881-1883*, p. 211.

[24]Costello, *The Siwash*, 151.

These stone weapons were also called "slave killer" or "skull crusher." The artifact at left was collected by Capt. James Cook at Nootka Sound. It was held by the rounded center portion and was also used for breaking copper pieces highly prized by natives. At right is a ceremonial axe believed to be of Nootkan origin of the type Capt. Cook called a "tomahawk." This type of club disappeared from the Northwest Coast soon after European contact. The wooden handle, carved to represent the head and neck of a bird, is decorated with human hair. Stone-clubbed weapons vary from six to eight inches with one pointed end protruding, and the other fitting into a wooden handle.
Courtesy, British Museum, London. Neg. #XXXVIII/40 (left); #PS 061381 (right).

which were like those the British explorer, James Cook, collected in 1778 along the British Columbia coast on his third journey to the Pacific. Part of his collection was auctioned off in 1806, its items appearing in various European museums in whose catalogues curators labeled them slave killers. Cook described these implements as consisting of "...short truncheons made of bone, and a small pick-axe, somewhat resembling the common American tomahawk." This, he went on to state, was a stone of the length of seven or eight inches; one end terminating in a point, and the other fixed into a wooden handle. This handle is intended to resemble the head and neck of a human figure; the stone being fixed in the mouth so as to represent a tongue of great magnitude. To heighten the resemblance, human hair is also fixed to it...and they have another weapon made of stone...about ten or twelve inches long, having a square point.

Cook further went on to state that one could reasonably conclude that the natives frequently engaged in close and bloody combat as evidenced by the number of their stone weapons, and the quantity of human skulls offered the crew for sale.

Anthropologist Erna Gunther, who visited many European museums, cataloguing weapons, states that one of the pickaxe type appearing in the British Museum, is labeled "Nootka Tomehawk for killing slaves." She also states that one from the Cook collection in Florence is similar to that illustrated by a cataloguer and labeled a "skull crusher." Cook noted crushed skulls along the British Columbia coast and the apparent "horrid [native] practice of devouring their enemies." Gunther confirms that descriptions of slave killings were absent from diaries of those collecting the weapons. One Vienna catalogue states that one piece was "used to kill prisoners of war." She does state that the labels were of a 19th century vintage of 18th century collections. These labels appear on the pickaxe type, which anthropologist Philip Drucker cautiously describes as of the "'slave-killer' type." The staff of Seattle's Burke Museum interprets Gunther's comments to apply to stone-fighting weapons. A letter from the curator interprets Gunther's comments to indicate that pointed and square-end stone clubs were the so-called slave killers. They were certainly used to break coppers in the 19th and 20th centuries after whites had forbidden tribal warfare in procuring slaves. Of value and substituted for slaves and treated like them, these coppers were used in ceremonials and trade and broken in the manner of killing slaves. Averkieva states that originally captives from raids were enslaved and put to death at festivals. Such would have occurred before coppers were substituted for slaves. She concurs in opinions of other scholars that elderly slaves were those most often killed as revealed in her comments on writings of Veniaminov who reported that since slaves became valued accumulations of wealth and exchange, only the "old, the ill and the small" were killed.[25]

Having spent a month among Kwakiutls, Cook wrote: "Among all the articles, however, which they exposed to sale, the most extraordinary were human skulls, and heads, with some of the flesh remaining on them, which they acknowledged they had been feeding on; and some of them, indeed, bore evident marks of their having been upon the fire. From this circumstance, it was too apparent, that the horrid practice of devouring their enemies is practiced here..." Traveling with Cook was the American John Ledyard, who wrote that the first Kwakiutls to visit Cook's ship, being hospitable "...brought us what no doubt they thought the greatest possible regalia, and offered it to us to eat; this was a human arm roasted. I have heard it remarked that human flesh is the most delicious, and therefore tasted a bit, and so did many others without swallowing the meat or the juices, but either my conscience of my taste rendered it very odious to me." Ledyard also wrote that the crew expressed displeasure of eating the human flesh to the disappointment of the Kwakiutls. Another accompanying Cook was Commander Charles Clerke of the *Discovery*. He was more cautious in his remarks. He noted the crew had a strong notion the Kwakiutls were cannibals because they "brought on board frequently...some human sculls and dried Hands, and one day a little Girl of 3 or 4 years of age in perfect health, which they want-

---

[25]Averkieva, *Slavery Among the Indians of North America*, 101n; Albert Parker Niblack, "The Coast Indians of Southern Alaska and Northern British Columbia," 275; James Cook, *A Voyage to the Pacific Ocean* 2, pp. 263-64, 211; Erna Gunther, *Indian Life on the Northwest Coast of America*, 39-43, 58-60; Drucker, *Indians of the Northwest Coast*, 94-95; Victoria Wyatt, anthropologist, letter to authors, June 28, 1988; Martine de Widersprach-Thor, "The Equation of Copper," 125; Averkieva, *Slavery Among the Indians of North America*, 103.

ed much to sell, and to enhance her Price, gave us to understand she was very good to eat…" The natives made motions "…seemingly of having eat the parts from the Heads and Hands…" Clerke noted that since communication was difficult between the natives and crew, there was grounds for misunderstanding.[26]

Commonly referred to as cannibalism, anthropophagy may have been part of a winter ceremonial originating among Kwakiutls. This practice brings to mind scenes of horror and revulsion among those made aware of it; yet, it was not without rationale in minds of its practitioners who believed that consumption of human flesh increased their contact with ancestors and also their own power and prestige rather than merely satisfying sadistic impulses.

In an article titled "Slavery" in the *Annual Review of Anthropology* (1982) Igor Kopytoff asks, "…why has modern anthropology which claims that nothing human is alien to it, consistently ignored so widespread phenomenon [as slavery]?"[27] And, he might have added, some of its harsh adjuncts. Prone to suppressing subrational forces in human behavior, anthropologists have tended to avoid characterizing Pacific Northwestern Coastal natives as cannibalistic. Some scholars, however, are aware that Wakashan-speaking Bella Bellas and Kwakiutls consumed animal or human flesh in their Spirit Dance which was so important in religious activities combined with non-religious ones such as feasting and potlatching.

Anthropologists revere Franz Boas as one of their number for his having contributed heavily to the study of North American natives in the initial stages of these scholars' discipline. Despite his reports that cannibalism did exist, skeptical anthropologists and others skirt the subject. Without moralizing Boas did write of accounts of the practice among northern natives, and of Kwakiutl use of slaves in their winter

---

[26]Cook, *A Voyage to the Pacific Ocean* 2, p. 211; John Ledyard, *A Journal of Captain Cook's Last Voyage,* 73; Charles Clerke, "Extracts from Officers' Journals," 1329.

[27]Kopytoff, "Slavery," 107.

ceremonials. In doing so, he relied on notes of an English-Tlingit native, George Hunt, whom he met at Fort Rupert on northern Vancouver Island in 1888. Although Boas observed on his own, Hunt, having grown up among Kwakiutls, was the primary source of reports of the Cannibal Dance, recording legends of his own people whom he interviewed. Boas stated that the element of cannibalism was probably added to the winter ceremonial about the time of the arrival of white men.[28]

Hunt related legends telling of slaves being eaten on occasions unrelated to the winter ceremonial; e.g. Cannibal Spirit pursuing slaves whom he killed at the throat for food, and as recorded by Boas, eating an entire slave. Bancroft stated that in some native groups dogs replaced slaves as victims in this dance. This use of dogs was practiced especially as the ceremonial distanced itself from Kwakiutls. At the southern extent of this secret society practice around Puget Sound dogs were torn to pieces during ceremonials. These animals were apparently sacrificed vicariously for slaves. The Dance was performed in recognition of one's ancestral heritage in which human flesh was consumed to symbolize ancestral encounters.[29]

Kwakiutl legendry tells of numerous spirits contacting natives and endowing them with one type of supernatural power or another. One such power was that of the Cannibal Spirit, the first to eat a man referred to as "he." Living on mountains, this spirit was always pursuing men to eat them. His wife and female slave procured his food by catching men and gathering corpses. His slave ate the eyes of those whom the spirit devoured. In the spirit's house lived a bird whose long beak broke men's skulls and ate their brains. The Cannibal Spirit was also supported by a grizzly bear whose strong paws killed people for him.

To acquire the protection of the Cannibal Spirit Kwakiutls

---

[28]Boas, *The Social Organization and the Secret Societies of the Kwakiutl Indians*, 664.
[29]Franz Boas and George Hunt, *Kwakiutl Texts*, 216-17; Bancroft, *Wild Tribes*, 203 and n.

An *hamatsa.* This sketch appeared in the Smithsonian Institution's Annual Report for the year ending June 30, 1895, written by anthropologist Franz Boas and George Hunt dealing with the latter's native peoples.

formed a secret society. Initiates for membership, known as the *hamatsa (hámacá)* performed a ritual of isolation with the Cannibal Spirit which was followed by a dance lasting several days. Feasts and giveaways were also featured in some of these dances. Older *hamatsa,* in impersonating the slave of the Cannibal Spirit, came to winter dances wearing bear skins to which were attached scalps of slaves they had eaten or slain. Some *hamatsa* wore masks around which were skulls carved from wood to represent skulls of slaves killed for the novice when the *hamatsa* were initiates. A Cannibal pole was erected in the middle of the rear of the dancing room.[30] In legendry the Cannibal Spirit gave initiates the Cannibal pole for the room, as well as songs which in part told of looking for many humans to eat; of tearing their skins and in doing so, becoming great magicians before whom people trembled. The Dance lasted for days, much of its routines in fours. Mistakes were believed to nullify a protégé's initiation, subjecting him to possible death for an error. Initiates usually

---

[30]Boas, *The Social Organizations and the Secret Societies of the Kwakiutl Indians,* 393-95, 447-46.

had blackened faces, although some had two curved lines on each cheek from the corner of the mouth to the ear in a wide concave sweep on the upper side representing streaks rubbed from the *hamatsa* skin to indicate they were living on blood.

With masks and ornaments protégés of the spirit impersonated it in these dances. As Boas has stated, "Thus the dance must be considered a dramatic performance of the myth relating to the acquisition of the spirit, and shows the people that the performer by his visit to the spirit has obtained his [own] powers and desires."[31]

In early times high-ranking Kwakiutl spirits summoned *hamatsa* initiates into the woods for three or four months preceding a dance. The pre-ceremonial disappearance of the initiates represented the "theft" of their guardians by the Winter Cannibal Spirit, in order to indoctrinate them into the secret society. Part of the indoctrination included human corpses prepared in a special way to be devoured. The one which the *hamatsa* always chose to devour was one of his relatives. Dead Kwakiutls where buried in coffins placed in trees where circulating air usually mummified them. Prior to the winter ceremonial corpses were hydrated by soaking them in salt water. Hemlock sticks were then pushed under the corpses' skins to remove decayed flesh, leaving only the bones encased in them.

Corpses were taken to the wooded area where they were placed atop small huts in which initiates stayed. Corpses' bellies were opened and placed over fires to smoke. Four days preceding scheduled dances the *hamatsa* sent for older ones of their society to join them, asking them which portion of corpses they wished to eat at the ceremony. Female slaves carried the prepared corpses into the house for the ceremonial, doing so moving backward and facing their masters. Each initiate used his own slaves to perform the ceremonial functions. These female slave helper-food procurers spent no pre-dance time in the woods with the *hamatsa* whom they

---

[31]Ibid., 405, 441; ibid., 434, 445; ibid., 396.

met as the former approached the house to commence the ceremonial. Rattles, which some attending female slaves carried, represented skulls indicating their wish to eat part of the human anatomy while other female slaves carried skulls in each hand. The *hamatsa* then took the skulls from them, breaking them and eating dry skins from them. Entering the dance house the wild, crazed and uncontrolled *hamatsa* bit flesh from any spectators in whom they could sink their teeth. Their ravenous pantomimed consumption of flesh was interpreted as satiation of their starvation during their absence. Body parts were bitten into as "pieces of flesh out of the arms and chests of the people" and when entering the house, the *hamatsa* bit everyone in sight.[32]

Decayed flesh of corpses of deceased *hamatsa* relatives, as well as bites of spectators at the dance, were not the only sources of human flesh consumed by young dancers. The flesh of slave women killed during the dance was a third source of flesh consumed. Traveling among Indians of the North in the 1880s, John Adrian Jacobsen confirmed reports of Boas and Hunt that bodies of the recently deceased (slaves) were consumed as well as that of "some that had been dead [corpses] for one or two years," but did not report the biting of flesh from dance spectators. Anthropologist Tom McFeat concurs, although his study seems to have been derived from much of Boas' work. Such cannibalistic practice, although modified, continued from the 18th well into the 19th century.

Biting of guests at the Cannibal Dance has been written about more in recent times than formerly. Perhaps this is because the practice was substituted for eating flesh of corpses and that of recently murdered slaves—a practice which was finally discontinued under the scrutiny and criticism of whites. Nevertheless, reports of the ingestion of bit-

---

[32]Ibid., 348, 394, 438, 441, 462; McFeat, *Indians of the North Pacific Coast*, 189; Boas, *The Social Organization and the Secret Societies of the Kwakiutl Indians*, 406, 438. More recent spirit-summoned *hamatsa* initiates are absent in the woods for but a few days prior to the Cannibal Dance.

ten flesh continued into the 20th century. Anthropologists have debated whether the issue of biting Cannibal Dance guests were real or simulated. Yet, such reports were fairly extensive among tribes of sounds and straits up to and along coastal British Columbia.[33]

Richly appareled Kwakiutl and Nootka *hamatsa,* imitating spirits, instructed others to maintain their singing. As asserted by Bancroft chieftains in these ceremonials grabbed participants, biting naked flesh from arms. Bancroft skeptically adds, however, that such might have been sleight of hand performances. Not embracing either Boas' or Hunt's observations of the consumption of flesh, Drucker is skeptical that cadavers were eaten, suggesting instead the use of a black bear's smoked carcass fitted with a human effigy to convince audiences of cannibalism. His skepticism extended to the biting of flesh, since he does not commit this metaphorical display of iconic representation at the Cannibal Dance as actually taking place. Although Drucker states that flesh may have been removed by trickery, he speculates that such dexterous maneuvering might have been effected with concealed knives excising the tissue, but stops short of stating that flesh was actually consumed. Instead of maintaining that pieces of flesh were bitten from victims, Boas stated that participants "merely pull[ed] the skin up with their teeth, sucking hard so as to secretly remove a piece of skin." "This," Boas states, "was not swallowed, but hidden behind the ear until after the dance, when it is returned to the owner, in order to assure him that it will not be used against him for purposes of witchcraft."[34]

Two tempos were beaten by the *hamatsa* in their dance, one representing great excitement signifying their search for human flesh to eat; the less exuberant other tempo, pacification of participants from having eaten flesh. During the

---

[33]Jacobsen, *Alaskan Voyage 1881-1883,* pp. 29-32, 64; McFeat, *Indians of the North Pacific Coast,* 189.

[34]Bancroft, *Wild Tribes,* 170-71; Drucker, *Indians of the Northwest Coast,* 151-52; Boas, *The Social Organization and the Secret Societies of the Kwakiutl Indians,* 440-41.

excitement of the dance *hamatsa* initiates lifted their heads to pantomime the looking for bodies held high in front of them while their attendants held these *hamatsa* by neck rings of hemlock branches. During the intensity of the frenetic part of the Cannibal Dance, slaves were killed and their mutilated bodies strewn on the dance floor. Edward Curtis wrote of Tsimshian *hamatsa* (whom he called "medicine men") tearing to pieces and devouring bodies of murdered slaves. One *hamatsa*, said Curtis' informant, purchased a slave from a companion for some blankets and then, dancing frenzily, leaped on her, pushing her on the back like a tiger pouncing upon the throat of its struggling quarry. Other participants held the slave's legs until she ceased struggling after which her master punched a hole about the umbilicus severing intestines. Then, placing one of their ends between his teeth, ran dragging it as though it were a rope. Pieces of the body were distributed for eating, the blood caught in a dish and passed around for communal drinking.[35]

Boas reported that when asked to dance for Kwakiutl *hamatsa* a female slave cried, "Do not get hungry, do not eat me..." She had scarcely uttered these words when her master, standing behind her, split her skull with an axe and she was eaten by the *hamatsa*. This dance as related by Boas was at Nahwitti. The participants, who related the dance to him, said that it was "exceedingly hard to eat fresh human flesh, more so than to eat dried corpses."[36]

Bones of these deceased slaves were stored at northern ends of houses where the sun could not shine on them. Later they were thrown into deep water instead of being inhumed from which state it was feared they might return to take their masters' souls. When mentioning the gender of slaves killed, Boas and others cited that they were females. However, Boas related an instance in which a male was butchered and eaten during a Cannibal Dance outside a house at Fort Rupert. The wife of the slain slave was said to have cast a spell on the

---

[35]Ibid., 443; Curtis, *The North American Indian* 10, pp. 239-40.
[36]Boas, *The Social Organization and the Secret Societies of the Kwakiutl Indians*, 440.

participants, predicting all would die in five years, such believed to have been their actual fate.[37]

Frequently uttered during the ceremony was the *hamatsa* cry, "hap, hap, hap," translated "eating, eating, eating," while their songs glorified the eating of flesh. They also signified the swallowing of food of live men and the circumnavigation of the world searching for human flesh, heads and corpses and the eating of dried human flesh. Following an elaborate ceremony older society members joined initiates for the feast of the corpse distributed to them to "count how many bites each of them swallows...[not being] allowed to chew the flesh, but...[to] bolt it." Between bites slaves brought participants water to drink. Boas states that "after the close of the ceremonial the *hamatsa*, by payment of blankets, indemnifies those whom he has bitten and the owner of slaves whom he has killed."[38]

Although modern anthropologists debate the actual existence of simulation of cannibalism among Northwest Coast tribes, their legends persist to tell of corpses robbed from coffins and eaten and, of the eating of brains of women whose skulls were broken. By the 1880s the killing of slaves to cannibalize them had largely ceased according to Boas who reported that much *hamatsa* cruelty had disappeared, but that the practice had actually existed.

Nootkans borrowed certain aspects of the winter ceremonial as it spread. Some Nootkans north of Barclay Sound modified a dance in which the performer made "gashes into his breast and arms." As late as December 1864 a female slave reportedly met a violent death at Alberni from being stabbed during a celebration. By that time, according to the observer, sacrificing victims did not occur annually, but perhaps every three years.[39]

Certain aspects of the winter ceremonial also spread to

[37]Ibid., 439.
[38]Ibid., 438, 459; ibid., 442-43.
[39]Ibid., 405-06, 632, 635-36; Sproat, *Scenes and Studies of Savage Life,* 155; Boas, *The Social Organization and the Secret Societies of the Kwakiutl Indians,* 636.

Coast Salish speakers around sounds and straits to the south. Their modified ceremonial involved a winter ritual excluding actual cannibalism. North of the Kwakiutls Salish-speaking Bella Coolas did not bite people; nor did they devour corpses, but did devour raw salmon and tore dogs to pieces. Salish-speaking Skokomishes were also said to have torn dogs to pieces. Through Northern Kwakiutls certain aspects of the winter ceremonial were adopted by Northern tribes. Among Haidas a slave was killed, its body thrown to a dancer who ate from it, but only after taking an emetic to insure vomiting after eating this human flesh, the process stimulated by tickling the throat with feathers. Boas writes that no doubt tribes peripheral to Kwakiutls "in the main derived [their ceremonial] from the same source." He also states that "the performances themselves were essentially the same from Alaska to Juan de Fuca Strait."[40]

Citing the Reverend William Duncan, who had the mission among Tsimshians, Bancroft wrote that "...Mr Duncan speaking of the Chimsyans in a locality not definitely fixed, testifies to the tearing to pieces and actual devouring of a body of a murdered slave by naked bands of cannibal medicine-men." He adds, "only certain parties of the initiated practice this barbarism, others confining their tearing ceremony to the bodies of dogs." Murdock told of Haida performers, one after another burying "...teeth in the flesh, sometimes eating it, but more only merely pretending to do so."[41]

Boas stated that origins of secret societies were closely connected with warfare. "The ceremonial of cannibalism," he stated, "which nowadays [in the decades prior to 1900] is the most important part of the whole ceremonial, is known to have been introduced among the various tribes recently, although its foundation, the idea of the existence of a spirit who is killing people, is present among all the tribes..." Boas further adds that among Nootkan and Coast Salish speakers

[40]Ibid., 644-46, 650-51, 658, 661.
[41]Bancroft, *Wild Tribes,* 171; Murdock, "Rank and Potlatch Among the Haida," 7.

the action of the cannibal was confined to his taking hold with his teeth of the heads of enemies, which were cut off in war. Boas further states that among Kwakiutls "the slave is the body of the cannibal or of his relatives, and by slaying him the victory is once more brought before the eyes of his admiring friends."[42]

Although the above discussion of cannibalism pertains primarily to its practice for ceremonial reasons, there were reports of bodies eaten by starving persons. In the Plateau hearts and other organs were cut from captives who were cunning, brave and outstanding by those seeking to assume qualities of these victims. The ethnologist Frederick Webb Hodge reports cannibalism as having been practiced among many tribes within the United States.[43] Revered scholars such as Franz Boas, George Hunt and others reported acts of cannibalism in the Kwakiutl winter dance without ever suggesting that they might have been symbolic performances. The literature of early explorer-fur traders, missionaries and other observers in the Pacific Northwest are full of reports of cannibalism among the tribes. There may be, however, some question as to the reliability of the reports of these visitors and of statements that cannibalism was practiced independently of the winter dance since the above persons appear to have been unaware of the ceremonial. We have the word of the 18th century mariner-trader, John Hoskins, that in 1792, natives of Clayoquot Harbor near the important settlement of Nootka were by their own admission involved in cannibalism.

On the other hand one must be aware of those who wrote of the practice of cannibalism from second hand accounts and exaggerated and dramatized their accounts. One such

---

[42]Boas, *The Social Organization and the Secret Societies of the Kwakiutl Indians*, 664.

[43]Hodge lists many American tribes which practiced cannibalism. Among these were natives in Maine; also Algonkins, Micmacs, Assiniboins, Crees, Foxes, Miamis, Ottawas, Chippewas, Illinois, Kickapoos, Sioux, Winnebagos, Tonkawas, Utes, Hopis, Caddo, Mohawks; tribes in Texas and California and others. *Handbook of American Indians North of Mexico* 1, pp. 200-201.

perpetrator having no first hand knowledge nor contact with Indians to the north was Hall J. Kelley, who promoted an American settlement of the Pacific Northwest on the lower Columbia. To punctuate the extremity to which he believed slave-owners would go, Kelley told of unfortunates herded into chiefs' houses and then compelled to join in singing and dancing before being cut to pieces. Then, wrote Kelley, "a reeking parcel is given to each of the guests, who, like dogs, seize the quivering flesh and while they devour it the blood runs from the mouth warm as in the current of life."[44]

Reverend Jonathan Green of the American Board of Foreign Missions believed a mission to be established near the mouth of the Columbia would be free of the violence which they claimed was so prevalent among the Northern Indians in alien British territory. Attempting to calm his readers, Green assured them that even among the Northern Indians the practice of killing slaves on the death of their master was "gradually growing out of custom" and, that "many now conceive manumitting their slaves..." His statements were made in 1829, although coastal slavery would not reach its maximum intensity until some years later.

The year Kelley recorded his observation Governor Simpson wrote that in the Northwest Coastal trade the principal articles were "Guns, Ammunition, Cloth, Blankets, Slops [loose smocks or overalls, or articles such as clothing sold to sailors], Liquor, Ornaments Toys &c. but we understand, that the Slave Trade in all its horrors, is here carried on to a considerable extent, and forms the most profitable branch of their American Business..."[45]

When Simpson visited Company posts in these northern quarters during a world tour (1841-1842) he found that slavery among the natives had not abated since his 1824-1825 tour. Of victims of its closely related carnivorous dance he wrote:

[44]John Hoskins, "The Narrative of a Voyage to the North West Coast of America and China on Trade and Discoveries by John Hoskins Performed in the Ship Columbia Rediviva 1790, 1791, 1792 & 1793." Typescript copy Ms. 119.1 G77 H82 p. 62; Hall J. Kelley, *A Geographic Sketch of That Part of North America Called Oregon*, 197.

[45]Jonathan S. Green, *Journal of a Tour of the North West Coast of America in the Year 1828*, pp. 30-31; Simpson, *Simpson's 1829 Journey to the Columbia*, 80.

These thralls are just as much the property of their masters as so many dogs, with this difference against them, that a man of cruelty and ferocity enjoys a more exquisite pleasure in tasking, or starving, or torturing, or killing a fellow-creature, than in treating any one of the lower animals in a similar way. Even in the most inclement weather, a mat or a piece of deer-skin is the slave's only clothing, whether by day or by night, whether under cover or in the open air. To eat without permission, in the very midst of an abundance which his toil has procured, is as much as his miserable life is worth; and the only permission which is ever vouchsafed to him, is to pick up the offal thrown out by his unfeeling and imperious lord. Whether in open war or in secret assassination, this cold and hungry wretch invariably occupies the post of danger.[46]

Simpson described "merry-making" masters at Sitka as "diabolically ingenious" in the work of murder, placing six slaves "in a row with their throats over a sharp ridge of rock, while a pole, loaded with a chuckling demon at either end, ground away at the backs of their necks till life is extinct."[47] Obviously aware that his London superiors had been influenced by evangelical-abolitionists who opposed black slavery, the question arises: "Did Simpson, as a point of duty or for some other reason as purposely exaggerating to impress them, cite such Indian excesses of which they may not have been aware?"

Without first-hand observation of British Columbia Indians the Reverend Demers described what he termed the Yougletas, a southern Kwakiutl (Lekwiltok) subdivision, as "fierce and cannibalistic."[48] Another Roman Catholic missionary, J.B.Z. Bolduc, stated how peoples living on Vancouver Island and on the continent north of Fraser River in southerly nocturnal sweeps destroyed villages, killing and massacring as many men as they could, taking women and children as slaves. According to Demers these fierce Northerners breathing only "blood and carnage" traded their victims to other northern peoples. On the basis of reports of fellow missionaries such as Demers, the Reverend Peter J.

---

[46]George Simpson, *Narrative of a Journey Round the Years, 1841-1842* I, 242-43.
[47]Ibid., 243.
[48]Demers is cited in *Notices & Voyages*, 99, 193.

De Smet, S.J., who came to the Pacific Northwest in 1842, wrote that white men were safe except on the North where natives did not "hesitate to feast upon the flesh of their prisoners."[49] Like Demers, his confreres Bolduc and De Smet, had not traveled as far north as the homelands of these Indians.

Ross Cox observed that in early times cannibalism as practiced among "savages on the coast to the northward" was unknown among natives of the Columbia.[50] His comment was one that was also based on hearsay. On similar word of early Pacific Coast white mariner-traders, Bancroft concluded that undoubtedly slaves of the Northern Indians were among those sacrificed in the "devilish" Cannibal Dance. He was uncertain if the bodies were then cannibalized.[51] The explorer, John Meares, among Nootkas in 1788, related that the Hawaiian Prince Tianna with him detested the "cannibalistic appetites," which statement did not, as such, mean the existence of cannibalism but suggests it.[52]

Robin Fisher and Hugh Johnston record that Europeans, intrigued by reports of Nootkan cannibalism, believed it a practice of these natives. On the other hand, Lieutenant John Williamson, dubious of the practice, wrote in his journal, April 25, 1778, that when he offered an Indian human flesh along with enticing him with iron and brass, the flesh was refused. Williamson took the refusal to mean such was not a custom. Fisher and Johnston cite cannibalistic acts among coastal natives, their citations ranging from American and British reports to Spaniards. The American, John Kendrick, characterized as "not entirely trustworthy," described butchered child captives, writing that he had been offered pieces of loin and a hand of a child. That he so report-

---

[49]Peter J. De Smet, S.J., *Oregon Missions and Travels over the Rocky Mountains, 1845-46*, p. 125.

[50]Cox, *Adventures* 1, pp. 310-11. Wasco informants, however, told how on a journey away from that river their ancestors unceremoniously boiled the head of a Paiute, which act, no doubt, was prompted by hunger and revenge. Lucullus V. McWhorter, "Paiute-Wasco Indian Tribal Warfare." Ms. 1538.

[51]Bancroft, *Wild Tribes*, 203 and n.

[52]Richard Nokes, "Patriot or Scalawag? John Meares' Exploits on the Northwest Coast," *Columbia, the Magazine of Northwest History* (Fall 1990), 42.

ed may have been to keep Spaniards away from natives with whom he traded. English seamen described for the Spanish navigator, Estéban José Martinez, how chiefs clubbed children's heads and ate the raw flesh.[53] Nevertheless, by 1880, reports of slave killings to cannibalize them on the spot had largely ceased. Within a decade cannibalism of the *hamatsa* became symbolic in their dances.

Some natives escaped being *hamatsa* victims when rescued by Spaniards and other whites or when freed at potlatches such as those of Haidas and Tsimshians as a favor honoring the slaves' relatives. Anthropologist Viola E. Garfield states that this rare gesture was comparable to the destruction of property. Potlatches, however, were scarcely instruments of slave manumission. Whatever the context, value grading, returning of gifts, or of interest collected on gifts returned, potlatches were better known than ceremonies of the *hamatsa*. Practiced in more simplified form by Chinooks, potlatching, which involved slaves and other properties, increased in complexity and severity in its northerly progression to the Tlingits. Such progression is understandable considering the wealth in slaves in that northerly region where ceremonials were calculated to oblige wealthy rivals to return greater wealth than did their competitors. Among the Northern Indian potlatches also served as public recognition of hereditary title-holders' claims to resource properties so as to establish their right to these places. Lasting up to a fortnight, sometimes longer, these ceremonials gave participants ample time to feast, gamble, sing and dance before formally distributing gifts to guests according to their ranking system in which no two persons were said to have shared identical status positions.[54]

Among Kwakiutls and others, potlatch and trade items such as martin skins were exchanged with at least a partial payment in slaves.[55] Such skins, woolen blankets and den-

[53]Fisher and Johnston, *Captain James Cook and His Times*, 85, 115-16.
[54]Garfield, *Tsimshian Clan and Society*, 274; Drucker, *Indians of the Northwest Coast*, 123-24.
[55]Curtis, *The North American Indian* 10, p. 5.

"Going to the Potlatch—Big Canoe, North-west Coast."
Sketch by Julian Ralph, from On Canada's Frontier.

talia, along with things from the forest such as canoes, were added to guns, coins from the mineral world, and like items. From the animal world the Northern Indians traded deer-skins for slaves. Among metal objects were shield-shaped "coppers," hammered from sheets originally acquired from trading with white merchants. Some coppers were engraved, some painted, and others plain. From multiple sources Leland Donald had catalogued the value of coppers ranging from one and a half to three feet in length as the equivalent of a slave. After native warfare and slavery were diminished, the destruction of slaves by contending native nobility was replaced by destruction of these highly prized coppers.[56]

Murdock calls this destruction a "vengeance potlatch" in

[56]Averkieva, *Slavery Among the Indians of North America,* 94; de Widersprach-Thor, "The Equation of Copper," 122-23; Donald, "The Slave Trade on the Northwest Coast," 142; de Widersprach-Thor, "The Equation of Copper," 122-23. de Widersprach-Thor stated that Indians made coppers from sheets of that metal obtained from maritime traders. Drucker states that coppers were first made from copper obtained in trade from natives of Alaska's Copper River, and made a dull sound unlike that of European sheet copper. *Indians of the Northwest Coast,* 131n.

"The Potlatch."
Potlatches were often ostentatious displays of the nobility to validate their own rank in a hierarchy of aristocracy. At these gather-
ings slaves were often given away or killed. *Sketch by Julian Ralph,
from* On Canada's Frontier.

which a slighted or insulted host invites the opponent for a
challenge. Whether or not the host killed slaves or broke
coppers or chopped up valuable canoes, the opponent had to
make similar sacrifices or suffer loss of prestige. The reputation of an opponent so poor as to be unable to sacrifice property was ruined. Aside from the vengeance potlatch
Murdock mentions four other types of potlatches among
Haidas; housebuilding potlatches where often a slave was
killed by being buried in the post hole of the house; the totem
pole potlatch held for families without means of holding a
housebuilding potlatch; potlatching given by parents
enabling their offspring to acquire status; the funeral potlatch given by relatives of the deceased in which slaves could
be killed, in some instances, to accompany the deceased to
the soul world; and lastly, the facesaving potlatch where one,
embarrassed by some act, hoped to regain his pride.[57]

While slaves were used in potlatch giveaways and in sea-

---

[57]Murdock, "Rank and Potlatch Among the Haida," 12-16.

sonal ceremonials such as the winter Spirit Dance, what practical day-to-day functions did they perform? Although apparently some tasks were of a servile nature, like providing comfort and other help for wealthy families, their work was similar to that of commoners, assisting masters in fishing and harvesting in tandem with other tribesmen since work at large was shared by all. Among the Tlingit providing comfort extended to women in labor, the slaves holding them to ease the pain. Women gave birth in a branch-covered hole dug behind the house, for they were not permitted confinement in the home. In sorting out contributions of slaves, anthropologists confirm the cooperative nature of engaging in such tasks. It has been maintained that the cost of keeping slaves outweighed what economic benefit masters received from them. Drucker is among those who believe their economic utility to have been negligible. Thus, it would appear that some scholars hardly term efforts of servile ones as "slave labor," since the latter assisted masters in various chores. Among scholars providing information about such work is Averkieva whose accounts are from her countryman, V. Romanov, who affirmed that Tlingit slaves occasionally performed chores.[58]

In some tribes male slaves participated in the hunt and prepared arrow tips so vital in hunting and warfare. In and out of season Tlingit slaves of both genders engaged in chores involving fishing which lay at the very core of tribal subsistence, preparing catches for winter consumption. Males joined masters in these piscatory endeavors, carrying catches and serving as oarsmen for masters' canoes, and maintaining such craft. Despite this association at the workplace, masters distanced themselves from slaves in many ways. Among these was the wearing of labrets which was forbidden to slaves, and sexual intercourse with slave women which disgraced free male Tlingits. Among Nootkas to the

---

[58]John R. Swanton, *Social Condition, Beliefs, and Linguistic Relationship of the Tlingit Indians*, 429; Philip Drucker, *Cultures of the North Pacific Coast*, 52; Averkieva, *Slavery among the Indians of North America*, 65.

south slaves joined commoners in fishing, but chiefs hunted whales and otters, leaving fishing chores to lesser persons. Tsimshian chiefs did not engage in hunting, expecting slaves to perform this activity.[59] Among other northern peoples slaves had lesser roles in hunting, often carrying arms for masters. At a more menial level they gathered wood, cut down trees, dragging to the water these aboreal products so important in tribal subsistence.

Female slaves assisted in cooking as well as serving chieftain families, watching over them and attending to their crying and hungry children and accompanying women of families. Young boys served as companion of chiefs' sons. Slaves also spread mats for masters' families and the guests whom these slave summoned to various events, announcing their arrival and entertaining them after they came. They also announced their masters' approach to houses of hosts. Slaves also had a part in preparing feasts at such occasions, having harvested crops such as root and berries which could have been consumed at these events. Other foods which could have been eaten on such occasions after their mid-19th century introduction were potatoes, which slaves cultivated and gathered.

Among those who perceive slaves as "more truly trophies of war..." is Elman R. Service.[60] Others question such contention, asserting that slaves did indeed perform important economic functions. Garfield, writes: "The economic value of slaves in the productive system has...been neglected, and the tendency has been to consider slaves from the point of view of 'prestige value' rather than as productive property and therefore basic economic assets...Nowhere, least of all on the Northwest Coast, can slavery be adequately explained as just another device for acquiring prestige, nor dismissed as of little economic importance."[61] Others contend that slave power

[59]Frederica De Laguna, "Tilingit." In Wayne Suttles, ed., *Handbook of North American Indians Northwest Coast* 7, p. 210; Sumner, *Folkways*, 271; Gunther, *Klallam Ethnography*, 214; Marjorie M. Halpin and Margaret Sequin, "Tsimshian Peoples." In Wayne Suttles, ed., *Handbook of North American Indians Northwest Coast* 7, p. 277.

[60]Elman R. Service, *Profiles in Ethnology*, 214-15.

in productive and storage activities freed title-holders for ceremonial "labor." Slaves, they contend, were among the most valuable and marketable of commodities in a trading system so important to local economies.[62]

Regardless of which contention is the more true, it must be admitted that slaves in the Northern zone, as well as those in other zones such as the Wakashan, performed numerous important tasks. This fact is supported by the information supplied by anthropologists such as Franz Boas and John R. Swanton, and by George Hunt. Besides examining the labor of slaves in real life situations, they cite examples in native legendry of such work. These accounts have been summarized by Averkieva.[63] Unlike anthropologists, early nonnative visitors among natives often overlooked slaves' work when recording various aspects of slave life, simply stating that it was menial. This void of data left present-day scholars to consider the reason for such paucity of information, and if slaves did indeed perform no more than everyday household chores in the regular rounds of subsisting.

Slaves of the Nootkas are reported in recent studies to have produced surpluses which enhanced the ability of upper classes to conduct managerial and socio-economic functions and maintain control by keeping aspiring commoners and rivals in check, even were it to involve murdering such aspirants. Overbearance of masters was tempered by the fact that, unlike slaves, commoners could change group allegiance by moving about. Such overbearance was also kept in check by masters' awareness that in their society commoners and slaves alike were important in food processing. This function was of great importance in the northern coastal area where there was such an abundance of natural flora and

[61]Viola E. Garfield, "A Research Problem in Northwest Indian Economics," 94. Garfield's position as stated in this work differs from that of her 1939 position when she wrote "...slavery was not of fundamental economic importance to the northwest coast tribes. While slaves did add to the wealth of their masters through their labor, the keeping of them for what they could produce was not a well developed concept." *Tsimshian Clan and Society*, 271.

[62]Donald Mitchell and Leland Donald, "Some Economic Aspects," 31, 32.

[63]Averkieva, *Slavery Among the Indians of North America*, 64-82.

fauna. Eugene E. Ruyle states that "feasts and potlatches, in addition to validating a chief's claim to titles and associated economic privileges, served to attract and hold a free labor force to enable the chief to exploit the productive resources he owned." Ruyle also states that "slaves formed an important captive labor force…" unlike commoners who freely came and went when unhappy, paying tribute to new superiors by yielding portions of harvests to them. "This ownership (or 'stewardship') of all productive resources," states Ruyle, "provided the ideological justification for the collection of rent and taxation. Since the chiefs," Ruyle explains, "supplied all the productive resources, they were justified in collecting a portion of all fish and game captured on their property." Up to half the seals and mountain goats hunted belonged to chiefs. Masters would not have welcomed commoners who moved about or lacked ambition and self respect, in which case they were categorized as "lazy men." After white contact, commoners, like those among Salish groups of the Strait of Georgia, gained some status and rank if they possessed talent and the ability to muster surplus goods. To maintain their status they had to give feasts and distribute goods. To keep from sliding down the social scale the nobility, like that of the Strait, had to maintain usual social customs, such as the observance of ceremonials and potlatching rules.[64]

---

[64]Donald, "The Slave Trade on the Northwest Coast," 124; "Was Nuu-chah-nulth-aht (Nootka) Society Based on Slave Labor?" 110; Ruyle "Slavery, Surplus and Stratification," 514-15. An example of the extreme to which the nobility attempted to maintian social class stability occurred among the Squamish Indians (immediately north of present-day Vancouver, B.C.) when a noble father, on discovering that a slave had irregular relations with his daughter, took them under pretense of hunting seals, far out to a rock exposed at low tide to be drowned by the incoming tide. Barnett, *The Coast Salish of British Columbia,* 208.

Barnett also writes that commoners were given the chance to better themselves, with intermarriage between the two free classes being permitted. He also writes that there were the despised persons, the "lazy men" who were without ambition. Ibid., 248. Among Coast Salish speakers such as those of the Gulf of Georgia, orphaned and impoverished children were not enslaved by families which sheltered them. In their society ransom was possible, usually for those captured and enslaved as adults. There was also less emphasis in their society on ceremonial counting of warriors' victims than there was in surrounding tribes. Ibid., 248-49. Barnett writes that while motives for carrying out warfare varied among Coast Salish peoples, they all engaged in war for slave-taking. *Culture Element Distributions' IX, Gulf of George Salish,* 266.

Ruyle, like Averkieva, over-emphasized exploitation of a slave "class" by "masters" in an internally structured and bonded "class" to validate grand themes of class struggle.

Potlatching, borrowed from Kwakiutls, evolved into a multi-functional institution among neighboring Indians in pre-contact times with distribution of native products. At contact, white mariner-traders brought goods which found their way into potlatches along with native ones. Trade with white men in the late 18th and early 19th centuries resulted in not only larger, but more numerous potlatches. By the same token, the natives' desire for imported goods fueled their involvement in war in order to acquire slaves. Exchanging them for furs to sell to white traders for the latters' goods helped solidify and stratify classes.

A more recent development of the potlatch was that of getting a return plus interest from potlatch distributions which occurred in the mid to late 19th century among Kwakiutls, when slave-produced surplus goods, along with blankets, were put out at interest instead of being stored for periods of time. Potlatches to distribute them became business transactions in social settings. Recipients of such "gifts" were obligated to return to donors at future times, the gifts plus interest which ranged up to seventy-five percent[65] of their value.[66] Potlatches were held not only to increase the prestige of their givers, but conversely in that competitive environment, to lessen that of visiting rivals. Among experiences of Commander Mayne was his attendance at a feast where eight hundred blankets were reportedly destroyed by one man and where a few days previously three otter skins (one of which had been sought in exchange for thirty blankets) had been cut in little pieces about the size of two fingers and distributed among the guests. Mayne also reported the destruction of property in instances other than in potlatching in which slaves were victimized by masters. "[I]t happens,"

---

[65]Boas says as much as 100% interest.
[66]Gunther, "The Indian Background of Washington History," 198.

wrote Mayne, "that some crime is atoned for by a present of three or four slaves, who are butchered in cold blood."[67]

At one time the human goods helping to fill the maws of the potlatch were acquired in blood and conflict. By the 1830s natives were deeply embroiled in what Mayne termed "a cruel system of predatory warfare."[68] In such conflict, writes Brian Ferguson: "many raids aimed at capturing food, property, or slaves... [creating a] clear picture...from available data...up to the 1860s" that Northwest Coastal peoples "were living in a constant 'state of war.'"[69]

When land based fur trading began in the 19th century, personnel at trading posts had greater opportunity to influence their native clientele than had maritime traders off their ships. Using this influence British, American and Russian fur men in the second and third decades of the century sought to halt the wars so as to deal a death blow to slavery. White traders, however, were caught up in a paradox in that the slavery they opposed was important in their acquisition of furs, for as Leland Donald writes: "...while Hudson's Bay Company traders often complained that fighting disrupted trade and deplored slavery and the traffic in slaves, both raiding for and trading in slaves helped maintain the flow of furs to Europe and eastern North America."[70]

Anthropologist Helen Codere noted as war decreased, noble natives increasingly vented their aggressions in potlatching. Among these were Kwakiutls, the nature of whose new type of giveaways is described by Wilson Duff:

> [They] became a substitute for war. Before the imposition of British law, war had been a major method of humbling enemy tribes and gaining prestige. During the 1850's and 1860's warfare decreased and potlatching increased. Energies formerly expended in war were now put into potlatches, which were organized like war campaigns and referred to in speeches as wars. One old Kwakiutl

---

[67]R.C. Mayne, *Four Years in British Columbia and Vancouver Island*, 263, 279.

[68]Ibid. 74.

[69]Brian Ferguson, "Warfare and Redistributive Exchange on the Northwest Coast," 134.

[70]Donald, "The Slave Tade on the Northwest Coast," 154.

said in a speech in 1895: "When I was young I saw streams of blood shed in war. But since that time the white men came and stopped up that stream of blood and wealth. Now we fight with our wealth."[71]

The Kwakiutl saying: "We fight our rivals with property" instead of weapons had not come easily to a people long involved in violence, but now relegated to non-warring. In an 1878 Canadian geological survey George Mercer Dawson reported that "...intertribal wars along the coast have now ceased...slaves, in consequence, are becoming scarce, and the custom is dying away."[72] This lessened but little the demeaning competition among rivals in which highly-valued copper pieces continued to be destroyed with the same intensity with which slaves were formerly sacrificed. Subsequent governmental bans against potlatching did not destroy the continuing subtle demeaning of rivals and the stigmatization of slaves. The change from slaves to coppers was prompted by no humanitarianism on the part of potlatch givers, but simply because slaves increased in economic value as their numbers decreased. Not unimportant in this change was pressure exerted by whites to try to stamp out the potlatch process.

Wars became less frequent when whites specifically pressured Haidas, Tlingits, Tsimshians, Bella Coolas and Haislas to cease their raids. At the same time potlatches, forums for competing, became more common among these tribes which substituted coppers for slaves in their ceremonials. Yet not only did slaves thus increase in value, but so also did the substitutionary coppers. Martine de Widerspach-Thor theorized that they were designed to represent human bodies. Painted with figures representing humans, they were broken to symbolize slave killing and were buried under house posts and poles as were slaves. In some instances figures of bodies and in other instances, of heads, were placed upside down on

---

[71]See Helen Codere, *Fighting with Property;* Wilson Duff, *The Impact of the White Man in the Indian History of British Columbia* 1, p. 59.

[72]Gunther, "The Indian Background of Washington History," 198. See also Codere, *Fighting with Property;* George Mercer Dawson, *Report on the Queen Charlotte Islands, 1878,* p. 132.

poles to signify the hanging heads of war victims. Sometimes bodyless captives were represented by carved wooden "coppers." Franz Boas noted a ceremonial in which a symbolic enemy head was placed on a pole. For captives killed, warriors burned hemlock wreaths to substitute for the hanging of captives' heads on poles. In later times they burned wreaths to represent coppers as evidence of donors' victory over rivals.

In substitution of slaves, coppers were placed on chieftain graves. At funerals they were broken and their pieces distributed to persons of rank, the practice said to symbolize bones and solidified blood of the deceased. More likely, they were distributed to symbolize the giving away of slaves as in earlier times. In initiation ceremonials they were now destroyed. In the Cannibal Dance they replaced knitted and wood-carved skulls attached to dancers' robes and were placed heads down to represent slave corpses already eaten. During this ceremonial coppers were held in front of dancers' mouths to symbolize the eating of slaves. Formerly challenged to kill slaves, it has been theorized that rivals were now challenged to break coppers given away by these competitors to enhance and flaunt their own prestige and affluence.[73]

Intrusions of the white man's socio-economic system created serious inroads in native cultures and their potlatching centerpiece. Despite government bans potlatching did not disappear quickly or easily since its participants continued demeaning their rivals.[74] Of the many legacies of potlatching not the least is the intrigue and puzzlement it bequeathed to students of the curious practice. Murdock writes:

> Whether viewed in psychological terms as an exaggerated and institutionalized expression of vanity or narcissim, or in economic terms as a disguised form of investment, insurance or exchange,

---

[73]de Widersprach-Thor, "The Equation of Copper," 124-26; Franz Boas, "The Social Organization and Secret Societies of the Kwakiutl," 522.

[74]An example of modified potlatching occurred when an agent permitted a Makah to wait until Christmas to put up a tree and gifts under it. Only then could he invite guests to this modified potlatch ceremony, doing so with the blessing of the agent and a missionary. Colson, *The Makah Indians*, 17.

or even in sociological terms as the conventional road to social recognition and prestige, the seemingly reckless distribution or destruction of property has appeared, at best, only partially understandable.[75]

The Northern Indians could not escape the axiom that among mankind all things change. Their contests whether in potlatching or in more physical conflict had reduced populations as they also had those of natives to the south. Declension also stemmed from devastating smallpox and venereal diseases which raced through native villages in chain reaction. In June 1791 Hoskins cited one consequence of the latter disease involving the Nootka chief, Cassacan, who sold a slave girl to a ship captain for several sheets of copper. After she apparently contracted the disease she was put ashore where she cohabited with Cassacan. Shortly he succumbed to it, passing it on to his wife. Hoskins believed they too would die and their village be destroyed by the malady. What one mariner-trader described as "amatory scenes" between these visitors and native women proved that the resulting venereal was no respecter of persons. "The result," writes Cook in his *Flood Tide of Empire* "was a commerce that loosed a crippling blight on the northwest coast, for the diseases contracted by slaves soon spread to their masters."[76]

The resulting decline of the lordly class left it with more available titles to bestow than there were persons of high birth to assume them; thus, those of lesser rank, unconnected from the line of chiefly descent, found themselves heirs to leadership positions.[77] This was unusual in earlier times

---

[75]Murdock, *Culture and Society*, 262. A similar assessment of potlatching is given by Eugene E. Ruyle who writes about controversy among professions, ethnologists, historians, anthropologists as to the origins, meaning and purpose of potlatches. See "Slavery, Surplus and Stratification."

[76]Hoskins, "The Narrative of a Voyage to the North West Coast," 62; Cook, *Flood Tide of Empire*, 353-54.

[77]The emergence of ranking of upper classes came about by environmental factors which permitted diversity and abundance of materials. Morton H. Fried, *The Evolution of Political Society: An Essay in Political Anthropology*, 110-18, 182-84. Then, by the mid-1880s there began to appear factors which dismantled the ranking system. Elman R. Service

when populations were in states of equilibrium. Now, native society, which in the 19th century had witnessed so much change through physical strife and debility, continued in a state of flux, its class structured society badly shaken.

---

writes, "the exaggerated status rivalry manifested in the North American Northwest Coast potlatches seems to have been caused by a breakdown in the social stucture (involving primogeniture, ranking by birth order, and the chiefdom form of organization), which left many hereditary statuses open for occupancy. Population loss due to European diseases was a large factor in this breakdown.

"In addition, the amount of European trade goods coming into the society in exchange for sea otter pelts created opportunities for ambitious potlatchers to achieve prestige." *Origins of the State and Civilization: The Process of Cultural Evolution,* 73n. Gilbert Malcolm Sproat's 1868 publication reinforces the belief that foreign imports were instrumental in breaking down the ranking system: "So great has been the disturbing force of contact with the colonists, that rank has lost much of its value, and as regards some of their ancient customs, they are now but little regarded by the natives." *Scenes and Studies of Savage Life,* 116. Ruyle states that although the ranks, which remained, had lost their original economic significance, they retained their prestige value, acquiring a new significance which allowed every Indian to "become a chief through potlatching." "Slavery, Surplus, and Stratification," 617.

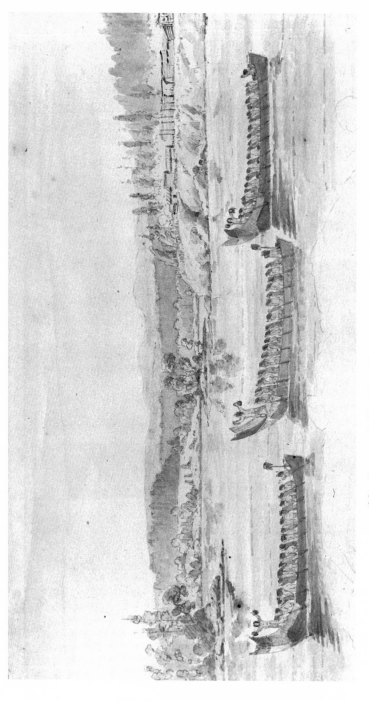

"The Return of a War Party," a watercolor by Paul Kane, 1846.
Setting is the Strait of Juan de Fuca. This strait and others between the U.S. and Canada were well traveled by Indians from the North raiding for women and children to enslave. As seen here, the heads of male victims were held aloft at bows of canoes to signify victory, and heads are also displayed on poles at the stern of two these craft. *Courtesy, Stark Museum of Art, Orange Texas. Neg. #31. 78/89. WWC 90.*

6

Slavery in the Sound and Strait

As the demand for enslaved natives increased, the Northern Indians expanded their raiding territory to include the southern extent of the sounds and straits of southwestern British Columbia and northwestern Washington. Here Coast Salish inhabitants were the focus of raids by the Northern Indians. As the demand for slaves continued, particularly after contact, these human commodities were brought from coastal Oregon and the Plateau through the Chinooks to the sound and strait Salish, and also to the Makahs, who acted as middle men, and transferred them north. The Coast Salish adopted the practice of slavery themselves, though in a milder form, just as they adopted a few of the less complex and less stringent rituals of Kwakiutl speakers. The potlatch of the Coast Salish was but a weak facsimile of the northern ceremonial. They did not adopt the rigid family structure of the northern matrilineal families. If slavery had continued with economic benefits to the Coast Salish, in time they might have taken on more of the intricate culture of the Northern Indians.

At its northernmost reaches the Coast Salish-Chinookan cultural zone encompassed both sides of the Strait of Georgia, the British Columbia mainland and the eastern portion of Vancouver Island to Kelsy Bay at the head of the small, short Johnstone Strait. The Central Coast Salish occupied the distal end of Vancouver Island and the mainland of Washington opposite it across the Strait of Juan de Fuca, with the Southern Coast Salish occupying most of the area around Puget Sound. Exceptions included the Chemakums at the confluence of the Strait of Juan de Fuca with Puget

Sound just east of the Salish Clallams. The straits of this area and Puget Sound composed the pool from which the Northern Indians raided for captives to enslave. Then, as has been noted, when the demand in the north for slaves increased, the flow of slaves was from south to north with Makahs at Cape Flattery acting as intermediaries so that slaves from the lower Columbia River were transported to Makahs and then relayed further north. Subsequently, with a desire of Plateau tribes to trade slaves east and south from the lower Columbia, there was also a north to south movement of enslaved Northerners. Some of them were shipped east across the Rocky Mountains through the trading process. The north-south trade continued to at least the 1820s, for the Britisher, Dr. John Scouler, observed that natives of the straits carried on an "inveterate war" to obtain slaves, many of which, he noted, the natives sold on "the South & arrive at the Columbia."[1] The movement was also from Puget Sound southerly to the Cowlitz as well as along the coast.

Tribes north of the Nootkas, such as the Tlingits, Haidas, Tsimshians and Kwakiutls, not satisfied with acquiring slaves through trade channels alone, continued adding to the inveteracy of a straits-Puget Sound war zone along complex trading and raiding routes. These Indians usually traveled along the Pacific Coast no further south than Cape Flattery in Makah country, and only rarely on to the Columbia River. Nootkas were said to have canoed south along the coast as far as Cape Mendocino, California, seizing natives and taking them north into thraldom.[2] If true, these journeys were certainly infrequent.

Natives of Sound and Strait were involved in inland conflict and concourse, but most of their slaving excursions and incursions were in salt water environs. Canoes transporting them were made by freemen with slave assistance. At first

---

[1]Scouler, "Dr. John Scouler's Journal of a Voyage to N.W. America" Pt. II, 195-96.
[2]Finlayson, "The History of Vancouver Island and the Northwest Coast," 16; Francis Densmore states that the Northern Indians traveled as far south as the Columbia River. *Nootka and Quileute Music. Smithsonian Bureau of American Ethnology Bulletin 124*, p. 10.

glance it might appear that the lesser slave role in canoe-making was due to their owners' fears that these slaves might develop a seamanship enabling them to escape or become involved in other troublesome situations. More importantly, their lesser role was due to their lack of status and spirit powers required in canoe-making and other pursuits.[3]

In native communities of Sound and Strait slaves and masters held a tenuous relationship despite their common goals of existence and coexistence. Religious beliefs and exercises, so important to non-slaves in communicating with the spirit world, were largely denied these servile ones. Slaves and non-slaves alike, however, faced the same threats from both violent nature and, more often, from violent men. As troublesome as was intertribal conflict within the region, conflict from incursions of fierce Indians to the north was equally, if not, more dangerous. For generations these bold northerners had attacked and counterattacked with spears, bows and arrows, knives and clubs and, at white contact, with firearms. That the record of such conflict in early times has been lost in misty antiquity might lead one to assume that it was only incidental. Archaeological evidence does not support this notion; neither does tribal legendry. Space does not permit an extensive cataloguing of this conflict involving natives of Sound and Strait, but a few examples cited herein give some idea of its cause, nature and extent.

As recorded by artist Paul Kane in the forepart of 1847, the Makahs in a retaliatory fight with Clallams to their east along the Strait of Juan de Fuca took eighteen prisoners, mostly women whom they enslaved, carrying home eight heads which they stuck on poles in front of their lodges. The Makah chief at the time was Yellow-cum whose father had piloted the Astorian ship, *Tonquin*, the one blown up off

---

[3]W.W. Elmendorf writes that Twana slaves "did not exercise any of the more specialized occupations such as canoe making, sea-mammal hunting, shamanistic curing, which depended on guardian-spirit support. A few slaves born in captivity acquired guardian spirits, but most lacked them. They were not, however, forbidden to seek spirit power." W.W. Elmendorf and Alfred L. Kroeber, *The Structure of Twana Culture with Comparative Notes on the Structure of Yurok Culture*, 345.

"Battle Between Clallam and Makah at I-eh-nus," a watercolor by Canadian artist Paul Kane. The primary objective of such intertribal warfare
was capture and enslavement of women and children.
Courtesy, Stark Museum of Art, Orange, Texas. Neg. #31.78/54, WWC 54.

Vancouver Island. Yellow-cum's human and inanimate possessions such as slaves and dentalia gave him great wealth.[4]
About a quarter-century later in the continuing revenge
cycle, the Makahs, belittled and goaded as inferiors by
Nootkan Nitinahts and Clayoquots, retaliated against Elwha
Clallams, killing two of their number. Had the United States
government by this time established its Makah Agency, such
an incident might not have occurred. An agent, at least, prevented Makahs from raising their victims' heads on poles in
celebrating their victory. No record exists as to how they
responded to Indians of the north under this goading, but
they did tell James Swan that they "could have taken plenty
squaws for slaves had they wanted to."[5]
    Like other leaders of Sound and Strait, those of the

[4]Kane, *Wanderings of an Artist*, 231-32.
[5]"Scenes Among the Mackahs, An Indian War Party," *Washington Standard*, Nov. 2,
1861.

Tatoosh, Makah leader and slave owner, after whom Tatoosh Island at the north-western tip of the Olympic Peninsula in Washington state was named. His people were intermediaries in tribal trade between natives of coastal Oregon, Washington and British Columbia.

Makahs became embroiled in conflict involving their own slaves. One who mistreated slaves was Makah Chief Tatoosh. Nearing the end of his life when mentally deranged, he beat them unmercifully with clubs.[6] Such inferior persons were naturally the first and most frequent objects of the wrath and vainglory of tribal leaders whenever their regal images became the least bit tarnished.

A root cause of conflict in native society lay in its highly structured nature. Fewer places was this more evident than among Makahs whose cultural roots lay with Nootkans to the north whose society was immersed in competition and status. Prerogatives of lordly chiefs and their lineage lay in ownership of fishing grounds, berry patches and strips of coastal beaches as well as in special privileges in ceremonials.[7]

---

[6]Information about Tatoosh's wrath and mistreatment of slaves came from the American, John R. Jewitt, the slave-captive of Maquinna, Tatoosh's brother-in-law. *Narrative of the Adventures and Sufferings of John R. Jewitt,* 108.

[7]Colson, *The Makah Indians,* 4, 203-04, 208.

Since Makah society centered around pursuit of the whale, daring exploits in that venture were requisites for leadership. Because of their special skills leaders almost automatically came into wealth in the form of canoes, blankets and slaves.[8] An example of skills qualifying one for leadership in Makah society was evidenced in the person of Tse-kauwtl (Sekowt'hl) whose mother was a slave and his father, a commoner. It was Tse-kauwtl whom Governor Isaac Stevens chose to speak for all Makahs at treaty sessions which he held with Indians on behalf of the United States. As the mid-19th century approached it was easier than previously for native leaders to acquire additional wealth in Euro-American products of which they had little before direct contact with whites.[9]

Like others, Makah chiefs did not wait for wealth to fall into their laps. One enterprising Makah chief designed a plan to not only retaliate against Nootkas of Clayoquot Sound, but to obtain wealth in the process. In 1860, when slave women were selling for from eighty to one hundred-fifty dollars, the chief propositioned the owner of a schooner to charter her to Clayoquot Sound to bring Nootkas aboard, ply them with liquor and then in their inebriated state, sail off carrying the entire lot into slavery.[10]

Among tribes of Sound and Strait their successful doctors, gamblers, hunters and fishers attributed wealth and position to powerful guardian spirits. Possibly the extreme danger of sailing into the broad Pacific to hunt earth's largest mammal, requiring as much spiritual as technical preparation, gave Makah chieftain candidates preeminence over those pursuing activities on a lower scale of danger and tribal importance. Valorous whale hunting was thus intimately interlocked with the structure of large extended families whose inherited slaves usually had little hand in the organizing and disposition of captured whales. At the bottom of the

---

[8]Ibid., 214.
[9]Ibid.
[10]*Port Townsend Register*, March 20, 1860.

social ladder, slaves were often relegated to catching lesser fish such as flounders, which one informant said they caught, cooked and served to villagers.[11]

As a rule Makah slaves were banned from marrying free-born persons, but lived in their houses and took part in social life. They defended masters in combat and dispatched those suspected of casting evil spells over them. Disposal was subtly administered with poison rather than with the violence. The Makahs classified poisons as those which killed victims and removed personalities from suspects so as to destroy their ability to influence others.[12]

If the end result of wars and raidings was not wounding and death, it was capture and enslavement. Capture of upper class persons (married within their own class to avoid contamination of commoner and slave blood) and commoner free men meant their perpetual stigmatization as slaves. Were they to return to their own tribe by escaping enslavement or by being ransomed or rescued, they suffered the same stinging insults from these tribesmen that they had once directed at their slaves.[13] Sound tribes held slaves who eventually escaped to their homelands as far away as Oregon, but once there they did not escape the disgrace of their former enslavement. When captured children among Teninos of north-central Oregon reached their majorities they could marry free persons, but like others, could not escape the stigma of their slave blood.[14] Among Sound tribes not even feasts or give-aways could mitigate the disgrace, dishonor, or guilt of those once in bondage.[15]

Anthropologist Wayne Suttles identifies "vassal villages" to which certain Sound tribesmen believed they had been

---

[11]Colson, *The Makah Indians,* 218; Warren A. Snyder, *Southern Puget Sound Salish: Texts, Place Names, and Dictionary,* 105.

[12]Colson, *The Makah Indians,* 202.

[13]Captured and enslaved persons suffered stigma like that of rape victims, both suffering such for life through no fault of their own. While rape victims are often counseled and comforted for their trauma, slaves had to fend for themselves, stigmatized to their graves.

[14]Murdock, *Culture and Society,* 216.

[15]Underhill, *Indians of the Pacific Northwest,* 160.

assigned by their deity, the Transformer. Such villages were also occupied by descendants of slaves no longer living with masters. They were also occupied by high-class persons who, under family pressure, were forced to sell themselves into slavery. Suttles states that when household thralls became too numerous, they could be turned out to form separate settlements.[16]

The Makahs and others such as the Upper Skagits[17] stressed the importance of blood lines to the extent that reference to another's slave ancestry was so insulting that only by killing the offender could the stigma of such ancestry be blotted out. In the face of such humiliation, ridicule, or unfortunate circumstance Makahs were always trying to upgrade their ancestry to nobility status when, in fact, slave blood had entered their lineage at some point.[18] Not even "cleansing rites" for those lacking close family ties among Coast Salish speakers could insure erasure of the taint of slavery.[19]

Geographic and social lines in Makah society were drawn between the high and the low. In shoreline villages beach and fishing rights were reserved for heads of noble houses. In more recent times admission that one's ancestors had lived south of the Strait of Juan de Fuca beach line makes a Makah suspect of having questionable ancestral blood or, in a manner of speaking, of living on the "wrong side of the tracks." Also in more recent times prestige, associated not only with lineage, but with wealth and displays thereof, is reflected in the ability to purchase commercial products. Inability to do so and dependence on handcrafted implements such as fish-

---

[16]Wayne P. Suttles, *Coast Salish Essays*, 9, 10.

[17]June McCormick Collins, *Valley of the Spirits: The Upper Skagit Indians of Western Washington*. Persons returning from slave captivity in other tribes were regarded by Twanas as social cripples, although such persons remained free. Elmendorf and Kroeber, *The Structure of Twana Culture*, 347.

[18]Colson, *The Makah Indians*, 208-13.

[19]Wayne P. Suttles, "Private Knowledge, Morality, and Social Classes among the Coast Salish," 503.

ing craft and gear has been equated with poverty and thus, with lower class.[20]

When tribes of Sound and Strait allied to war against one another their contests were often bilateral with power balanced and broken by alliances as in modern peace and war. The Snohomish Indians, among those bordering Puget Sound (in the vicinity of Everett, Washington) were perennial foe of the Chemakums near Hood Canal and the Strait of Juan de Fuca. According to their tradition, the Chemakums in the distant past were a remnant of a Quileute band of Chemakuan speakers fleeing from high Pacific tides to settle in their new homelands.[21] The latter was virtually a war zone between warlike Clallams to their west and equally warlike Snohomishes and other Sound tribes to their east. Chemakum strategy, like that of their aggressive neighbors, was to overpower their foe with sheer numbers, killing by stealth and surprise.[22] That they continually raided Clallams and Makahs for slaves and vice verse emboldened tribes such as the Snohomishes to move into this breach to raid for slaves. This did not mean that Clallams and Snohomishes were allied against the Chemakums, for Clallams fought both Snohomishes and Lower Skagits just as they did the Makahs.[23] Chemakum attrition was especially severe as a result of internecine raidings. In a September 1, 1852, report to Anson Dart, Oregon Superintendent of Indian Affairs, Edmund A. Starling, Indian agent for the Puget Sound District, attributed the decline of the Chemakums to death and enslavement at the hands of the Clallams.[24]

The famous Duwamish-Suquamish Chief Sealth, or

---

[20]Beatrice D. Miller, "Neah Bay, the Makah in Transition," 271-72.

[21]Ruby and Brown, *A Guide to the Indian Tribes of the Pacific Northwest,* 171.

[22] Gibbs, *Tribes of Western Washington and Northwestern Oregon* 1, Pt. 2, p. 191.

[23]Curtis, *The North American Indian* 9, p. 59; Albert B. Reagan, *Archaeological Notes on Western Washington and Adjacent British Columbia,* 6.

[24]Edmund A. Starling, Indian agent, District of Puget Sound, Wash. Terr. to Anson Dart, Supt. Indian Affairs, Oregon Terr., Sept. 1, 1852. *Annual Report, Secy. Interior, 1852,* Serial 658, p. 462.

Seattle, gained prominence and eminence around 1810 when in his early twenties he led an expedition eastward against mountain-dwelling Green and White River (Skopahmish, Smulkamish and Skekomish) Indians who were preparing to resume raiding saltwater tribes for slaves. With warfaring credentials this son of a chieftain father became chief not only of his own people, but reportedly, of others.[25] Regardless of his fame, much of it posthumously bestowed on him by the white community he befriended, his reported slave maternity stigmatized him for life. According to reports this did not prevent him from acquiring up to eight slaves, six of whom he inherited and two which he purchased.[26]

Also involved in wars and raidings for slaves and other booty were the culturally similar Puyallups and Nisquallys of southern Puget Sound. According to a student of their culture, by acquiring slaves they sought prestige more than economic gain. One of their main concerns, however was avoiding enslavement by Northern Indians, whose practice was to strike at pre-dawn to catch them unawares,[27] for should they let down their guard their women and children could be enslaved by these fierce Northerners. Like these attackers, the Puyallup-Nisquallys raided distant tribes for women and child slaves, seldom taking adult males. They considered their slaves as chattel, passing them on through inheritance; yet, they were accepted into family circles and treated as members were they of reasonable demeanor and industry in performing routine and heavy work. That they bore their owners' children prevented these offspring from being sold or gambled away.[28]

---

[25]Clarence B. Bagley, "Chief Seattle and Angeline," 246-47; Frank Carlson, *Chief Sealth*, 7. Seattle was reported to have had a slave mother and this was a "stigma on him;" nevertheless, he was a free man. Starling to Stevens, Dec. 10, 1853. *Records of the Washington Superintendency of Indian Affairs, 1853-1874, No. 5, Roll 9.*

[26]Clarence B. Bagley, ed., "Attitude of the Hudson's Bay Company During the Indian War of 1855-1856," 263. In an article, "Types and Characteristics of Puget Sound Indians," *The Northwest* 12, no. 9 (September, 1894), p. 5, E.I. Denny stated that Chief Seattle often bought slaves out of pity for their condition and then set them free or retained them in his "kindly employ."

[27]Marian W. Smith, *The Puyallup-Nisqually*, 154.   [28]Ibid., 52 and n.

Despite their inferior status, Puget Sound slaves seldom escaped, were we to take the word of an Indian agent who on December 10, 1853, reported: "There seems to be a code among slaves or among the people at any rate, against running away; but few do, although there are many chances to do so."[29] Among Puyallup-Nisquallys shamans who prevented girls from enslavement received from grateful families their daughters as wives. Warriors were given additional mates were they to rescue or prevent family members of these girls from becoming enslaved. Despite remaining within their physical environs, slaves remained outside what one scholar has termed "the social struggle for prestige," apparently few in number with distinguishing features "so shadowy that they cannot be said to have constituted a social class in a caste sense."[30]

There was little variation in percentages of slave numbers of Puget Sound tribes near the mid-19th century. Again, were we to take the word of an Indian agent in 1856 the Nooksacks had "no slaves whatever and no Indian more than one wife."[31] Such small tribes, living in relative isolation in hill country east of saltwater (in their case, inland shortly below the Canadian border at that time), had fewer slaves than did those nearer coastal waters. This did not mean that they made no incursions against other tribes to acquire slaves, for they did so usually in retaliation against coastal peoples who raided them. White men visiting these more remote peoples around mid-19th century recorded instances of their involvement in slavery. An American, Samuel Hancock, was among mountain-bordering Snoqualmies when they enslaved a neighboring Snohomish woman. He wrote

[29]Starling to Stevens, Dec. 10, 1853. *Records of the Washington Superintendency of Indian Affairs, 1853-1874, No. 5, Roll 9.*

[30]Smith, *The Puyallup Nisqually*, 47, 168.

[31]E.C. Fitzhugh, Special Indian agent, to Col. J.W. Nesmith, Supt. Indian Affairs, Wash. and Oregon Terrs., June 18, 1857. *Annual Report, Secy. Interior, 1857,* Serial 919, p. 616. Fitzhugh also wrote that after the initial white contact period the Nooksacks and Semiahmoos were greatly endangered due to raids by the Northern Indians. Ibid., 32. Arthur D. Howden, ed., *The Narrative of Samuel Hancock, 1845-1860,* pp. 100-101.

that when the Snoqualmies were brought to task by her Sno-homish people, her captors paid them two blankets and two muskets and then departed in friendly fashion which was typical of small-scale slave-taking so common among natives of that region. When Hancock was among the much-raided Stillaguamish Indians living shortly north of the Snohomish peoples, they believed he had come to raid them, and some of them wanted to enslave him.[32]

Former high-ranking persons enslaved by Upper Skagits (along the upper Skagit River) were permitted to marry into that tribe's middle class, were such marriages second ones for the latter. Although not treated as slaves, children of such second marriages were marked for life as offspring of slave mothers.[33] Less warlike and with fewer slaves than were held by saltwater Lower Skagits, the Upper Skagits have been described as relatively peaceful, their only motivation for warring being to retaliate in the manner of the blood-feud by taking slaves from those who raided them.[34] In their retalia-tory journeys their women navigated their canoes and their men did the fighting. Where Sound and Strait tribes feared attacks from Indians to their north, the Upper Skagits feared those to their north from the Thompson River of the British Columbia interior who swept down on them, leaving bodies rammed through with pointed sticks and placed upright in visible locations so that relatives on returning to their villages could easily find them.[35] This treatment was similar to that administered by Paiutes of the lower Plateau.

One anthropologist suggests that in pre-contact times the Upper Skagits were too poor to buy slaves. Their social stra-tum was weak and social control held fighting in check among villages within the tribe, which tended to restrict blood-feuds and travel. After white contact, the Upper Skag-its achieved more wealth involving potlatch give-aways. This

---

[32]Arthur D. Howden, ed., *The Narrative of Samuel Hancock, 1845-1860*, pp. 100-01.
[33]Collins, *Valley of the Spirits*, 126.
[34]Ibid., 115.
[35]Ibid., 118.

expansion, enabling them to capture slaves from surrounding tribes, posed the problem of how to treat captives who might be their own relatives. Marriage of free upper-class Skagits to slaves was a source of contention among these tribesmen. "Honored names" of the wealthy few Upper Skagit nobility were transmitted to families. At name-giving potlatches and other ceremonials these nobles were restrained in demeanor, avoiding quarrels, loud talking and violence, believing that such befitted only those of lesser class. Wealth was accumulated through personal effort rather than through inheritance.[36]

Southwest of both Upper and Lower Skagits were the Twanas who, in their Hood Canal homeland, enjoyed a measure of isolation lacking in tribes of the Sound who were constantly raided by Indians of the Straits as well as by those further to the north. The Twanas had no organized raiding ventures; consequently, captives were not their primary source of slaves. Nor did they enslave their own people for social infractions. Like their neighbors they did purchase slaves. These occupied the bottom of their social ladder on whose rungs above them were commoners, medicine men, headmen, subchiefs and chiefs.

Twana slaves lived in winter households with masters. South of present-day Hoodsport on Hood Canal there were special quarters for them and they were humanely treated so they would not run away. A student of the Twanas states that a few slaves born in captivity and having guardian spirits were permitted to seek spirit powers. They were also fed and clothed by their masters who treated them as family, addressing them in fictitious kinship terms.[37]

Free Twana persons performed few menial tasks or hard labor. In 1848, for instance, some of them for the first time saw white men making camp nearby. On noticing one of them doing chores, they assumed him to be a slave, offering

---

[36]June M. Collins, "John Fornsby: The Personal Document of a Coast Salish Indian," 126; Collins, *Valley of the Spirits,* 124-25.

[37]Elmendorf and Kroeber, *The Structure of Twana Culture,* 345.

to purchase him from his companions for some pelts, muskets, blankets and two native slaves.[38]

The taint of slave strain in one's ancestry served to bar wealth-power acquisition.[39] Upper class "blood" meant membership in a bilaterally reckoned line of freemen forbears of high social reputation with no trace of slave blood.[40] For the wealthy there was largess other than the giving of wealth in food feasts, for foods accumulated in Twana society were separate from accumulations of wealth. Feasts were usually held in autumn during the height of salmon fishing when subsistence was abundant. Secret society initiation ceremonies held in winter, were equated in form with intercommunity give-aways in which slaves were not permitted to participate, as they were unqualified for wealth distribution.[41] Potlatches to which recipients were invited validated one's social status and displayed importance to neighbors and acquaintances.[42]

Many lower class Twanas were recruited from ranks of offspring of liaisons of upper class slave owners and their female slaves. This too was at variance with the customary practice in which offspring of such liaisons were usually slaves. Some males tried to force social recognition of "half-slave" sons as being of the upper class. Because of such recruitment they were suspected of having bad, or slave blood, and were thus barred from acquiring wealth.[43] Free persons, captured by foes and escaping to rejoin their own people, remained free, but their descendants were subjected to covert disparagement.[44]

Behind the moat-like Hood Canal the Twanas were fortunate to be buffered from attacks of Chemakum, Clallam and

---

[38]J.C. Rathbun, *History of Thurston County, Washington*, 14.

[39]Elmendorf and Kroeber, *The Structure of Twana Culture*, 334.

[40]Ibid., 327.

[41]Twana giveaways were unlike those of several other tribes because in them there was no concept of twofold return of fixed interest on gifts which were not loans. Ibid., 345.

[42]Ibid., 323.

[43]Ibid., 334.

[44]Ibid., 347.

Makah raiders. Also sheltering them from attack was their own lack of raiding, which did not evoke revenge cycle incursions of their foes. Tribes along the Strait did not buffer Sound Indians in like manner from Indians from the north who came down as they had for generations to plunder and kill Sound men and capture their women as slaves.

To retaliate against such incursions a coalition of Sound tribes under Suquamish Chief Kitsap in 1825 undertook a northern expedition of a reported two hundred or more warrior-canoe armada against Cowichans. Finding the Cowichan men gone from their village, the Sound tribesmen killed the elderly and enslaved their young women. On their return south they ran into thick fog near Dungeness Spit (near present-day Port Angeles, Washington). When it lifted they discovered a host of Cowichan warriors canoeing northward with Sound women and children whom they had enslaved. In an ensuing fight both forces reportedly lost half their warriors.[45]

The conflict occurred between what Leland Donald describes as two major slave-trading networks—one among Indians from the north and the other, among those of the lower Columbia River. Charting the complex trade patterns from Prince William Sound in the north and from there southward (including the northern interior) to northeastern Vancouver Island, he finds no connection between this northern network and that of the Columbia River. Within these two networks the practice of slavery was more intense than in that region between them; yet, in the interregional slave trade there is the matter of preference of Indians from the north for the Kiskimo-type head-deformed slaves from Vancouver Island as cited in an 1840 report crediting Tlingits with having war-captured slaves from that region.[46]

---

[45]Edmond S. Meany, "The Indian Chief Kitsap," 298.

[46]Donald, "The Slave Trade on the Northwest Coast," 127-35; Aurel Kranse, *The Tlingit Indians*, 105. Bancroft writes that the Northern Indians carried on slave trade with southern tribes and, that when first noted by early-day white travelers, these northern tribes had mostly flatheaded slaves which would indicate trade with natives to the south. *Wild Tribes*, 108.

In a letter to Governor Stevens, December 10, 1853, E.A. Starling, Puget Sound district Indian agent, confirmed a southerly flow of slaves into his district from Vancouver Island and points further north.[47] Three decades later Jacobsen observed an incident in the southerly flow of slaves in which Indians of a village near Vancouver Island's Clayoquot Sound were virtually imprisoned by other villagers. When they tried to escape they were captured and sold into slavery at Cape Flattery.[48]

During the first half of the 19th century the numbers of Sound and Strait Indian victims of raids by northern tribesmen is believed to have run into the thousands since these northern marauders had acquired more guns and ammunition from the Hudson's Bay Company and other sources in the north than had Indians to the south, from Fort Vancouver and other Company posts in that region.[49] A most important advantage of the northern raiders were their navigational skills, enabling them to move swiftly over long distances in craft outdistancing sailing ships and later, steamers.

Tribes of the Sound sought not only to defend themselves, but to strike back as had those under Chief Kitsap, to kill as many foe as possible and return to their villages with the visible wealth of slaves and human heads, the symbolic evidence of their success.[50] These attempts weakened over time. To protect themselves from retaliatory attacks they fortified their dwellings with stockades of heavy twelve to fifteen-foot puncheons set in the ground and strengthened by posts and crosspieces in these structures which were similar to fortifi-

---

[47]*Records of the Washington Superintendency of Indian Affairs, 1853-1874, No. 5, Roll 9.*

[48]Johan Adrian Jacobsen, *Alaskan Voyage 1881-1883 An Expedition to the Northwest Coast of America.* Erna Gunther, trans., 61.

[49]Fitzhugh to Nesmith, June 18, 1857, *Annual Report, Secy. Interior, 1857,* Serial 919, p. 616. Henry L. Oak wrote of the advantage of the Northern Indians with their swift canoes and Hudson's Bay Co. guns. "Notes on Indian Wars in Washington Territory." Ms. P-A 69.

[50]Bancroft wrote that "Sticking the heads of slain enemy on poles in front of their dwellings, is a common way of demonstrating their joy over a victory." *Wild Tribes,* 215.

cations they had seen at fur posts.[51] In 1841 Lieutenant Charles Wilkes reported such a fortress erected by Lower Skagits in a great raiding area to prevent attacks from Indians from the north and those closer home as Clallams against whom they had long been at odds. The fort was four hundred-feet-long of thick planks, each about thirty feet tall and well set in the ground with barely enough space between them to fire a musket. Wilkes believed it rendered its defenders impregnable to attack.[52]

Other government representatives supplied information pertaining to encroachments of Indians from the north. One Indian agent reported that Semiahmoos living near the Canadian border by the Strait of Georgia entrance to the United States "were formerly a powerful tribe, but have suffered from the hostilities of the north Indians to such an extent that they hardly number one hundred now."[53] The agent also stated that Indians from the north told him that one flatheaded Indian was worth more than two with round heads.[54]

Coast Salish Lummis and, formerly, Nooksacks were among the first below the Canadian border to feel the wrath of northerners on their southerly sweeps. Mention has been made of their method of attack carried out when villagers were sleeping or when their men were preoccupied with fishing and unable to gather weapons to counterattack. Rushing past fishermen the attackers made for their houses to capture women and children. Haidas and Tlingits often attacked mothers who had little time to protect their children. Those fortunate enough to escape grabbed their children and ran off with them into the woods or shoved them into berry bushes warning them not to whimper so as not to reveal themselves. Enemy raiders were aware of this stratagem. A

---

[51]Gibbs, *Tribes of Western Washington and Northwestern Oregon* 1, Pt. 2, p. 192.

[52]Charles Wilkes, *Narrative of the United States Exploring Expedition, during the years 1838, 1839, 1940, 1842,* iv, p. 481.

[53]Fitzhugh to Nesmith, June 18, 1857, *Annual Report, Secy. Interior, 1857,* Serial 919, p. 616.

[54]Ibid., 615.

response to enemy calls meant lives of enslavement for these children.[55]

Tribes north of the Strait of Juan de Fuca were aware of intertribal squabbling among tribes to the south across the Strait whose contestings they sought to use to their own advantage. On one occasion seven warriors from north across the Strait, hearing that the Ozettes (a Makah subtribe) and Makahs at Neah Bay were quarreling, pounced upon a Makah village at night, killing, plundering, enslaving some of its people and forcing others to flee.[56] Afterwards when the two contending Makah peoples became friends, they turned their combined fury against others including nearby Quileutes.[57]

Sweeping down various straits, Indians from the north continued probing deep into Puget Sound. On the way there they attacked Indians such as the Lower Skagits who lay exposed near the mouth of their river off the northern end of nearby Whidbey Island. When some raiding Kwakiutls killed a Lower Skagit, his Upper Skagit relatives, joined by some Sound tribesmen, canoed north seeking revenge. They were successful in this venture, killing a number of Kwakiutls and taking heads as well as enslaving young boys.[58] In the north the Skagits saw one of their women enslaved by Kwakiutls, but could not rescue her since she was carefully guarded by her captors.[59] Southern Kwakiutl Lekwiltoks, whom Reverend Demers called "the terror of the other nations, whom it pillages, massacres, and reduces to slavery," occasionally surprised and carried off victims from Whidbey Island and places in Puget Sound, taking them north into slavery.[60] Occupying lands in the general area of present-day Seattle, the Duwamishes continued as objects of annual plundering by Tlingits. Such incursions helped reduce Duwamish num-

[55]Thomas Talbot Waterman and Ruth Greiner, *Indian Houses of Puget Sound*, 45, 46.
[56]Helen W. Clark, "Chips From an Old Block." Typescript copy of ms.
[57]Ibid., 2, 3.
[58]Collins, *Valley of the Spirits*, 115-17.
[59]Ibid., 117.
[60]*Notices & Voyages of the Famed Quebec Mission to the Pacific*, 99.

bers from roughly five hundred to a mere handful huddling near Seattle's Shilshole Bay.[61] In earlier times natives of the Sound were also victims of the Cowlitz Indians raiding north for slaves to take back to their Cowlitz-Columbia River homeland.[62]

The Anglo-American boundary, established in 1846, extending no further west than to an area of several straits, permitted the free passage of Indians in what was essentially an international no man's land. The result was trouble between Indians and whites, not to mention trouble between Americans and Britons, during a quarter-century hiatus until the 1872 San Juan Island boundary settlement in the straits. Prior to the 1846 boundary settlement the Indians found Hudson's Bay-British control of the Oregon country more to their liking since it had not involved the danger of large scale influx of whites as it might have under American control.

From early times natives of Sound and Strait believed that white men, especially Americans, were coming to take their lands and enslave them.[63] The 1846 boundary settlement only confirmed this belief. Moreover, it has been speculated that an earlier settlement of the San Juan Islands could have taken place had there not been such a dread of the Northern Indians marauding southward along these island shores.[64] One story circulating among Indians below the Canadian border was that Americans planned to transport them in "fire-ships" (gunboats) to some distant country where the sun never shone and leave them there to die. [65] Helping perpetuate this notion, credited to Nisqually chief Leschi, were John Taylor, a Snohomish-Snoqualmie chief, and Sno-

---

[61]Costello, *The Siwash*, 86.

[62]The 19th century ethnologist, George Gibbs, termed the north to south movement of slaves an exception, that Dr. William Fraser Tolmie of the Hudson's Bay Company's Fort Vancouver and Nisqually had informed him that the course of the slave trade had always been south to north. *Tribes of Western Washington and Northwestern Oregon* 1, Pt. 2, p. 189.

[63]Tribes of the interior had similar fears of loss of their lands and enslavement at the hands of whites. Gustavus Hines, *Wild Life in Oregon*, 147.

[64]H.R. Crosby, "The San Juan Difficulty," 205.

[65]Rathbun, *History of Thurston County, Washington*, 14.

qualmie head man Patkanin, both of whom led what were
called the "Big Tribes" which raided smaller ones for slaves.
Some chiefs were not so ill-disposed toward Americans. One
of these was the Nisqually Gray Head who believed they
would protect his people from powerful chiefs as Patkanin.
In response to a Duwamish chief who said he would protect
the Nisquallys, Gray Head said he would rather have one
rifle with a Boston [American] behind it protecting him than
the entire Duwamish tribe. Neighbors to the Nisquallys, the
Chehalis Indians shared the same sentiment.[66]

After Washington Territory was organized in 1853, Governor Stevens as Superintendent of Indian Affairs set out in
1854 to effect treaties with American tribes of Sound, Strait
and Coast. One treaty provision required Indians to cease
their warring and then free slaves, and neither purchase nor
acquire others.[67] Besides the provision forbidding slavery and

---

[66]Evans, *History of the Pacific Northwest: Oregon and Washington* 2, p. 530. A.B. Rabbe-
son, who was associated with the Hudson's Bay Company at Fort Nisqually, revealed that
to have Indians around the fort abandon the practice of killing slaves and binding live ones
to bodies of the dead in canoes on high poles, Company officials assured Gray Head they
would protect his people from raiders. *Mason County Journal,* February 7, 1890, p. 6.

[67]The treaties were: those with Nisqually, Puyallup, Steilacoom, Squaxin, Sahewamish,
etc., December 26, 1854; with the Duwamish, Suquamish, Snoqualmie, Snohomish, Skagit, Kikiallus, Swinomish, Nuwaha, Lummi, etc., January 22, 1855; with the Chemakum,
Clallam, Skokomish, January 26, 1855; with the Makah and Ozette, January 31, 1855; and
with Quinault, Quileute, Queets and Hoh, July 1, 1855 and January 25, 1856.

In correspondence to the authors, June 14, 1989 Patrick A. Dunae of the British
Columbia Provincial Archives, Victoria, writes concerning Indian treaties of western Canada: "As it happened, very few treaties were made with native people of this province-hence
the ongoing litigation between the provincial and federal governments and various Indian
bands re: native land claims. A number of treaties were made between the Hudson's Bay
Company and Indian bands on southern Vancouver Island in 1850-1852. Known as the
"Fort Victoria Treaties," these agreements dealt solely with the question of land title. None
of the treaties contained any "anti-slavery" provisions. [For details, see Wilson Duff, "The
Fort Victoria Treaties," *B. C. Studies* no. 3 (Fall 1969).] The only other formal treaty which
effected British Columbia was Treaty 8, made between the federal government of Canada
and various northern Indian tribes in 1899. Treaty 8 dealt with lands in the Peace River
area. And while it was more detailed and comprehensive than earlier agreements, it contained no "anti-slavery" provisions either. [For details see Rene Fumoleau, *As Long As This
Land Shall Last: A History of Treaty 8 and Treaty 11, 1870-1939.*]

Holding that Indians had title to lands, the United States set out to extinguish that title,
defining in its treaties the Indian realties. On the other hand, north of parallel 49° Great
Britain held that Canadian Indians had only "qualified Dominion" over the lands, or the

its trade the treaties called for surrender of tribal lands, establishment of reservations, schools and medical facilities. Provision was also made for instruction in agriculture with
accompanying implements. Also to be provided were
sawmills, teachers, doctors, and annuities.

The Indians largely ignored the provisions calling for the
abolition of slavery and its trade. Such practices, carried on
for generations, were not as easily abolished as the United
States government wished. There were several reasons why
Indians continued trading in Canada in violation of their
pacts with the government: their strong desire to purchase
things in Victoria such as slaves, blankets, liquor and fish and
fur products; failure of the governments to settle the international boundary in the straits between Vancouver Island and
the American mainland unlike that settled inland from the
straits at the 49th parallel; the four-year failure of the American government to ratify and fulfill its obligations under the
treaties; its failure during this hiatus to supervise the Indians;
and its difficulty in enforcing trade restrictions due to the difficult terrain and the deceptive nature of the many bays and
inlets in the straits between the United States and Canada.

Slavery would wane only through attrition and a natural
flow of events, especially the ebbing of tribal warfare by
which many had been enslaved. Writing in the late 1860s,
James Swan observed that formerly "these battles were sanguinary, numbers being killed on both sides and prisoners
taken, who were invariably made slaves; but of late years they

"right of occupancy but not title to the land," and until the "uncivilized inhabitants" established a "settled form of government and subjugate the ground to their own uses by the cultivation of it," they had no individual ownership of property. All lands save those with
houses on them and under cultivation were regarded as "waste and therefore available for
colonization." For the Hudson's Bay Company James Douglas made eleven treaties with
Indians of the Fort Victoria area and two at Fort Rupert and one at Nanaimo. Little account
of Indian realties was noted except for village sites and enclosed fields. In the Saanich area
there were numerous claimants; thus, a fifty square-mile tract was purchased, the Indians
being paid in blankets with a 300 percent markup over the wholesale price for surrendering
their lands. They were allowed to hunt on unoccupied lands and fish in special places. Robin
Fisher, *Contact and Conflict Indian-European Relations in British Columbia, 1774-1890*, pp.
66-67.

have confined themselves to occasional murders only, fearing lest any more extensive warfare would call down upon them the vengeance of the whites."[68] With these changes ex-slaves among the Makahs preferred to remain with their owners' families. Despite resistance of prominent families, some of their people married slaves who were even admitted into certain tribal societies. Prominent Makah families opposed government policies restricting their sources of wealth in what had been their vested resource-producing waters such as fishing places, and in lands on their Makah Reservation (established under the January 31, 1855, Makah treaty). Ownership of these places passed from these families to others, including former slaves.

The Yakima-Puget Sound phase of the Indian War, which broke out in 1855, was a consequence of Indian unhappiness with the Stevens treaties. The treaties involved land-taking more than they did peace-keeping, thus adding a complex ingredient to the existing strife between Sound tribes and Indians from the north.[69] Leading the anti-American faction, Nisqually Chief Leschi in December 1856, reportedly warned the Sound tribes that if they did not join the war coalition, powerful Yakima-Klickitats would cross the Cascade Mountains to enslave them. [70] After leading the war faction for a time, Patkanin was approached by American officials to gather head trophies of "hostile" Indians for a bounty of twenty dollars per warrior head and four times that amount for that of a chief. The heads were to be delivered to the sloop-of-war *Decatur* whose officers were instructed to send them to be recorded in Olympia, the Washington Territorial capital. Lieut. T.S. Phelps of that ship recorded that "several invoices of these ghastly trophies were received, and sent to their destination..."[71] Mrs. Margaret Brown Busby

---

[68]Swan, *The Indians of Cape Flattery*, 51.

[69]For an account of this war, see Ruby and Brown, *Indians of the Pacific Northwest*, 145-46.

[70]Wesley B. Gosnell, Special Agent for the Nisqually, Puyallup and Squaxin reservations, to Governor Stevens, December 31, 1856, *Records of the Washington Superintendency of Indian Affairs, 1853-1874, No. 5, Roll 11.*

[71]Admiral T.S. Phelps, *Reminiscences of Seattle, Washington Territory,* 41, 42.

stated that her pioneer neighbors on Whidbey Island understood at that time that Patkanin, finding the business of taking enemy heads to be dull, took to killing his own slaves to
increase his bounty.[72]

Some Indian factions refusing to join the war party wished
the Americans to protect them from tribes from the north
who took advantage of the turmoil occasioned by the war to
increase their raidings into the Sound and Straits. White settlers on the Sound initially feared that its Indians would join
those of the north in joint attacks on them.[73] Military posts
such as Fort Steilacoom (established in 1849 below present-
day Tacoma) offered little protection for both whites and
Indians from their common northern foe, and army officers
admitted their inability to provide protection to settlements
beginning to spring up in the region. Writing in 1855 Capt.
George Stoneman and Lieut. W.H.S. Whiting (both
U.S.A.) reported that "It is not too much to say that in event
of an outbreak the northern Indians are able to exterminate
every white man dwelling on the waters of Puget Sound."[74]

In the summer of 1856, when Indian agencies had been
established around the Sound, E.C. Fitzhugh, special agent
at Bellingham Bay below the Canadian border, called on
Governor Stevens for help. Fitzhugh warned that seventy-
six canoes of Haidas, Bella Bellas, Tsimshians, Stikine and
Tongass subdivisions of Tlingits were "preparing to descend
on the Sound to plunder the Bostons and take slaves among
the flat heads..."[75]

In 1857 Col. T. Morris, U.S.A. opined that by retaliating
against aggressive Indians from the north, those of the
Sound might not only prevent their attacks, but protect the
white community as well.[76] In that time of hysteria the white

---

[72]Meany, *History of the State of Washington,* 183.

[73]Ibid., 204.

[74]Capt. George Stoneman and Lt. W.H.C. Whiting to Maj. E.D. Townsend, July 5,
1855 (50 Cong., 1 sess., *Sen. Exec. Doc. 165*), Serial 2513, p. 72.

[75]Fitzhugh to Stevens, July 8, 1856. *Records of the Washington Superintendency of Indian
Affairs, 1853-1874. No. 5, Roll 10.*

[76]Col. T. Morris, "Army Officer's Report on Indian War and Treaties," 140.

community was more concerned with its own safety than with that of their Indian neighbors. Between attacks of Indians of the north and diseases, Indian population decrease was severe. Although failing to stress the disease factor, an agent among Samish Indians on strait lands below the Canadian border in 1857 issued a report with figures unsupported by those of a Hudson's Bay Company census:

> Their total number now I do not think exeeds two hundred, whereas ten or twelve years ago they were one of the most numerous tribes on the Sound, and at that date numbered over two thousand. But, like the other tribes living contiguous to the Gulf of Georgia, (the great northern thoroughfare,) they have been nearly annihilated by the hordes of northern savages that have infested, and do now, even at the present day, infest, our own shores. They formerly came down for the purpose of taking slaves... They were supplied at an earlier day with [more] fire-arms than our Indians, and therefore had a decided advantage over them—killing all they could not carry away. They told me last summer that they had among them over two thousand Flathead slaves, and had traded off with those living still further north. They have taken several during the past spring and summer, and are prowling around the [Lummi?] reservation now for the same purpose.[77]

Shortly after mid-19th century the son of a band chief of the Sookes of southern Vancouver Island (whose people spoke a Salish dialect similar to that of Clallams) stabbed and killed the relative of a Clallam chief. The blood-feud propitiatory offering for the deed was a slave (acquired from another tribe) along with canoes and blankets thrown in to seal the transaction.[78] Old Dan, a Nootka slave, whom Makahs had captured on Vancouver Island and then sold to Quinault chief Capt. Mason, was later freed by the Quinaults thanks to the anti-slavery provision in the Stevens treaties. Once free, he built a house near Point Grenville along the Pacific Ocean where he made a living escorting tourists.[79] For every instance

---

[77]Fitzhugh to Nesmith, June 18, 1857, *Annual Report, Secretary Interior, 1857,* Serial 919, p. 615.

[78]Col. W.C. Grant, "Description of Vancouver Island."

[79]Olin D. Wheeler, "A Day with the Queniut Indians," 60.

Old Dan, once the property of
Captain Mason, a Quinault
chief, and Mason's father.
*Courtesy, Special Collections,
Univ. of Washington Libraries.
Neg. NA 1246.*

of adherence to the treaties, however, there were several instances in which they continued being disregarded.

Relations between Clallams and Sookes and other tribes of Vancouver Island were indeed stormy during the immediate post-treaty period when they did not let a piece of treaty paper dissuade them from abandoning the deep rooted revenge cycle mentality in which they were enmeshed. Occupying lands on the southern shores of the Strait of Juan de Fuca, the Clallams lay as exposed as ever to Canadian tribes crossing canoe sea lanes to the American side to raid and plunder. Resolved to wreak vengeance on these Canadian bands were two Clallam chieftain sons who devoted their full energies to the task.[80] Proof of the Clallam thirst for revenge were the more than a hundred enemy skulls lining their beaches above the highwater mark.[81] Such trophies were

[80]Curtis, *The North American Indian* 9, p. 22.
[81]Ibid.

grim reminders of conflict not only with fierce northern Indians such as Tlingits, Haidas and Tsimshians, but with nearer Canadian Coast Salish Indians such as Sookes, Songishes and Cowichans. Rather than raiding their more powerful Indian neighbors to the north these Coast Salish peoples attacked Indians of the American Sound and Strait.

In his *Hyda Land and People* (1884), Newton H. Chittenden stated that in the previous thirty years Haidas had captured and enslaved several white men. Among these was an American party which included James McAllister, whose problem of bad teeth was solved by an elderly slave woman who chewed his food so he could eat it. McAllister did not get off Scot free for this service, for his party was held captive until ransomed. The British government, which furnished about a thousand dollars worth of goods which the natives appropriated, was reimbursed by the United States.[82]

We may never know how many natives fell to attackers and counterattackers in the conflict to raid for slaves and other goods, and seek revenge. That populations of the Coast Salish of British Columbia, the most numerous of tribes to the north, remained fairly constant into the 1830s despite losses from smallpox and slave raids, was of little comfort to victims of their aggressions. By August 1855, the Clallams were distraught over an anticipated attack by those Salish and other northern speakers. A sophisticated captain aboard an American warship reported that they cut and lacerated their own bodies and invoked the evil spirit to do "very naughty things" to their enemies, and the good spirit to watch and protect them in the manner of "one of our revivals of tent meetings." The captain lost his flippant attitude on learning that northern Indians had killed some white men.[83]

Troubles within tribes continued, embroiling those of Sound and Strait as though there was not enough trouble

---

[82]Newton H. Chittenden, *Hyda Land and People—Official Report of the Exploration of the Queen Charlotte Islands for the Government of British Columbia, 1884*, pp. 15-16; Sarah Hartman, "Pioneer James M'Allister's Family," *Weekly Ledger*, March 24, 1893.

[83]Philip C. Johnson, Jr., "Private Notes of Philip C. Johnson, Jr. on Board U.S.S. Active 1855-56," pp. 5, 6. Typescript copy of ms.

from tribes further north. When advised that a Samish "tyee," General Pierce, had killed one of his slaves, United States District Court Judge Francis A. Chenoweth observed that "they could commit murder on one another and that, our courts could not interfere… The Indians themselves," he observed, "seem to consider the murder of a slave as a matter of course and that a Tyee has a right to put to death his own slave, just as the fancy takes him."[84] With greater responsibility for keeping peace among the Indians than Judge Chenoweth, and with long-standing disputes such as that between the Lower Chehalis and Quinault Indians in mind, Special Indian agent Sidney S. Ford in June 1857, suggested that the government bring contending parties together. Then, by listening to both sides in an arbitration-like hearing, have the wronged tribes receive presents from the other.[85]

Judge Chenoweth came to change what had apparently been an indifference or inability to settle the problem of strife and killing among tribes after Indians killed a prominent white man on August 11, 1857. The victim, I.N. Ebey, a resident of Whidbey Island, was killed and decapitated in a revenge attack by Northern Indians, said to be the "Kakes" of a central Tlingit division.[86] The killing occurred shortly after the Kakes' losing confrontation with the gunboat U.S.S. *Massachusetts*, which sailed from the Sound much to the consternation of American settlers. After a meeting, presided over by Chenoweth, to see what could be done to protect American citizens from "incursions of a savage and foreign foe,"[87] Governor James Douglas of Vancouver Island was asked to deliver the murderers. He responded by stating that he would be happy to see them brought to justice and would not fail to communicate with Northern Indians through

---

[84]Fitzhugh to Stevens, Feb. 7, 1857. *Records of the Washington Superintendency of Indian Affairs, No. 5, Roll 10.*

[85]Sidney S. Ford, Special Indian Agent, to Nesmith, June 30, 1857, *Annual Report, Secretary Interior*, 1857, Serial 919, p. 630.

[86]Crosby, "The San Juan Difficulty," 206.

[87]Charles M. Gates, ed., "Defending Puget Sound Against the Northern Indians," 70.

Hudson's Bay Company post personnel, adding that a law forbade the British Indians from entering Washington Territory. He also expressed the wish that the law force them to suspend their visits to the American settlements and "remain quietly in their own country." He also maintained that the Ebey killers were from Russian Alaska, not from British territory, a fact acknowledged by the Washington Territorial Legislative Assembly, January 20, 1860.[88]

Continuing incursions from the north were brought to the attention of President James Buchanan by Washington Territorial Governor Fayette McMullin, October 20, 1857. The governor advised the president that he had visited the territory bordering Sound and Strait and had crossed over the Strait to Victoria on southern Vancouver Island to confer with Governor Douglas about adopting a policy to prevent what he described as further incursions of the "northern hoardes of savages" inhabiting Russian possessions and British America.[89] In 1859, Haidas captured passenger schooners *Ellen Maria* and *Blue Wing* sailing between Steilacoom on the Sound and Port Townsend on the Strait, murdering passengers and crews.[90] Americans accused Douglas of not apprehending the perpetrators because his wife was an Indian.[91] The pioneer, Charles Prosch, wrote that in the first and subsequent issues of *The North-west*, a newspaper of Port Townsend which lay vulnerable on the Strait, its editor appealed to the government to protect settlers who were unsafe in small boats any distance from shore.[92]

Shortly after mid-19th century a Port Townsend resident visiting in Victoria recognized a young Indian girl taken from a tribe in Washington Territory and enslaved by Songish Indians. The visitor took her home, but a short time later Governor Douglas' clerk came down with a statement requiring her to return to Canada. On investigating the mat-

[88]"Decapitation of Colonel Eby," 74, 75.
[89]Gates, "Defending Puget Sound Against the Northern Indians," 70.
[90]Meany, *History of the State of Washington*, 205.
[91]Prosch, *Reminiscences of Washington Territory*, 40.   [92]Ibid., 40, 41.

ter Washington Territorial justice, James Swan, determined that she not be returned since she had been enslaved to Songish Indians and there was no fugitive slave law between the United States and Canada. Swan's decision made her family happy, but not so her former owners who had lost a drudge.[93] In 1838, a Bay Company chief trader, James Murray Yale, had released a Snohomish woman captured by Indians near his Fort Langley post on the lower Fraser River. Since they had not only enslaved her, but killed her husband, Yale believed the two incidents would likely cause a war.[94]

On July 1, 1860, Washington Territorial Indian agent Michael T. Simmons wrote the Oregon and Washington Superintendent of Indian Affairs, Edward R. Geary, that "some few weeks since" a party of Haida Indians, en route to Port Orchard (west across Puget Sound from Seattle) to retrieve a woman living with a white man, was discovered by some Snohomish and Suquamish Indians. Being a much stronger party than the Haidas and having old grudges to settle with them, the two tribes attacked, killing two Haida men and a woman and capturing seven other women. The attack was in retaliation for a Haida attack on Snohomish Indians in which three of the latter were captured, enslaved and taken to the Queen Charlotte Islands. Of the seven Haida women captured, white persons took two of them from the Suquamish Indians. They also took two others from another point on the sound. Two of them were brought to local agent R.C. Fay. Missionaries sent one to Simmons.

Simmons returned the Indians to Victoria not solely as a humanitarian gesture, but to demonstrate to Northern Indians that the United States tolerated neither war nor the taking of slaves.[95] He reported accompanying the prisoners to

[93]MacDonald, *British Columbia and Vancouver's Island,* 137-38.

[94]Dee, "The Journal of John Work, January to October, 1835," pp. 86, 87.

[95]Michael T. Simmons, Indian Agent, Wash. Terr., to Edward R. Geary, Supt. Indian Affairs, Wash. Terr. and Oregon, July 1, 1860, *Annual Report, Secy. Interior, 1860,* Serial 1078, pp. 414-16. It was stated in the *Weekly Oregonian,* June 20, 1860, that Simmons had rescued the two "squaws" from the Snohomish Indians, returning them to the Haidas.

show them that his government did not wish to injure them should they stay home; and furthermore, that the United States did not encourage its Indians to take slaves. He also helped arrange the securing of three enslaved Snohomish Indians. Former chief trader at Fort Nisqually, Dr. Tolmie, assisted him in having a "satisfactory" talk with the Haida chief. Simmons reported the chief as having appreciated the return of his people, promising to return the Snohomish prisoners as soon as they could be brought down from the Queen Charlotte Islands.[96]

This was the best arrangement Simmons could make since the Victoria government appeared to him as having little control over its Indian tribes. In fact, he reported that when in Victoria, gunfire from two native factions erupted on her outskirts.[97] He also warned the Snohomish and Suquamish Indians involved in international troubles that they had breached two provisions of their treaties with Stevens: warring on other tribes and taking slaves.[98]

Like other government agents, Simmons was concerned with the many matters which in one way or another were related to slavery. Many official tasks stemmed from acculturative changes resulting from white contact. With that contact former wealthy families decried the fact that they no longer had the necessary resources to hold potlatches or to purchase, let alone destroy, slaves to display their wealth. Other grievances involved their inability to travel on former lands now occupied by white settlers. There was also the annoying agency pressure for them to abandon long-established practices such as slavery, shamanism, polygyny, head-flattening and gambling. Occasional atrocities kept cropping up to worry the agents. For example, an incident of a slave buried alive with a Duwamish chief proved that much more

---

[96]Simmons to Geary, July 1, 1860, *Annual Report, Secy. Interior, 1860,* Serial 1078, p. 415.

[97]Ibid.

[98]Ibid.

work was needed to complete what these government officials termed the "civilizing" process.

With the coming of white men new practices such as that
of mixed marriages were added to the native culture, sometimes bringing down on heads of couples involved the wrath
of their respective races. Such unions continued into the settlement period, but not to the extent of the practice in the
earlier fur trading era. Struggling westward to the Columbia
River in 1839, Thomas J. Farnham narrated a marital com-
plication involving the Indian slave wife of a white trapper.
Returning from a beaver trapping expedition, the trapper
discovered that another white man had run off with her.
Catching up with them the trapper killed the interloping
paramour.[99]

In early 1863 the Makahs planned to send a slave to kill
some whites whom they blamed for the deaths of two of their
subchiefs from chronic diarrhea. Fearing that a man-of-war
had come to retaliate, they planned to deliver the slaves to
save their own necks. On the other hand the Indians ambivalently hoped that whites would protect them from Northern
Indians. On the other side of the coin the excitement of sanguinary activity was not easily assuaged among tribes such as
the Makahs who lived further from most white settlers who
might try to impede them. When in August 1862, the
Makahs killed a native of Barclay Sound on Vancouver
Island, his people threatened to raid them in return. In such
instances the Makahs were happy to have white men around
to protect them in the face of this threat.[100]

When a Nootkan band of Nitinahts planned to raid
natives near Victoria, British warships in her harbor prevented them from carrying out their plans. Not to be deterred,
they canoed south across the Strait after nightfall. Ashore,
they waited until morning to attack a band of Elwha Clal-

[99]Thomas J. Farnham, *Travels in the Great Western Prairies, The Anahuac and Rocky Mountains, and in the Oregon Territory,* 308-09.

[100]Swan to Webster, March 31, 1863. *Records of the Washington Superintendency of Indian Affairs, No. 5, Roll 14.*

lams. Before sunrise the Elwhas were out fishing from canoes at some distance from shore. Suddenly the Nitinahts rushed from the forest, intercepting the unarmed fishermen before they could reach land. Their women and children ran shrieking. There was no battle, only silence. In short time, headless Elwha bodies lay in canoes of the victors who paddled homeward across the Strait singing a death song.[101]

Bad blood existed between Clallams and Tsimshians, who made the long sea journey down to the Strait of Juan de Fuca. In 1865 the Tsimshians murdered two Clallam women and two girls and enslaved a boy for whose release his father paid three hundred dollars. At the same time, the wife, daughter and mother of one of the captives was taken by Tsimshians and carried north where they were enslaved for five months. They would have been imprisoned longer had the wife's husband not paid a thousand dollars in gold coin for their release.[102] In 1866 the Tsimshians attacked a party of ten Clallams, cut the throats of six and carried off the remaining four as slaves. To ransom them their relatives paid four hundred blankets, or the equivalent of twelve hundred dollars at the time.[103]

Burning under such attacks against their persons, pride and pocketbooks, the Clallams itched for revenge. Their opportunity came on September 21, 1868, when they fell upon a ten-man, eight-woman and one-child Tsimshian band encamped near the Dungeness Spit lighthouse on the Strait. Indiscriminately they thrust knives and spears through the tent in which the Tsimshians were sleeping and seized their guns and revolvers, shooting and killing all of them except a woman hiding under a mat. Before the attack ended, a Clallam woman was killed when a Tsimshian, taken for dead and being robbed by a Clallam, jumped up and grabbed the Clallam's gun, killing him before suffering death herself.[104]

---

[101]Sproat, *Scenes and Studies of Savage Life*, 153-54.
[102]C.S. King, Indian Agent, to T.J. McKenney, Wash. Supt. Indian Affairs, Oct. 7, 1868. *Records of the Washington Superintendency of Indian Affairs, No. 5, Roll 13*.
[103]Ibid.   [104]Ibid.

The attack, occurring over a dozen years after the Stevens' no-slave, no-slave-trade provisions in his treaty, was a serious violation by Clallams, as were those of other signatory tribes. Consequently, a month after the attack, C.S. King, agent for the Skokomish Reservation at the southern end of Hood Canal, with help from Justice James Swan, arrested and imprisoned in the reservation blockhouse twenty Clallams from Port Discovery, Dungeness and Sequim bays, all of which were on or near the Strait of Juan de Fuca. One prisoner, a young lad, was immediately released and enrolled in the reservation school. His frightened incarcerated people, wanting their families brought down the Canal to the reservation, agreed to restore properties they had stolen from the Tsimshians.[105]

That same year, 1868, Washington Territorial Superintendent of Indian Affairs, Thomas J. McKenney, struck at a very important cause of troublesome intertribal relations when he reported that

> Among these evils may be enumerated the institution of slavery, to which they have clung with great tenacity, even those whose treaty stipulations forbid it. This system of slavery is one by which they make merchandise of their women, and support the polygamy so common among them. I have made it a point to enforce the conditions of the treaties in regard to slavery among all the tribes, to discourage, by all the means in my power, the practice of polygamy.[106]

In his solicitousness for the welfare of native women caught up in slavery and polygyny, McKenney apparently overlooked the fact that their men suffered the far worse fate of death in raids and warfare. As he wrote, slavery was passing away and although it did not do so instantaneously on the heels of the treaties, their importance should not be minimized too severely in helping effect its demise. After the treaties the Nisquallys, who in times past practiced such

---

[105]Ibid. Not all Northern Indians coming down into Puget Sound were intent on raiding. The *Oregonian*, Feb. 7, 1878, cited a band of about thirty Wesleyan missionary converts employed at a Port Blakely sawmill who held regular church services on Sundays and week-day evenings.

[106]T.J. McKenney, Supt. Indian Affairs, Wash. Terr. to N.G. Taylor, Commr. Indian Affairs, Aug. (n.d.), 1868. *Annual Report, Secy. Interior, 1868*, Serial 1366, p. 549.

hideous practices as burying favorite slaves with dead masters and thus "consigned [them] to a living tomb,"[107] discontinued the practice after the treaties.

Despite the negative aspects of reservation life, slavery was either stopped or slowed there, especially since the changed economies and lifestyles of their native inhabitants could not support it. One of many former slaves, John Kettle, a Nootkan by birth, was sold to a Suquamish, but freed after establishment of Port Madison Reservation on the Kitsap Peninsula on which he married and raised a garden.[108] Despite its humanitarian benefits, the passing of slavery disrupted old tribal patterns. Among tribes there was the question of what to do with freed slaves since under the cloud of stigma they could not marry as easily as John Kettle. This is but one example of the many dislocations occasioned by the compulsory unshuffling of a society once rigidly stacked with slaves and non-slaves—rich and poor. It was difficult to wash from ex-slaves their tainted blood like that which had been so copiously shed to enslave them. After their freeing, their condition, not unlike that of Negroes freed after the Civil War, was reminiscent of words of James Oppenheim's poem, "The Slave:"

> They set the slave free, striking off his chains...
> Then he was as much of a slave as ever.

---

[107] *Tacoma Ledger*, May 23, 1866.
[108] Costello, *The Siwash*, 24.

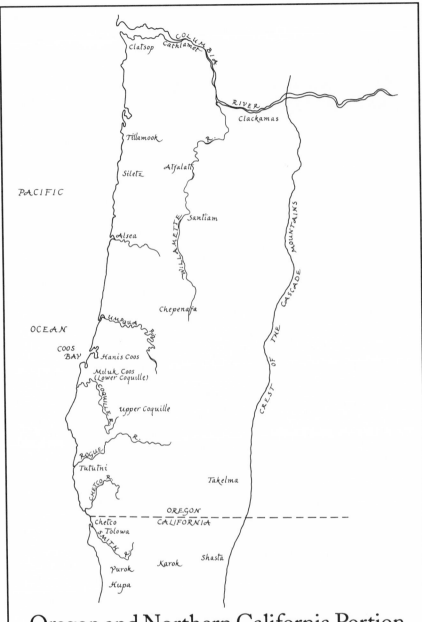

COLUMBIA

Clatsop Cathlamet

RIVER

Clackamas

Tillamook

Atfalati

Siletz

Santiam

PACIFIC

WILLAMETTE

Alsea

Chepenafa

UMPQUA

OCEAN

COOS
BAY Hanis Coos

Miluk Coos
(Lower Coquille)

COQUILLE R.

upper Coquille

R.

ROGUE

Tututni

CHETCO R.

Takelma

OREGON
CALIFORNIA

Chetco
Tolowa

SMITH R.

Karok Shasta

Yurok

Hupa

CREST OF THE CASCADE MOUNTAINS

Oregon and Northern California Portion
of the Northwest Coast Culture Area

7

The Northwest California Slave Cluster and Western Oregon Tribes

The slave trade in the Northwest California zone at the southern extent of the Northwest Coast culture area differed from that in the remainder of the culture area, with the exception of some characteristics seen in a few Willamette Valley tribes. The zone covers the tips of northwestern California and southwestern Oregon. Three language groups made up the slave cluster. Slavery here is less well recorded, perhaps because of fewer contacts with whites until later times. It was a less violent activity. Misfortune often placed one in enslavement through no fault of his or her own. Slaves were less likely to be acquired by raiding. Rather, they came into bondage by the incursion of debt and accident.

Numerous language groups occupied western Oregon, a large area at the southern part of the Coast Salish-Chinook zone south of the Chinook slave cluster who, with exception of Tillamooks, were neither Salish nor Chinookan speakers. These tribes were resources for slaves destined for the north. John Dunn, a Hudson's Bay Company fur man, referred to these tribes as "the original kidnappers" for initiating passage of slaves north to the slave arc stretching nearly two thousand miles northward.[1] The western Oregon tribes were less aggressive than the Chinooks, resulting in a lessened ownership of, and traffic in slaves.[2] Increasing, albeit mildly until the Columbia River and its approaches were reached, slavery activity gained momentum and intensity in its continuing

---

[1]Dunn, *History of the Oregon Territory*, 273.
[2]Verne F. Ray, "The Historical Position of the Lower Chinooks in the Native Culture of the Northwest," 369.

northerly passage into British Columbia. Writing on Indian slavery, Gilbert M. Sproat states that most of the Indians in the southern region preferred acting as middlemen selling slaves and taking a markup on them instead of keeping and using them. This is not to say they were spared raids by others who would enslave them. A pre-reservation branch of Tillamook Indians of the middle Oregon coast, for instance, were contemptuously called "slaves" by more warlike tribesmen who were said to have captured more slaves from them than from any other tribe. A similar situation existed on northern Vancouver Island where, writes Sproat, some smaller tribes were so frequently attacked and raided for slaves that they were considered slave breeders.[3] Whether the southern Indians acquired slaves or lost their people to slavers, their societies, like those to the north, were painted with the same primary colors of nobility, freemen and slaves. The latter were treated less severely than were slaves among tribes to the north. This was especially true of those in northern California.[4]

Because of their geographic proximity and cultural similarity to the Chinooks, slavery among Clatsops of the Columbia River left bank near its mouth shared in the Chinooks' monopolistic slave trade. Both peoples acquired slaves from their Tillamook neighbors to their immediate south who fell upon weaker peoples further south, killing them with knives and guns and imprisoning others. The Tillamooks killed captives whom they did not enslave.[5] They were also known to have conveyed slaves directly to Chehalis peoples living north of the Clatsops and Chinooks. Like others living along the slave arc, the Tillamooks did not pass all slaves through their hands, but brought adopted, purchased, or captured children into their families, treating them as their

---

[3]Sproat, *Scenes and Studies of Savage Life*, 92; Spier and Sapir *Wishram Ethnography*, 223.

[4]The Tolowas, Tututnis, and Yuroks, the southernmost tribes of the slave trough, mark the lower end of the tribal lower class in which slavery paled as compared with that among tribes of northern British Columbia. Elmendorf and Kroeber, *The Structure of Twana Culture*, 318n.

[5]Lee and Frost, *Ten Years in Oregon*, 103.

own.[6] They also permitted the ransom of slaves not killed on deaths of their masters. These thralls were much like the poor; yet, they could be traded or sold.[7] The artist, John Mix Stanley, shortly before mid-19th century wrote: "It is a very common practice of the Shaste, Umpqua, and Roque River Indians, to sell their children in slavery to the tribes inhabiting the banks of the Columbia River [some of whom arrived there having perhaps passed through Tillamook hands]. During my tour through the Willamette valley in 1846," continued Stanley, "I met a party of Tlickitacks [Klickitats] returning from one of these trading excursions, having about twenty little boys, whom they had purchased from the Umpqua tribe."[8] The middlemen Tillamooks supplied others in the middle like the Chinooks with human articles to pass along in the trade.

Inhabiting the Coquille River, a Pacific Ocean affluent of southwestern Oregon, the Hanis and Miluk Coos Indians (the latter, also known as Lower Coquilles), and the Upper Coquilles (Mishikhwutmetunnes) held slaves in their structured society of nobles, commoners and bondsmen. The Coquilles raided Hanis Coos peoples at Coos Bay of the Pacific, enslaving their children only to experience retaliation in kind from Hanis Coos elders.[9] When the American fur trapping party, led by Jedediah Smith, moved north along the Oregon coast in June 1828, they frightened off a band of Coquille River Indians (most likely the Miluk Coos) who hastily retreated, leaving behind a young Kalapuyan slave.[10]

Smith preceded American miners entering Indian lands of southern Oregon seeking gold, and settlers trekking into the Willamette valley seeking farmlands. Had these trespassers closely examined the natives, which is unlikely since they were usually at odds with them, they might have noted their

[6]Thwaites, ed., *Original Journals of the Lewis and Clark Expedition, 1804-1806*, IV, pp. 120-22.

[7]John Sauter and Bruce Johnson, *Tillamook Indians of the Oregon Coast*, 26.

[8]J.M. Stanley, *Portraits of North American Indians*, 62.

[9]Ruby and Brown, *A Guide to the Indian Tribes of the Pacific Northwest*, 131; John Yoakam, "Coos Bay, Notes on," 1. Ms. P-A 85.

[10]Dale L. Morgan, *Jedediah Smith and the Opening of the West*, 265.

involvement in slavery. Earlier in northern Oregon three erstwhile employees of another American, John Jacob Astor, were rudely introduced to native ways when they deserted Fort Astoria only to be captured and enslaved by Chinookan speakers of the lower Willamette River. To purchase their freedom the clerk, Gabriel Franchère, paid their captors eight blankets, a brass kettle, a hatchet, a small pistol and powder-horn and some rounds of ammunition.[11] Thanks to Franchère's action the deserters, among the natives but a short time, were happy to return to the fort. In some ways their experience was typical of slavery in this area, where slaves were often only temporarily among the particular tribe before being traded to others. A case in point were the Alseas of the middle Oregon coast who seldom raided for slaves,[12] but bought and sold them so rapidly that they were in Alsea households but briefly, giving them little opportunity to demonstrate their real value.[13]

Like natives of Sound and Strait, those of Oregon used the element of surprise in taking captives; but unlike those of Sound and Strait, they did not behead their foes. Most of the roughly dozen groups of peoples of the Kalapuyan linguistic family of the Willamette valley to the east raided for, or purchased, their slaves of other Kalapuyans. Sometimes they sold children as slaves to tribes such as the Cowlitz Indians to their north across the Columbia River, who in turn sold them further north to tribes of Puget Sound.[14] About 1844 an Atfalati (or Tualatin) chief near present-day Portland, led his warriors against "Wallawallas" (local Sahaptins). Should they be killed, he promised the warriors, he would recompense their survivors with slaves.[15] Motives for the Atfalati action are sketchy.

Sometimes Atfalatis were joined by their Upper or North-

---

[11]Franchère, *Narrative of a Voyage to the Northwest Coast of America*, 137.

[12]Philip Drucker, *Contributions to Alsea Ethnography*, 91.

[13]Livingston Farrand, "Notes on the Alsea Indians of Oregon," 242.

[14]Curtis, *The North American Indian* 9, p. 75.

[15]Albert Samuel Gatschet, Leo J. Frachtenberg, and Melville Jacobs, *Kalapuya Texts*, 196.

ern Molala neighbors who had also been raided by inland tribes like the Cayuse seeking slaves. Together the Molalas and Atfalatis warred against, or traded with, Kalapuyan Santiams, Calapooyas proper and Chepenafas, striking in early mornings, killing and enslaving not so much for the glory of conquest as for profits to be made in selling captured slaves.[16] Chepenafa legendry tells of their predecessor on earth, the trickster Coyote who, gambling with other animals, parlayed five slaves he had won from Whale into eighty more.[17] Lacking the cleverness of Coyote these tribesmen took their slaves by force rather than by guile, using stratagems like attacking in early mornings. As with many aggressors, they killed those they did not enslave perhaps because they were unfit for servitude, or perhaps because it was difficult to escort them to homes of these captors.[18]

Indians of southwest Oregon most frequently acquired slaves through purchase or trade. Athapaskan speaking Chetcos, Tututnis and Hupas traded slaves that may have reached The Dalles through intermediaries, but these tribes rarely traveled there if at all, unlike Lutuamian speakers east of the Cascade Range, the Klamaths and Modocs who, after contact, were frequent visitors bringing Shastan speaking Shastas and Pit River slaves to be sent further north through intermediaries.[19]

Offspring of slaves in tribes such as the Alseas and Tillamooks inherited their slave status.[20] Impoverished Alsea parents sometimes sold children into slavery to cover their debts as did Siletz and Yurok Indians.[21] Debts among Siletz Indians would be incurred by mentioning names of the dead, requiring heavy fines to be paid to relatives of the deceased in what amounted to economic servitude.[22]

---

[16]Melville Jacobs, *Kalapuya Texts* Pt. 1. *Santiam Kalapuya Ethnologic Texts,* 41; Albert Samuel Gatschet, "The Molale tribe raided by the Cayuses." Ms. 2029.

[17]Gatschet, Frachtenberg and Jacobs, *Kalapuya Texts,* 211-15.

[18]Jacobs, *Kalapuya Texts* Pt. 1, p. 41.

[19]Slaves were moved not only south to north, but after contact, north to south as well.

[20]Homer G. Barnett, *Culture Element Distributions:* VII, Oregon, 185.

[21]Farrand, "Notes on the Alsea," 242.

[22]A.W. Chase, "Siletz or Lo Reconstructed," 431.

Among Kalapuyan speakers families of murdered victims in some instances received up to twenty horses or five slaves. Failure of murderers to pay survivors could result in forfeiture of their own lives.[23] Kalapuyan Santiams also enslaved orphaned children. Their male slaves could marry free women.[24] Slaves among Atfalatis were permitted to marry other slaves or even free persons on payment in horses to the slaves' owners. Such payment often allowed slaves to gain their freedom later on. Their offspring, however, remained enslaved.[25] One Kalapuyan shaman, accused of witchcraft in the death of a patient, was forced to pay indemnity in the form of an orphaned niece who was traded several times, finally living among Chinooks at Bay Center, Washington. She eventually married a white man, but to her dying day resented the actions of her uncle who precipitated the various trades in which she was involved.[26] In his *History of the Willamette Valley, Oregon* (1927), Robert Carlton Clark stated that Indians of the Willamette valley considered their slaves no better than dogs, much in the manner of Indians to the north who had an expression, "like a slave or a dog."[27]

The path to enslavement took many turns. Girls from poor Oregon coastal families were sometimes blackmailed into marrying wealthy tribesmen by being threatened with slavery.[28] The children of free Kalapuyans eager to buy things were sometimes sold by their parents at market places.[29] Children of Atfalatis of the Willamette Valley, caught in slavery by accident of heredity, usually were not

---

[23]Gatschet, Frachtenberg, and Jacobs, *Kalapuya Texts*, 193.

[24]Harold Mackey, *The Kalapuyans: A Sourcebook on the Indians of the Willamette Valley*, 36.

[25]Ibid., 24.

[26]Only in the contact and post-contact periods do we have a picture of the feelings of ex-slaves about their servitude and involvement in slavery and its trade, for with the passing of their bondage they were able to express their feelings and tell of their experiences to white persons who recorded them.

[27]Robert Carlton Clark, *History of the Willamette Valley*, 1, p. 56; Pamela Amoss, "Man and Dog on the Northwest Coast, Ancient Man's Best Friend," 17.

[28]Stephen Dow Beckham, *The Indians of Western Oregon: This Land Was Theirs*, 77.

[29]Curtis, *The North American Indian* 9, p. 75.

sold to keep families intact.[30] Slaves of Willamette tribal chiefs usually did not suffer death at the decease of their masters. The multiple marriages among these chiefs precipitated considerable conflict among families as to who should inherit their slaves.[31] Among Atfalatis slaves were frequently offered along with dentalia, beads, and with white contact, coins and horses. Should slaves acquire horses, they were permitted to marry slaves of their same households and even, in some cases, free persons. Occasionally by trading horses they could gain their freedom.[32]

Clackamas Indians of the northern Willamette watershed on one occasion paid an unusually high bride-price of ten slaves, while out on the coast Alseas reckoned a slave to be the equivalent of the bride-price of a girl of good family. Perhaps few slaves at any one time were involved in the reckoning of this equivalency. Primary Alsea wealth was measured in slaves and dentalia.[33] Anthropologist Melville Jacobs records that in transitional times a Clackamas slave girl fled with a freeman after stealing valuables from her villagers. Unable to locate the stolen items with the help of a shaman, two slaves were sent to search out and destroy her and return the purloined items. The two slaves duly performed their grisly task.[34] In a similar incident, when a man could not be cured, two Molala slaves were sent to fetch a medicine woman. They were ordered to shoot her should she fail to respond.[35]

In his *Information Respecting the History, Condition and Prospects of the Indian Tribes of the United States...*, Henry R. Schoolcraft stated that among certain tribes of southern

---

[30]Albert Samuel Gatschet, "Various Ethnographic Notes. The Kalapuya People," 214.

[31]John Minto explained the complications arising from inheritance involving slaves and other property. "The Number and Condition of the Native Race in Oregon When First Seen by White Men," 301.

[32]Gatschet, "Various Ethnographic Notes. The Kalapuya People," 214.

[33]Melville Jacobs, *Clackamas Chinook Texts* Pt. II, 601; Drucker, *Contributions to Alsea Ethnography,* 91.

[34]Jacobs, *Clackamas Chinook Texts* Pt. II, 610.

[35]Ibid.

Oregon west of the Cascade Mountains the "revolting custom" had prevailed of "putting out an eye of a slave, in order
that if he escaped, he might be marked and known as such by
the surrounding tribes."[36]

The cluster of debt slavery was in the Northwest California
zone. Its debt slavery, varying from the general pattern in the
rest of the Pacific Northwest culture region, was at and below
the California border in the northwestern corner of that state.
In this zone, writes A.L. Kroeber, were those slaves who had
"invariably entered this condition of life through debt, not
through capture in war." One way to become indebted to
another, thus leading to enslavement, was through destruction of another's property. For example, a man of northwestern California was enslaved when he was unable to
recompense another whose property, including some valuables, he inadvertently destroyed when firing some brush.[37]

In the common debt slavery form of bondage persons were
unwittingly and unwillingly involved. Ethnologist George
Gibbs described indebtedness and insolence as ways of
becoming so enslaved:

> …If one Indian has wronged another, and failed to make compen-
> sation, or if a debtor insolent he may be taken as a slave. Their
> mode of procedure is characterized by their wonted deliberation.
> The plaintiff comes with a party to demand satisfaction, and holds
> out to the other the option of payment or servitude. If no satisfac-
> tion is given he must submit unless he is strong enough to do battle.
> And this slavery is final degradation. The rule of once a slave always
> a slave extends so far that if the debtor should have given up some
> relative in his power, and subsequently redeems him, he becomes
> his slave in turn. If a man purchase his father or mother, they
> become his slaves, and are treated as such…Even if one purchases
> his own freedom, he is yet looked upon as an inferior.[38]

The missionary Samuel Parker described how gamblers
sold themselves into perpetual debt slavery by alienating first

---

[36]Henry Rowe Schoolcraft, *Historical and Statistical Information Respecting the History,
Condition and Prospects of the Indian Tribes of the United States* 5, p. 654.

[37]Kroeber, *Handbook of the Indians of California*, 33.

[38]Gibbs, *Tribes of Western Washington and Northwestern Oregon* 1, Pt. 2, pp. 12, 188.

their hands then their arms, other parts of their bodies and finally, their heads. This practice was especially reprehensible to him and to other missionaries like the Father De Smet who also reported the anatomical dismemberment stemming from gambling losses.[39] What would have been as reprehensible to them were elders selling children in order to cover gambling debts. Poor persons failing to compensate others on whom they inflicted wrongs fell into debt slavery, and sought wealthy persons to redeem them. Were persons to kill others and be unable to pay blood-feud compensation for their deeds, the victims' relatives could force these killers into slavery. Masters did not kill slaves in this zone, which contrasts sharply with that practice at the other end of the culture area, as did the absence of secular unions with family slaves.[40]

Despite such differences in slave-holding practices among tribes, their bondsmen were still property and as such, means by which their owners paid debts or purchased favors. As chattel they were moved about the coast or through the Willamette and other valleys like cattle; and like cattle their value rose or fell depending on prices at the market place where economic value was dictated by the quality and quantity of the product as well as by the times and places of such transactions and by the tastes of those involved in them.

Northwestern California tribes were part of the Northwest Coast culture area as evidenced by "prestigious" behavior, albeit mitigated from that in the north. Writes Suttles of the Tolowas of California:

> It has been implicit in the previous discussion of the Coast Salish that items of 'wealth' (blankets, canoes, hide shirts, etc.) did not constitute all-purpose money. As in several other parts of the world, there were restrictions on the occasions when wealth items could properly change hands. These restrictions seem to have been less severe among the Tolowa [whose wealth came from selling

---

[39]Parker, *Journal of an Exploring Tour Beyond the Rocky Mountains*, 251; Peter J. De Smet, S.J., *Letters and Sketches*, 171. *See* William Christy MacLeod, "Debtor and Chattel Slavery in Aboriginal North America."

[40]Harold E. Driver, *Indians of North America*, 245-46, 387-88.

food items], but still present in that only exchanges that related to marriage and litigation were publicized, while those that were purely commercial were not, hence the appearance of a separate "prestige economy."[41]

Suttles states that Yurok slaves were not taken through war or purchase, but only enslaved for debt. Kroeber states their worth as being one to two strings of dentalia, their relatively low value possibly attributed to the fact that they were not utilized to their full capacity. In citing their value he states that Yuroks did not know how "to exact full value from the labor of their bondsmen, not because the latter could not be held to work, but because industry was too little organized." Among Yuroks, if daughters of slaves were to marry men of means, bride-prices were paid, but to the slaves' owners. Brides then merged into classes to which their husbands belonged.[42]

Among Hupas of the southern periphery of the Northwest (Pacific) Coast culture area, bastards became slaves for life under ownership of their mothers' male relatives for whom they were compelled to perform menial tasks. Such slaves, however, were entitled to purchase their freedom were they able to accumulate sufficient wealth, yet were never permitted to marry free persons. Among most tribes of the region when marriages were arranged among the wealthy there was much largess in things offered, varying from slaves to shell money and woodpecker scalps. Families of lesser means gave their brides' parents with fewer items. There was a category, "scarcely married at all," when but a few items were presented as a formal sign of marriage. In such "half marriages" where payments were not considered, offspring were regarded as illegitimate and became enslaved.[43]

Tolowa commoners could be enslaved for swearing at a

---

[41]Suttles, *Coast Salish Essays*, 61.

[42]Ibid., 59; Kroeber, *Handbook of the Indians of California*, 27; Elmendorf and Kroeber, *The Structure of Twana Culture*, 321n.

[43]Hodge, *Handbook of American Indians North of Mexico* 2, p. 598; Curtis, *The North American Indian* 13, p. 23.

wealthy man, or for violating mourners' rights, or for not compensating someone for damage claims. They could even be enslaved for failing to rescue persons from perilous situations such as drownings.[44] Should Tolowas inflict injury on others the injured were entitled to indemnity. Were persons too poor to pay this debt, wealthy persons might pay it for them, but then these wealthy ones became their owners. In some instances poor men sold their sisters and other relatives into slavery in their stead.[45]

With the onset of diseases and increasing numbers of white men on Indian lands, the number of slaves by the 1840s decreased sharply, reducing the tribesmen's ability to conduct successful slave raids. This forced them to more carefully husband their human prizes,[46] thus reducing cruelties of former times. Enslavement was less a cause of the decline of Willamette Valley and adjacent tribes than were devastating diseases. In his *Sketch of the Oregon Territory Or, Emigrants' Guide*, P.L. Edwards described the effects of the "fever and ague" sweeping the western region as though he were assuring emigrants that the malady had removed much of the Indian threat to their emigration to Oregon.[47] Of its devastation, which did not discriminate between native nobility and those trapped in slavery, he wrote:

> Over this vast region did the dark angel of death moves
> his leaden sceptre—
> The children of the forest knew no remedy and died—
> Died the stalwart chieftan and his slaves—
> The frenzied mother and her babe.[48]

Indians of southwestern Oregon, who once held and

---

[44]Philip Drucker, *The Tolowas and their Southwest Oregon Kin*, 250.

[45]Curtis, *The North American Indian* 13, pp. 99, 100.

[46]The initial Oregon-bound immigration of 1842 consisted of from 112 to 137 persons. Before the decade of the "forties" ended, the number had risen to about 10,000. Diseases, which white men introduced into the region nearly a century earlier, continued with succeeding immigrations. Robert H. Ruby and John A. Brown, *The Cayuse Indians: Imperial Tribesmen of Old Oregon*, 94n.

[47]P.L. Edwards, *Sketch of the Oregon Territory*, 15.

[48]Ibid.

passed slaves on in trade, succumbed to a new form of "slav-ery" in the 1850s when they were rounded up and put on the Alsea, Grand Ronde and Siletz reservations. Crowded out by whites in the lower Willamette Valley, Indians, like others of their race defeated by whites in the "Rogue Wars" (1853-1856) to the south, had but two options: to blend awkwardly into an alien culture or to remove to reservations. A Siletz Reservation visitor in the 1860s observed that those profan-ing names of the dead had to be enslaved for a year to their surviving relatives.[49] Such traditionalism was also evidenced in the instance of ex-slave, John Adams, one of the first to embrace Christianity on the Siletz Reservation. When Agent J.W. Fairchild supported him for the head chieftain-cy, non-Christian traditionalists in 1875 threw their support to Adams' former owner, George Harney, their incumbent chief.[50] Old stigma and new faith had cost Adams the posi-tion. As slavery and other traditional practices ebbed, so did the memory of what had been good for reservation Indians now victimized by the culture-shattering trauma of confine-ment.

East of the Cascade Mountains natives soon faced similar confinement as white men pressured for their removal from ancestral lands in the vast Columbia Plateau. As their char-acteristics and that of their homelands differed from those of coastal regions, so did the slavery practiced by these native inhabitants.

---

[49]Chase, "Siletz or Lo Reconstructed," 431.

[50]J.W. Fairchild, Agent, Siletz Reservation, to Commr. E.P. Smith, July 6, 1875. *Records of the Siletz Indian Agency. Press Copies of Letters Sent to the Commissioner of Indian Affairs, 1873-1914.*

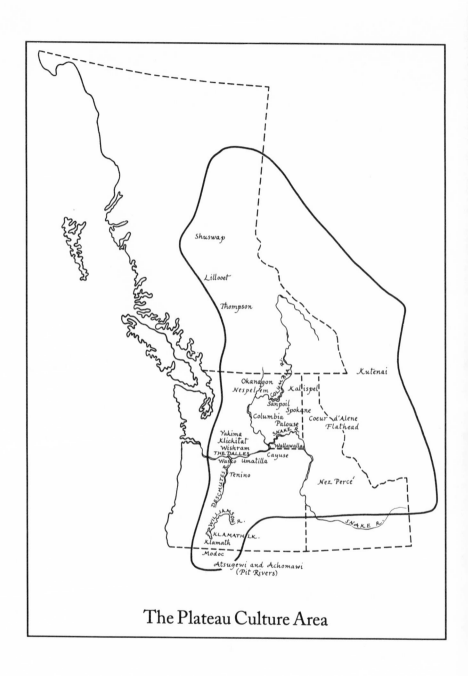

Shuswap

Lillooet

Thompson

Kutenai

Okanagon
Nespelem
Sanpoil
Columbia
Palouse
Yakima
Klickitat
Wishram
THE DALLES
Wasco Umatilla
Tenino

Kalispell
Spokane
Coeur d'Alene
Flathead

SNAKE R.
Wallawalla
Cayuse

Nez Percé

DESCHUTES R.

SNAKE R.

WILLIAMSON R.
KLAMATH LK.
Klamath
Modoc

Atsugewi and Achomawi
(Pit Rivers)

The Plateau Culture Area

8

The Plateau: Free Riders and Captive Slaves

Plateau warfare was equally violent to that found along the Northwest Coast, although in a different manner. Until historic times enslavement of captives was less common than along the coast because of much different subsistence patterns not conducive to supporting an aristocracy. Before historic times captives were humiliated and subjected to initial persecutions and to menial rules. In time, however, they regained some freedoms, often becoming socially integrated with captors. With the increase in demand for slaves following white contact, Plateau peoples began supplying chattel for coastal markets.

Cradled between the Cascade and Rocky mountains, the Plateau cultural area rarely produced abundant harvests like those on the coast. In pre-horse times travel afoot often took them great distances for game, fish, roots and berry harvests. Such food had to be preserved, packed, carried and cached in wintering quarters. It would appear that such laborious food preparation would have required services of slaves, but such was not the case. In traveling, Plateau tribesmen would have found it difficult to capture, control and maintain captives. This contrasts sharply with natives of the populous coastal areas, where abundant flora and fauna did much to help create and support a servile class for the benefit of masters capitalizing on the beneficence of nature in their rich environment. Conditioned by the severity of their own natural environment Plateau societies tended toward egalitarianism in which all were required to participate equally in order to survive.

The coming of the horse to Plateau peoples near mid-18th century enabled them to move swiftly, striking their foe, taking and riding off with captives before their surprised foe could recover and retaliate. No longer could captives escape from victorious Plateau horsemen as they had in pedestrian times. These horsemen were among the greatest equestrians in history. Among those with special acumen in horsemanship were Nez Percés, Columbia Sinkiuses and Cayuses, the latter providing the name of their fast moving mounts. Plundering, booty taking and avenging enemy encroachments were now facilitated and in the process tribal boundaries were maintained or changed. Sedentary salmon peoples such as neighboring Wallawallas were intimidated and forced to perform menial tasks for their Cayuse captors. Moreover, the Cayuses found their captives to be useful items of trade as well as symbols of wealth along with horses, bolstering their own imperiousness.

As defined by William Christie MacLeod the lower portion of the Plateau, encompassing areas of Washington, Oregon and but a small portion of northern California, was "marginal to the hereditary slave area of the Northwest Coast" whose natives, "being little interested in keeping slaves themselves, were always active in raiding their neighbors to the east and south for captives whom they might sell to the Chinooks in the great intertribal mart at The Dalles of the Columbia River."[1] The anthropologist, Verne Ray, states that for the most part slavery in the Plateau was a by-product of war and in its upper reaches, of slight importance compared with the well established institution of the coast. Slaves, however, were found in the upper Plateau, which includes southern reaches of interior British Columbia. To this latter region, and to lands of Athapaskan speakers to the

[1]MacLeod, "Economic Aspects of Indigenous American Slavery," 645-46. The Plateau of the Columbia intermountain area between foothills of the Cascade and Rocky mountains is one of the largest areas of volcanic upheaval on earth, covering more than 200,000 square miles. Otis Freeman and Howard H. Martin, *The Pacific Northwest: An Overall Appreciation*, 65.

north of it, slaves could conceivably have come in a 360 degree circle of itinerancy.

The Lillooets, Thompsons and Shuswaps in the upper most reaches of the Plateau dealt in slaves where, according to Aubrey Cannon, "the structure and slavery relationships on the Fraser Plateau was very much a function of salmon resource availability." Raiding for slaves paralleled the shortage of salmon. The fewer the salmon, the more raiding for slaves and salmon booty. Cannon questions the value of having taken so many captives on raids other than for the prices realized for them in trade. Their functional value to captors as a labor source "does not appear to have been of paramount importance," writes Cannon, except for the Lillooet, who used slaves to assist in salmon harvests.

The value of slaves seems to have been as hostages with which to procure more salmon. Cannon has not considered that soon after contact, as the demand for slaves on the coast market increased, the Plateau was looked to as a resource for this commodity. Fraser Plateau slaves were traded to tribes to their south. Though there was trade to the west, traffic up and down the Fraser River did not compare to the volume of trade on the Columbia. This may have been because there was no one tribe dominating the mouth of the Fraser and controlling the river trade as at the mouth of the Columbia and the Skeena. These chattel as hostages brought high sale prices, and acquisition of salmon appears to have been the most preferred trade item for slaves. As for Plateau tribes, with exception of the Klamaths, there was no permanent class of slaves. Few Shuswap households kept slaves. Shuswap sold their chattel back to the tribe of origin. The Thompsons captured many slaves, but turned around and sold them quickly. Lower Lillooets were prime targets for Shuswap and Thompson raids. They sold slaves of Lower Lillooet origin to Upper Lillooets, who in turn sold them back to the Lower Lillooets. Writes Cannon, "in this area the institutions of trade, warfare and slavery inter-related very

effecting the movement of salmon from areas of stable abundance to areas where the salmon resource was much less stable and abundant... Trading, raiding and taking captives were all available strategies for obtaining salmon when supplies were needed."[2]

Unlike coastal slaves, who were captured, bought and sold as property, most slaves in the Plateau retained their personal identities and were adopted into tribes. In their new domiciles they were allowed to marry and their children fathered by free men attained free tribal member status. While captive women added new blood to captor tribes, young male slaves were adopted into them more often than were elder males who, not easily submitting to enslavement, preferred death to capture. Plateau tribesmen took captives less to enslave them than to prove their own valor in seeking revenge and tribal honors. Thus, their victims were less chattel than prizes. By contrast, captives in coastal areas were sought for enslavement to enhance the coffers of their master-owners who held or disposed of them as they did other products of their rich coastal environment.

Plateau raiders for generations had taken captives in aquatic and pedestrian raids. It was only the scope, not the pattern of conflict, that changed with the acquisition and use of horses during their buffalo-hunting era (c. 1780-1870), since these animals gave them more mobility to travel to the Plains and in some instances, even beyond. By the same token this increased mobility brought them into conflict with bands of Blackfeet and other Plains peoples who regarded the Plateau peoples as poachers on their lands. Although hunting was the primary objective of Plateau tribes in going "to buffalo," they also went there to trade their products such as salmon pemmican to the plainsmen for objects like highly-prized buffalo robes. During trading sessions trouble sometimes erupted, opening old wounds and renewing the

[2]Verne F. Ray, *Cultural Relations in the Plateau of Northwestern America*, 30, 31; Aubrey Cannon, "Conflict and Salmon on the Interior Plateau of British Columbia," 515-17. See also James A. Teit, *The Salishan Tribes of the Western Plateaus*.

revenge cycle. When numbers of Plateau and Plains hunters were uneven, the precarious balance of power was broken resulting in short but vicious encounters.[3] Animate objects— men, horses and buffalo then combined with knives, bows and arrows and guns to make the Plains a maelstrom of conflict. For Plateau peoples to have traveled to the Plains without firearms acquired in the early 19th century, despite having earlier acquired horses, would have proven dangerous. This was because Plains peoples had obtained guns from white traders in the fourth decade of the previous century. Ironically, it was from the Plains that Plateau tribes such as the Flatheads living just west of the Rocky Mountains acquired certain war-cultural elements with trappings to match. Christopher L. Miller summarizes this conflict, stating in his *Prophetic Worlds...* that "the meeting of the horse and gun frontiers combined with a shared economic investment in the buffalo plains to create a persistent state of war."[4]

Slavery on the Plateau resulting from such conflict bore certain characteristics of that of the Coast. Since Plateau peoples, unlike buffalo hunters of the Plains, were also salmon fishers and gatherers, their enslaved captives, like those of the Coast, would have performed subsistence tasks in non-violent settings. This was in sharp contrast to the violence of their initial capture and that attending initiation into some captor tribes.[5]

Despite the largely non-chattel status of Plateau captives, there were instances when they were traded at places such as The Dalles, where the slave trade among tribes like the Nez Percé-Cayuses was precipitously halted by the culturally upsetting arrival of fur people, missionaries and government agents. Further to the south slavery was slower in coming to Klamaths due to their relative isolation.

---

[3]The Salish-speaking Flatheads maintained their right to hunt on the Plains in keeping with their belief that their tribe had previously lived in that region.

[4]Christopher L. Miller, *Prophetic Worlds: Indians and Whites on the Columbia Plateau,* 38.

[5]An example of such initiation is cited below in Ross, *The Fur Hunters of the Far West,* 203-04.

Slavery among specific Plateau tribes is more fully examined below. It should be pointed out here, however, that to the extent that Plateau tribesmen were hunters, especially in distant places such as the Plains, their slave-holding was not the well-established practice of that in coastal areas. Their horse-borne sorties to the Plains forced them to experience the similar problems of Plains tribesmen in managing not only their captives, but their mounts as well. Acquisition of more captives also created a need for more horses. That captives were tempted to escape on the more sparsely populated Plateau and Plains than in coastal areas increased the probability of their owners contesting with tribes to which they could escape, or with tribes from which they were originally taken. Unlike many coastal slaves, who were passed from tribe to tribe, those captured by Plateau hunters on the Plains were often returned directly to the Plateau without passing through intermediary bands.

Much of our information about Plateau slavery has come down from non-Indians visiting the area in the 19th century and recording their observations with varying degrees of accuracy. Although numerous examples of such may be cited, those of two American Board missionaries may be noted. One of these was the Reverend Elkanah Walker, who labored among the Spokane Indians from 1838 to 1847. He understandably evidenced greater concern for their spiritual welfare than for their social structure. This is seen in his statement to his board secretary that their morals were "debased as any heathen people," adding that "the more wives they have, the richer they consider themselves." He concluded that "their wives are to them what slaves are to the planter as it is their business to provide the provisions" since "a man without a wife is in great danger of being hunger."[6]

---

[6]Clifford M. Drury, *Nine Years with the Spokane Indians: The Diary, 1838-1848, of Elkanah Walker*, 113. Teit states that it seems that a little extraneous blood was introduced, particularly among Spokanes, by marriage of that tribe's males to slave women and war captives, some of whom were of Snake lineage. This is particularly significant since intermarriage between free people and captives was customarily accepted in Plateau tribes, but on the coast, for the most part, frowned upon, and any children of such unions were usually

He often mistook for slavery the physically demanding tasks
which both captive and free women uncomplainingly performed.

It was on the basis of other reports that Walker's American
Board colleague, Samuel Parker, who was in the mid-Plateau
region in 1835-36, believed slavery to the north (possibly to
or beyond its upper reaches) was practiced in early times, but
not so later on.[7] On the basis of records (rather than on
hearsay) modern researchers, Donald Mitchell and Leland
Donald, trace a steady slave trade from coastal to interior
regions during the 1830s (as well as the 1840s) during the
very time Parker was in the Plateau. They point out how
interior tribes even north of the Plateau played an important
role in the demand for coastal slaves which possibly resulted
from population losses from smallpox among many Athapaskan speakers.[8]

In what he terms the "Salish network," Donald explains
how three Interior Salish groupings in the northern Plateau,
the Lillooets, Shuswaps and Thompsons, were tied to Coast
Salish peoples in the slave trade. He writes that although
James Teit, in his study of the Lillooets (1906), reported
rather full information, he did not supply slave trade data of
quality in his other reports. Despite having access to more
information on slavery than most previous student-observers
of the practice, Donald admits the need for more information in order to obtain a satisfactory picture of that activity in
the North. He writes:

This points out how much our picture of the slave trade depends on

---

slaves by inheritance. *The Salishan Tribes of the Western Plateaus,* 323. Coastal tribes also
entertained the idea of infusing their veins with foreign blood. Sproat theorized that "Intermarriage with other tribes is sought by the higher classes, to strengthen the foreign connections of their own tribes, and, I think also, with some idea of preventing degeneracy of
race..." *Scenes and Studies of Savage Life,* 99. Albert Buell Lewis states that there were no
classes in the Plateau where prisoners of war were commonly held as slaves, but were usually
well treated and frequently adopted into the tribes; and furthermore, that slavery was an
incident of war rather than the recognized institution as found among Chinooks. *Tribes of
the Columbia Valley and the Coast of Washington and Oregon,* 180.
[7]Parker, *Journal of an Exploring Tour Beyond the Rocky Mountains,* 251.
[8]Mitchell and Donald, "Some Economic Aspects," 31.

our luck with sources. Where slave trade links are reported, we can be fairly confident that trade in slaves occurred. But when our sources are silent—and they rarely explicitly deny trade links—we often cannot choose between the alternatives of no slave trade and missing information about slave trading that did go on.[9]

Of Nez Percés of the eastern Plateau anthropologist Herbert J. Spinden writes that it was "the necessity of united defense against invading warparties from the Plains which probably brought about the tribal integrity..."[10] It would be unfair to demean earlier observers of Plateau peoples since these observers in the Pacific Northwest lacked the benefit of hindsight enjoyed by later ones. It should also be noted that not all earlier observers in the region lacked insight into its native cultures. On the basis of his visit in the early 1840s, Charles Wilkes, for instance, shrewdly detected complex organizational upheavals among tribes as varied as Interior Salish Flatheads and Waiilatpuan-speaking Cayuses. We are indebted to even earlier 19th century fur men in the region such as Alexander Ross and Alexander Henry whose observations reveal a modernity surprising for those times.[11]

The American failure to establish fur factories on the Plateau denied its tribes some protection from continuing incursions of Blackfeet and other tribes. Without these posts and their personnel, aggressive southern Plateau and Great Basin tribesmen such as the Shoshonis and Bannocks (the "Snakes") whose appetites had been whetted by the acquisition of Euro-American goods, were forced to turn to Spanish settlements to the south to obtain them. To acquire the means to purchase the goods, the Shoshoni-Bannocks were forced to raid Plateau and Plains tribes for slaves.

To counter these raids and protect themselves, Blackfeet, Assiniboin, Sarsis, Atsina, Cree peoples and other Plains tribes coalesced in common effort against the Shoshoni-

[9]Donald, "The Slave Trade on the Northwest Coast," 133-35.
[10]Spinden, *The Nez Perce Indians,* 271.
[11]The ability was shared by other early Britishers as David Thompson, John McLoughlin, James Douglas, John Work, Peter Skene Ogden and others.

Bannocks. The latter were known for their severe treatment of captives, killing male prisoners after subjecting them to what a former army captain described as "pitiless and prolonged torture." Not the least of this cruelty was inflicted by women with "fiendish ingenuity." Captive children, he stated, were frequently adopted into the tribes, the girls eventually marrying into them, and the boys being trained as warriors, were they not soon killed after capture.[12]

Among Plateau tribes long at enmity with the Shoshoni-Bannocks were the Nez Percé-Cayuses who played the same deadly game of giving and taking lives and captives as did their "Snake" adversaries, speeding off on fast-moving mounts with their prizes. Although initially of a different linguistic family, the Cayuses, before the end of the 19th century, adopted the more flexible Nez Percé tongue. There was much cultural exchange between the two peoples, each sharing mutual traits of pride and imperiousness. The Nez Percés received their gallicized name when strangers saw dentalia worn in nose perforations, a practice involving only slaves in the tribe, writes anthropologist George Pierre Castile. Ethnologist James A. Teit states that the Nez Percés and other Plateau tribesmen wore nose pins, but does not indicate if their wearers were slave or free.[13] The Nez Percés were also reported as having a slave jargon, words of which, according to one source, were foreign to them having originated "through their intercourse with prisoners of war, and contain[ing] expressions for *eye, horse, man, woman,* and other most common terms, which are entirely foreign to Sahaptin."[14] Castile does not explain why slaves wore items of the wealthy.

The Nez Percé-Cayuses acquired their wealth in slaves through sale of horses, unlike the Klamaths of southern Oregon highlands who sold slaves in order to purchase mounts.[15]

---

[12]J. Lee Humfreville, *Twenty Years Among Our Savage Indians,* 282.

[13]Castile, *The Indians of Puget Sound,* 287; Teit, *The Salishan Tribes of the Western Plateaus,* 82.

[14]W.W. Beach, ed. *The Indian Miscellany: Containing Papers on the History, Antiquities, Arts, Languages, Religions, Traditions and Superstitions of the American Aborigines,* 444.

[15]Stephen Powers, "The California Indians: No. VII—The Modocs," 541.

"Nezperee Indian," an oil portrait by Paul
Kane, based on sketches and watercolors
he prepared while traveling in the West,
1846-1848. Visiting the Nez Percés in
July 1847, Kane painted a watercolor on
the spot of this Nez Percé without a nose
pin, but reportedly added it to the oil using
the tribal name as artistic license to do so.
Though Lewis and Clark told of seeing
natives among the Nez Percés wearing
such nose pieces, it is unlikely that they
wore them when Kane visited since mid-
19th century accounts make no mention
of them. Anthropologists differ as to
whether the nose pins were worn by both
freemen and slaves on the Plateau, or by
slaves only. *Courtesy Royal Ontario Museum, Toronto. Neg. #912.1.72.*

Poor was the Cayuse who owned a mere fifteen to twenty
horses.[16] Bancroft may have had in mind horse-rich Cayuse
head men such as Quahat when he stated that certain individual tribal members possessed bands of up to three thousand head. Journeying westward through Cayuse country,
Thomas Farnham observed that one Cayuse had more than
two thousand horses.[17] It was Farnham who gave the tribe
their sobriquet, "The Imperial Tribe," which name they
gained on the backs of their horses.[18]

    Although slave-holders, the Nez Percés, unlike most war-
ring Plateau tribesmen, usually did not kill their male foe in
combat. A white man, observing slaves traveling "to buffalo"
with their Nez Percé masters, learned that they were shorn of
their hair shortly after capture in southern Oregon and
northern California.[19] War-captive women, who became

    [16]Farnham, *Travels in the Great Western Prairies*, 341.
    [17]Bancroft, *Wild Tribes*, 272; Farnham, *Travels in the Great Western Prairies*, 341.
    [18]Farnham, *Travels in the Great Western Prairies*, 340.
    [19]Frank W. Woody, "From Missoula to Walla Walla in 1857 on Horseback," 284-85.

Nez Percé wives, were not considered personal property; yet, they could be disposed of in any manner their owners chose.[20] Disposal was not perfunctory since they performed many chores in the numerous Nez Percé villages. Their treatment contrasted with that administered by Flatheads, who reserved special cruelties for their most persistent Blackfeet foe. It was the Flathead practice to assemble their captives at certain times daily to remind them of their servile status and punish them by having them hold poles topped with scalps of their unfortunate tribesmen while, in Bancroft's words, Flathead women exerted "all their devilish ingenuity" in tormenting their victims.[21] Among Nez Percés on the other hand, the practical outweighed the revenge factor, for they knew that dead or abused captives would deny them a source of labor, although they could have destroyed their human property any time they wished. Unlike their men, Nez Percé women could gamble away their freedom.[22]

Where coastal nobles, the Maquinnas, the Comcomlys and the Casinos, displayed their wealth in canoes and slaves, the Cayuses continued measuring theirs in horses, their means of acquiring slaves. They originally acquired horses from Shoshonis to their southeast in the 18th century, but subsequently, through breeding and trade, their skill in horse husbandry increased into the 19th century.[23] In the 1840s Quahat's successor, Five Crows, was said to be the wealthiest man in the Plateau with nearly a thousand horses, some cattle, and like coastal nobles, possessor of many wives and slaves.[24] As late as 1893 the nearby Palouse Chief Wolfe (Harlish Washomake) owned over two thousand horses.[25]

The Indians' horses were small, surefooted and hardy. From their introduction into America they diminished in

[20]Spinden, *The Nez Perce Indians*, 245.
[21]Bancroft, *Wild Tribes*, 269.
[22]Spinden, *The Nez Perce Indians*, 245.
[23]Thomas R. Garth, "Early Nineteenth Century Tribal Relations in the Columbia Plateau," 50-51.
[24]Simpson, *Narrative of a Journey Round the World* 1, p. 164.
[25]Clifford E. Trafzer and Richard D. Scheuerman, *Renegade Tribe: The Palouse Indians and the Invasion of the Inland Pacific Northwest*, 133.

size to about thirteen hands. The Cayuses found their name-sake "cayuses" better suited to their equestrian life style than for agriculture, since less mobile and more bulky draft animals required more care and attention.[26] Like horses of Interior Salish speakers to the north, these animals brought Cayuses into contact with Plateau and Plains tribes and all that implied, not the least of which was conflict and capture. From their meeting with Lewis and Clark the Nez Percés received the American stamp of friendship, manifesting it throughout the 19th century. During this time some of their people helped the Americans while others remained at least neutral during the Indian wars of the 1850s. Their reputation among Americans was marred only by the Nez Percé or (Young) Joseph's War (1877), which in reality was the flight of but a portion of that tribe from American troops. The Cayuses, on the other hand, although initially friendly to whites, were branded by them as not only haughty and imperious, but villainous after their involvement in the 1847 Whitman massacre.

The Nez Percé-Cayuses were not always well regarded by others of their own race—not only by their ancient Paiute and Shoshoni foe, but by neighboring Wallawallas. These peoples subserviently caught and supplied the Cayuses with fish, the catching and preparation of which the Cayuses demeaned as work of inferiors. In exchange, the Cayuses supplied Wallawallas with horses and other things at "a highly inequitable rate of exchange."[27] Samuel Parker was told that these Wallawallas were slaves formerly owned and liberated by Nez Percés.[28] After 1750 the Nez Percés and their Cayuse allies raided down the Columbia and southerly up its Willamette River tributary to Willamette Falls, a gathering place similar to, but smaller than, The Dalles. From there they carried off captives of Chinookan speakers downstream at The Cascades. The native inhabitants would flee their vil-

---

[26]Garth, "Early Nineteenth Century Tribal Relations in the Columbia Plateau," 47.
[27]Ibid., 50.
[28]Parker, *Journal of an Exploring Tour Beyond the Rocky Mountains*, 251.

lages for the sanctuary of the woods when these raiders tra-
versed their homelands, and sedentary dwellers at The
Dalles cowered before them. Cayuse-Nez Percé raids against
these lower riverine peoples, although spasmodic, was not
without dangers to themselves. When Lewis and Clark tra-
versed Nez Percé lands these tribesmen would not accompany them beyond The Dalles, fearing retaliation from natives
below that place. In 1814 Alexander Henry reported that
Nez Percés-Cayuses still raided for slaves at Willamette
Falls.[29]

The image of horse-riding Cayuses wielding whips,
knives and later, guns might lead to the false conclusion that
their use of arms disqualified them as traders. They were, in
fact, "the Chinooks" of the Plateau, trading in old mercantile
haunts such as the Grande Ronde Valley of northeastern
Oregon.[30] After mid-19th century, when the tribe tumbled
from its former preeminence, it was surpassed in the interior
slave trade only by Klamaths whose late acquisition of horses
facilitated their travel and commerce, enabling them to
acquire and trade slaves.

In coastal fashion Cayuse families owned hunting territories as well as slaves. Major Benjamin Alvord, commanding
an army garrison at The Dalles in the early 1850s, was well
positioned to observe and evaluate the Cayuses and other
area tribes. His statement that half the Cayuses were slaves,
mostly of Shastan and Wallawallan extraction, seems excessive. Nevertheless, considering the fact that in the aftermath
of smallpox, measles and massacre Alvord's word that only
"fifty pure Cayuse warriors" remained, makes the large number of slaves in proportion to masters more likely. "Two-
thirds of the remnant of this tribe," wrote Alvord, "are
descendants of chief families, and are, therefore, haughty,
disdain labor, have many slaves, and like the modern Poles,
their people are all nobles."[31] His observation of their wealth

[29]Coues, *Henry-Thompson Journals 2*, p. 853.
[30]Farnham, *Travels in the Great Western Prairies*, 341.
[31]Benjamin Alvord, *Military Report* (34 Cong., 3d sess., *House Exec. Doc. no. 761*), Serial 906, p. 11.

in horses and cattle is ironic indication that their livestock had flourished better than they.

The Cayuse warlike disposition as noted by Alvord was as sharply honed as were their weapons wielded against Shoshoni-Bannocks, Klamaths and especially Paiutes in acquiring slaves.[32] During an early 19th century raid the Paiutes captured the child, Egan, on headwaters of central Oregon's John Day River when his people were hunting elk. One source claimed him to be of Umatilla parentage.[33] General O.O. Howard, U.S.A., described him perhaps more correctly as being of Cayuse parentage.[34] Nevertheless, that he later became a Bannock-Paiute head war chief against American forces in 1878 indicates that slave captives could rise to leadership positions among the Great Basin peoples.

The Cayuses had long feared attacks of the Paiute *twelka* (foe) lying in wait to snatch their women and children on rootdigging and berrypicking journeys near their temporary villages. They also feared loss of their horses for which they exchanged slaves, as did Modocs theirs to Shastas for these animals. Traders of the North West Company's Fort Nez Percés, established in 1818 near the confluence of the Columbia and Walla Walla rivers, sought to maintain good relations with the temperamental Cayuses who controlled entry to the vast rich Snake River fur hunting grounds. Fur men also sought to remain on good terms with Wallawallas and other tribes near the fort. Understanding tribal dispositions and tactics, these traders knew that condemning natives for slavery and other barbaric practices on grounds purely moralistic rather than mercantilist was of little avail, only jeopardizing the trade in the process. Pushed to the limits of objectivity, Alexander Ross has left a lengthy, but vivid description of captive treatment by natives (very possibly Cayuses) in the vicinity of the fort. It is one of the most

[32]Ibid.
[33]J.W. Redington, Col., "Honest Chief Egan." Ms. 175.
[34]Ruby and Brown, *The Cayuse Indians*, 283.

graphic to be found in the annals of western American history:

The subject next to be considered is the treatment of the slaves taken in war. On their return from an expedition of this kind the warparty keep in a body and observe the same order as at starting, until they reach home. And if successful their shouting, yelling and chanting the war song fill the air. The sound no sooner reaches the camp than the whole savage horde, young and old, male and female, sally forth not however to welcome the arrival of their friends but to glut the desires of implacable revenge by the most barbarous cruelties on the unfortunate captives.

The slaves, as is customary on such occasions, are all tied on horseback, each behind a warrior. But the squaws no sooner meet them than they tear them down from the horses without mercy, and then begin by trampling on them, tearing their hair and flesh, cutting their ears and maiming their bodies with knives, stones, sticks, or other instruments of torture. After thus glutting their revenge, they are driven to the camp.

It is then settled unalterably what the slaves are doomed to suffer. Every afternoon, some hours before sunset, the camp makes a grand turnout for dancing the scalps. For this purpose two ranks or rows of men, a hundred yards long or more, arrange themselves face to face, and about fifteen feet apart. Inside of them are likewise two rows of women facing each other, leaving a space of about five feet broad in the middle for the slaves, who arranged in a line occupy the centre in a row by themselves. Here the unfortunate victims, male and female, are stationed with long poles in their hands and naked above the waist, on the ends of these poles are exhibited the scalps of their murdered relations. The dancing and chorus then commence, the whole assemblage keeping time to the beating of a loud and discordant sort of drum. The parties all move sideways, to the right and left alternately, according to Indian fashion, the slaves at the same time moving and keeping time with the others. Every now and then a general halt takes place when the air resounds with loud shouts of joy and yell upon yell proclaim afar their triumph.

All this is but a prelude to the scenes that follow. The women placed in the order we have stated, on each side of the slaves, and armed with the instruments of torture, keep all the time jeering them with the most distorted grimaces, cutting them with knives, piercing them with awls, pulling them by the hair and thumping them with fist, stick or stone, in every possible way that can torment without killing them. The loss of an ear, a tooth, the joint of a

finger or part of the scalp torn off during these frantic fits are nightly occurrences. And if the wretches thus doomed to suffer happen
not to laugh and huzza, which in their situation would almost be
contrary to the efforts of human nature, or fail to raise or lower
according to caprice the scalps in regular order, they are doubly tor-
mented and unmercifully handled.

On these occasions a termagant often pounces upon some victim, who not unfrequently falls senseless to the ground under the
infliction of wounds. And if any of them happens from a sudden
blow, to start back a little out of line, another in the rear instantly
inflicts another wound, which never fails to urge the same victim as
far forward. So that they are often kept pushed backward and forward, till at last they are insensible.

The men however take no part in these cruelties but are not
silent spectators. They never interfere, nor does one of them, during the dancing, menace or touch a slave. All the barbarities are
perpetuated by the women! These are the only examples I have ever
witnessed among savages wherein the women out-do the men in
acts of inhumanity: and where sympathy is not regarded as a virtue
by that sex. But then we must take into consideration that it is part
of the law of the land. It is a duty the females, according to the customs of war, are bound to perform.[35]

Ross also described warfare of unidentified Sahaptian speakers against the "Snakes" after which the latter came to within
three miles of the fort where they killed a man and nine
women and children whom they scalped, taking a man and
two women to enslave.[36]

These thralls accompanied fur company employees on
treks into the Snake River country. On one of these journeys
Ross alluded to "our Snake slave," who was perhaps the property of an Indian in the party which took him along to guide
it in his former homelands,[37] as did coastal slaves in theirs.
Ross stated that on one occasion a chief presented Nor'Westers a slave to confirm a promise his people had made. Should
his people renege on that promise the chief vowed that the
Nor'Westers could treat them as slaves. The fur men

---

[35]Ross, *The Fur Hunters of the Far West*, 203-04.
[36]Ibid., 155-56.
[37]Ibid., 244.

returned the slave, who was a bondsmen in every sense of the word.[38]

Nez Percé-Cayuse relationships became strained when American Board missionaries Dr. Marcus Whitman and wife Narcissa established their mission on lands at Waiilatpu (Place of the Rye Grass) in 1836. The Nez Percés believed their Cayuse neighbors had first chance to receive the missionaries' new "medicine." Shortly thereafter the Nez Percés received other American Board missionaries, the Reverend and Mrs. Henry H. Spalding, on their lands at Lapwai (Idaho). At Waiilatpu Mrs. Whitman employed Wallawalla women to work for her, since she thought the "Kayuse ladies are too proud to be seen usefully employed." That she employed Wallawallas confirmed more deeply in Cayuse thinking that those working for missionaries were of a servile nature. Their response was similar to that of Koloshi Tlingits, who regarded Aleuts as slaves after being baptized by Russians. On the other hand, there were instances of natives escaping to mission houses to avoid confinement.[39]

In their correspondence and reports American Board missionaries made few allusions to slavery among their red parishioners, possibly because slavery was such a sensitive issue in the East at the time or, that reference to it might discredit their labors. Possibly they failed to clearly distinguish slave from free women who performed similar tasks. Their meagre remarks about slavery among Nez Percés may also be credited to the free-mingling of peoples in that tribe, which also facilitated and widened missionary endeavor. An example of this was the May 14, 1843, reception of a Shoshonean ex-slave war captive into the Presbyterian Church.

Charter members of the Oregon Presbyterian Church, organized, August 18, 1838, at the Whitman Mission, were

---

[38]Ibid., 77.

[39]Archer Butler Hulbert and Dorothy Printup Hulbert, eds., *Marcus Whitman, Crusader. Part Two, 1838 to 1843*, p. 268. Innokentii Veniaminov, "The Condition of the Orthodox Church in Russian America: Innokentii Veniaminov's History of the Church in Alaska," 47.

primarily Nez Percés-Cayuse men and women. Nine years later the mission was the scene of the infamous Whitman massacre. In later years Kate McBeth, a Presbyterian missionary to the Nez Percés, explained from the Cayuse point of view an important motive for the massacre: "The whites are going to take away our land, and make us slaves." In other words the Cayuses feared they would suffer from white men the same slavery they had inflicted on the tribe's own red foes. Details of the massacre have been too often narrated to repeat here. One assisting in burying the Whitmans and other massacre victims was a Cayuse slave. The Cayuses even treated the forty-five survivors as enslaved hostages, just as they did their native captives, until their rescuer, Peter Skene Ogden, promised the tribesmen fifty blankets, fifty shirts, ten guns, ten fathoms of tobacco, ten handkerchiefs and a hundred rounds of ball and powder.[40] For his part, Five Crows received indemnity in the form of sexual favors by forcing one of the captive women to sleep with him in partial fulfillment of his wish for a white wife to add to his five-native-woman harem. On one occasion he indicated that he would dismiss all of them if he could marry the daughter of a Hudson's Bay Company official. When the lady refused the offer, he married one of his female slaves.[41]

From their exalted position in the Plateau the Cayuses spiraled downward after the massacre, eventually losing the Cayuse War against Oregon Territorials. In 1851, the Oregonians hanged five of those they deemed guilty of the Whitman murders. The Cayuses suffered further defeat in 1858 when Young Chief (Weatenatenamy) was killed skirmishing Shoshonis who had captured many Cayuse men and some of their women.

After the Indian treaties and wars of the 1850s it may have been fortuitous for the Wallawallas that the Umatilla Reser-

---

[40]Kate C. McBeth, *The Nez Perces Since Lewis and Clark*, 64, 70; Garth, "Early Nineteenth Century Tribal Relations in the Columbia Plateau," 48; Ruby and Brown, *The Cayuse Indians*, 120.
[41]Simpson, *Narrative of a Journey Round the World* 1, p. 164.

vation, established for them, the Umatillas and Cayuses, lay on the latter's lands; otherwise, these Cayuses, disgruntled at being forced to live on lands other than their own, might have continued making life miserable for the Wallawallas whom they traditionally demeaned. As it was, the stigma of the latter's servility remained with them well into the reservation era. On their reservation there was trouble aplenty. There was the ever-present danger that, like so many other confines, it would be altered by the government seeking to satisfy whites wanting to eliminate or, at least, reduce the size of the reservation.

It was in an August 11, 1871, meeting with Special Indian Commissioners headed by Felix R. Brunot, seeking to alienate some reservation land, that Young Chief's successor, also named Young Chief, told them that "...we do not try to make slaves of anybody red or white men."[42] He was certainly aware that his Cayuse people had enslaved other tribesmen or had cowed them into submission. Now the government was the master driving his people into their prison-like Umatilla Reservation seeking to take its lands.

Although Cayuse resistance to the government had broken down, there was much concern among its officials over contentions among tribes of the Umatilla Reservation. Its Roman Catholic Indians were pitted against (Marcus) Whitman Presbyterians, with nativist Dreamers helping keep the reservation pot boiling. In their bickerings the Cayuses may have brushed aside the fact that it was the former chief of their Wallawalla neighbors, Peopeomoxmox, whom trigger-happy territorials had killed in the Indian War. After that conflict the slave-owning Chief Kamiakin, who unsuccessfully led the fight against soldiers in the war, had abandoned his Yakima Reservation. Some of the Yakimas did not recognize his chieftaincy partly because of his non-Yakima paternity. He spent the rest of his life in exile,

---

[42]Thomas K. Cree, Secy., *Record of Council August 7-13, 1871, accompanying report of Felix R. Brunot, Umatilla Reservation, Appendix A c. Annual Report, Secy. Interior, 1871*, Serial 1505, p. 528.

refusing benefits from the government. His chieftain son, Tomeo, who joined the Nez Percés, told an historian of the Yakimas, Lucullus V. McWhorter, that his father often traded with tribes as far south as California. On one trip there, said Tomeo, the elder Kamiakin purchased a slave captive. Bearing the name Attween, he became known as Seeskomkee (Askoomskee) or No Feet. Tomeo also told McWhorter of a custom among the tribes (presumably among those such as Yakimas and Nez Percés) that slaves were freed after sufficiently serving their owners to repay the price of their purchase.[43]

In Yakima society prisoners were said to have been more nearly true chattel than bondsmen among other Sahaptian peoples. They were said to have eaten at their masters' "tables," but from separate trays. They were excluded from ceremonials, held no properties, and performed menial tasks.[44]

In early times Yakimas were said to have raided extensively. Among objects of their aggressions were peaceful Interior Salish Sanpoils and Nespelems of the Columbia River in the middle Plateau. Edward Curtis stated that in pre-contact times Yakimas also raided Nez Percés from whom they captured slaves.[45] It was also said that for one slave from the

---

[43]Thomas Garth writes: "The friendly relationship between the Cayuse and the Walla Wallas makes it unlikely that Cayuse slaves came from this group but rather from downriver [the Columbia] Sahaptins, such as the Tenino or Klickitat, who were all lumped under the term 'Walla Walla' by most whites of the period." "Early Nineteenth Century Tribal Relations in the Columbia Plateau," 47.

Information about Tomeo, his father, Kamiakin, and the slave, No Feet, are found in McWhorter's *Yellow Wolf: His Own Story*, Appendix II, 50-53. No Feet's story is also found in Alvin M. Josephy, Jr., *The Nez Perce Indians and the Opening of the Northwest*, 524. He received his name after the elder Kamiakin punished him for stealing by clapping steel traps on his wrists and ankles, then placing him outside the tipi one winter night. From this experience he lost both feet and a hand. This did not immobilize him. As a good rider and horse breaker he managed to escape from soldiers at the Battle of Big Hole in the 1877 Nez Perce War after warning the camp of their coming. Subsequently, he joined the camp of Sitting Bull in Canada from which time his life among the Sioux continued to be marked by violence.

[44]One explanation of the meaning of the name, Yakima, is that of a phonetically similar word denoting an incident in which a youthful Columbia River slave left two young girls in a family way when their parents were away at The Dalles. Lucullus V. McWhorter, "Origin of Yakima," 180. Ms. 1518.

[45]Curtis, *The North American Indian* 7, p. 14.

upper Columbia the Yakimas traded five horses at a time when these animals were in short supply.[46] Were such the case, these slaves would have been valuable, for after 1800 when horses were more plentiful, one of them was exchanged for a slave.

Like other tribes between the Rocky and Cascade mountains the Yakimas, situated on the western fringes of the Plateau, were not immune from tribes raiding for horses, scalps and slaves. To prevent such incursions in the forepart of the 19th century Yakima Chief Owhi posted guards to intercept the foe. When a party of Indians from Montana, possibly Kalispels (Pend d'Oreilles), invaded Yakima territory, his guards knifed them, leaving few alive. In the attack two women were captured and enslaved.[47]

Formerly captured by Kalispels, Yakima Chief Ta-kill traded furs at Fort Nisqually in 1835.[48] Most Yakimas at that time, however, traded more frequently at the nearer and more accessible Dalles, acquiring their slaves through trade which largely replaced their raidings for them. Yakimas continued trading occasionally at Fort Nisqually and during the Yakima phase of the Indian War (1855-1857) threatened Indians in the area of the fort with enslavement should they not support them in their fight against American soldiers.[49]

Closely allied with Yakimas were the Klickitats, one branch of which did enough slave raiding in the 19th century for both tribes. Klickitat excursions extended as far west as Oregon's Coast Range and southerly into the Willamette valley and beyond. Passing gingerly through Rogue River country, whose natives were known for their fighting abili-

[46]Ibid.

[47]Lucullus V. McWhorter, "Chief Owhi's Only Crime," Ms. 1530.

[48]Bagley, "Journal of Occurrences at Nisqually House, 1833-1835," p. 161. Some ethnologists classify Kalispels in two divisions of one tribe in the manner of others separated by slight dialectic variations. They divide them into Upper and Lower Kalispels, or Upper and Lower Pend d'Oreilles. Other scholars classify the Upper Kalispels as Pend d'Oreilles and the Lower, as Kalispels. The present Kalispel Indian Community (Washington) was formerly composed of Lower Kalispels or Pend d'Oreilles. The Upper Kalispels of the tribe are now incorporated within the Confederated Salish & Kootenai Tribes (Montana).

[49]W.B. Gosnell, Special Indian Agent, to Isaac I. Stevens, Dec. 31, 1856. "Indian War in Washington Territory," 296.

ties, the Klickitats pounced upon the Shastas, who spent much time and energy trying to defend themselves from these Klickitats and raiders from the Columbia River.[50]

The journeying of a Klickitat band to California to work for Spaniards was not unusual, for Plateau peoples such as the Wallawallas went there around mid-19th century to trade and buy horses. When the Klickitats returned after spending a year or so in California some of their horses were stolen by Rogue River Indians. In response, Klickitat Chief William Spencer organized a foray against these Rogues, killing three chieftain sons and others of that tribe.[51] The Klickitats slipped away with Rogue women and children to enslave. During the 1855-1858 Indian War one of these Rogue women married the paymaster at the United States military post, Vancouver Barracks. Fearing she might tell her superiors that three Klickitats were helping the Yakimas in their war against the Americans, the three, to silence her, tied rocks to her body and threw her over a high cliff into the Klickitat River. The victim left a son who went on the Yakima Reservation with the Klickitats and received from its agent, the Reverend "Father" James Wilbur, the name "Abe Lincoln."[52] Spencer went on to become head chief on the Yakima Reservation.[53]

Some Plateau tribes apparently had no history of acquiring or using enslaved captives. Among these were the closely related Sanpoil-Nespelems.[54] Even after neighboring tribes acquired slaves, these two peoples made no concerted effort to take on horse culture (so important in the acquisition of captives) until about contact time, roughly a quarter-century

---

[50]Spier and Sapir, *Wishram Ethnography*, 222-23.

[51]Lucullus V. McWhorter, "Chief William Spencer's Foray Against the Rogue River Tribe," 112-13. Ms. 1548.

[52]Ibid.

[53]Ruby and Brown, *Indians of the Pacific Northwest*, 230. Mrs. Kate (Caesar) Williams of the Yakima Reservation told of the enslavement, a decade later, of Paiute women by other Indians who, most likely, were from the Umatilla Reservation. Lucullus V. McWhorter, "Incidents of the Paiute War 1878." Ms. 1542.

[54]Verne F. Ray, *The Sanpoil and Nespelem: Salishan Peoples of Northeastern Washington*, 25.

later for them than for their neighbors. Wayne Suttles and certain other scholars take issue with Verne Ray's characterization of the Sanpoil-Nespelems as a peaceful people.[55] To their west lived the Okanagons with whom they were allied.

In pre-contact times these Okanagons acquired and enslaved young women captives in raids. They also held slaves which they had purchased at The Dalles, especially Paiutes as well as from Shastas and Rogue Rivers.[56] Some Okanagon slaves came from coastal and northern interior tribes like the Lillooets through the Ntlakyapamuks, or Thompson Rivers, who traded them on to the Okanagons.[57] At one time, stated Bancroft, the Okanagons sacrificed slaves, but more commonly, horses killed over their owners' graves unlike their slaves whose dead bodies were sometimes bound upright to tree trunks.[58] Captured women were readily accepted by Okanagons, who seldom mistreated them or their children, whom they accepted as societal members. Only in times of stress and quarrels were they called "slaves." Apparently referring to later times, Ray states that Okanagons held no slaves, and indicates that their Senijextee, or Lake, neighbors to their east held none.[59] This tends to confirm the fact that the Lakes "had hardly any slaves," which were also called such only during quarrels.[60] The statements of Ray and anthropologist James A. Teit do not preclude the possibility that they might have held slaves in earlier times.

The same holds true for the Columbia, or Sinkiuse Indians (later, the Chief Moses tribe) whom Ray states did not practice slavery.[61] According to Bancroft, further north in

---

[55]Suttles, *Coast Salish Essays*, 282-86.

[56]Teit, *The Salishan Tribes of the Western Plateaus*, 277.

[57]Ibid.

[58]Bancroft, *Wild Tribes*, 288.

[59]Ray, *Cultural Relations in the Plateau of Northwestern America*, 30. According to fur man Alexander Ross the Okanagons were not war minded, and had but few slaves which were adopted as children and treated "in all respects as members of the family." *Adventures of the First Settlers*, 320.

[60]Teit, *The Salishan Tribes of the Western Plateaus*, 277.

[61]Ray, *Cultural Relations in the Plateau of Northwestern America*, 30.

245   INDIAN SLAVERY IN THE PACIFIC NORTHWEST

Canada there was no slavery among the Shuswaps. Commander Mayne confirmed this view, stating that the absence of slavery among them and the Okanagons contributed "much to their superior moral condition."[62] Archaeologist Rodger Hegler states that Shuswaps and other upper Plateau peoples such as the Thompson Rivers and Takullis, or Carriers (so-named because their widows were obliged to carry ashes of dead husbands in bags around their necks for several years as tokens of servitude) participated in periodic raidings, although such appear to have been of little importance to Shuswaps.[63]

Another slave-holding people were the Spokanes in the watershed of the Spokane River, many of whose slaves were captured in war or acquired in trade at The Dalles.[64] Like other Interior Salish peoples like the Flatheads and Okanagons, they preferred female slaves, and like that of many Plateau peoples their slavery fell off well after contact as noted by the Reverend Walker in 1841, who found but one "genuine" slave among them.

The Spokanes' near neighbor to the east, the Coeur d'Alenes, like several other Plateau peoples, procured slaves from capture in war and through purchase. Teit states that although Coeur d'Alene slaves were purchased mainly and originally from Paiutes and Shoshonis, they had previously been enslaved to tribes to their south as Nez Percés, Cayuses, Wallawallas and others. He states that very few of their slaves procured from the south ever returned there. The Coeur d'Alenes did not permit their slaves to purchase their freedom, nor did they sell them for other trade items. Some of their slaves escaped, but on the whole they were well treated and it was reported that their owners' families sorrowed

---

[62]Bancroft, *Wild Tribes*, 276; Mayne, *Four Years in British Columbia and Vancouver Island*, 300.

[63]Anthropologist Rodger Heglar also states that the Shuswaps visited other plateau tribes not always to trade, but to capture slaves. *A Racial Analysis of Indian Skeletal Material from the Columbia River Valley*, 69. Thesis 813020; Dunn, *History of the Oregon Territory*, 79-80.

[64]Teit, *The Salishan Tribes of the Western Plateaus*, 380.

when they died.[65] Women bearing their masters' children became free members of the tribe, as did the children who were never taunted as being "slave children." The Coeur d'Alenes cut their slaves' hair short in the coastal manner, but when these slaves became full-fledged tribal members, they were permitted to let it grow. Before contact some Coeur d'Alenes were enslaved by Kalispels who in time allowed them to return to their homelands.[66] When the Coeur d'Alenes began going "to buffalo," they rarely kept slaves and when buffalo hunting ended for them so had the vestiges of slavery.[67] They were aware of it in earlier times, for in 1858 they looked upon army scouts as slaves serving their military masters.[68]

Among Flatheads to the east of the Coeur d'Alenes slavery was less an economic institution than a paramilitary activity. That they lived just west of the Blackfeet on the front line of Interior Salish defense from these aggressive tribesmen might explain the semi-military caste in which they held captives taken in war, rather than acquired through purchase. The Flatheads were said to have learned their patterns of revenge from the Blackfeet from whose lands they claim to have migrated, and when provoked, unleashed their anger on their Plains tutors.[69] In early times the aggressive Blackfeet were said to have learned the arts of torture from Iroquois.[70]

Female captives were the sole property of Flathead captors, who regarded their taking almost as highly as they did enemy horses. Treatment of Flathead captives, harsh by Interior Salish standards, must be explained in the bitterness of the revenge cycle in which they became involved in conflict with Blackfeet and other Plains tribes. With the dwin-

---

[65]Ibid., 158.

[66]Ibid.

[67]Teit states that "slaves were of little value to a people who were not fairly sedentary, and they could easily be kept captive," ibid., 159.

[68]Hiram Martin Chittenden and Talbot Richardson, *Life, Letters and Travels of Father Pierre-Jean De Smet, S.J. 1801-1873*, p. 750.

[69]Olga Wedemeyer Johnson, *Flathead and Kootenay*, 37.

[70]Ibid.

dling of the buffalo herds in the 19th century, the contests of Flathead and their allies against the plainsmen did not decrease accordingly since Indians on both sides of the Rocky Mountains competed for the last kills. The passing of the herds rendered moot the question of which peoples, Plains or Plateau, had the priority to hunt them.

Initiating women captives into humiliating submission, the Flatheads cut their prisoners' hair and painted their faces with charcoal, often staking them down at night and tying bells and rattles to them, as they did their horses, to prevent their escape and recapture. Once initiated, they performed duties like those of Flathead women. Their children were treated as free persons, but considered a step below their owners. Flathead males kept female war captives as concubines that Olga Johnson calls slaves.[71] These female captives were of far more economic value than were their men, most of whom had been killed in Flathead-Blackfeet fighting.

Around Flathead campfires stories were told of ancient cruelties inflicted by their Blackfeet foe and how these Flatheads and their Kutenai allies had retaliated against them, celebrating their victories in blood curdling scalp dances and torching of prisoners—cruel lessons learned on the Plains. Among incidents likely remembered was that of Christmas Day, 1813, when their predecessors tied a captive Blackfeet to a tree, heated a gun barrel to burn his legs, thighs, neck, cheeks and abdomen and then cut flesh from his nails which they extracted before severing his fingers joint by joint. The Blackfeet was said not to have winced as his tormentors scalped him and scooped an eye from its socket, presenting, wrote eyewitness Ross Cox, a "horrific appearance."[72] Before the victim was put to death by a bullet through the heart, he had sufficient life remaining to boast that it was he who the previous fall had put out the eyes and torn the tongue from his captor's wife. Cox was known to have embellished his accounts. Such violence exceeded that of Coastal tribes raids.

---

[71]Ibid., 113.   [72]Cox, *Adventures* 1, pp. 232-34.

Stirred as much as their men by such stories, female Flat-heads continued treating Blackfeet women more cruelly than their men did their Blackfeet foe.[73] Among those recording the murderous competition between the two tribes was John Work, who in 1824 wrote that the Blackfeet retaliated against both Flatheads and Nez Percés and fought Paiutes for slaves, especially women and children. For Plateau tribes-men to have returned with large numbers of male captives would have been as impossible as it was for those of coastal regions, which helped account for the numbers of natives, especially males, killed at scenes of conflict. Although Flat-head numbers fell off precipitously with wars and raids, they would have preferred extinction to the adoption of Blackfeet males to bolster their own numbers. Male captives that they did have were abused and subject to death should their lords tire of them. They could be sold[74] which was a lesser fate than remaining with their Flathead captors. Like some Plateau tribes, the Flatheads did not practice debt slavery; nor did they purchase slaves or sell their own wives and children into bondage for payment of debts, which left debtors to repay creditors in other ways.[75]

It was to protect themselves from similar troubles that

---

[73]Ibid.

[74]Harry Holbert Turney-High, "The Flathead Indians of Montana," 120.

[75]Ibid. Turney-High states that in the Flathead language the word for "slave" and "cap-tive" is the same. Among Flatheads slavery was not an economic, but a socio-military insti-tution. Male captives were returned to their Flathead captors' villages, where they were abused by both men and women; yet, Flatheads spoke proudly of the gentle character which white explorers ascribed to them. Some male captives were made "camp slaves," but were never sent out to perform chores in situations from which they could escape. Ibid., 129-30.

Among the various linguistic groups suffering Blackfeet incursions were Shoshonean people who experienced such inroads well into the 19th century. It was from an incursion of Blackfeet proper and Gros Ventres that the Lemhi Shoshoni Sacajawea became well-known in history for serving as entree for Lewis and Clark traversing her country en route to the Pacific Coast. When encamped earlier with her people at the Three Forks of the Mis-souri River, they were raided by Blackfeet and Gros Ventres who killed many Lemhis and carried off a number of boys and girls to become their property to be sold or gambled away. Through this process Sacajawea reached Mandan country of North Dakota where she joined the Lewis and Clark party wintering there (1804-1805) as it prepared for its long westerly trek. Had Sacajawea been elderly she might have been the victim of the scalping knife, or even suffered death.

Flatheads, strengthened by other Salishan and Sahaptin hunters, crossed the Rockies to the Plains; but unlike their Blackfeet foe, they were without firearms.[76] On a warring expedition against the Kutenais the Piegans, a Blackfeet sub-tribe, took with them a well-treated Flathead slave. When the Piegans fled the battlefield he managed to remain behind. The Kutenais were about to kill him when the Nor'Wester, David Thompson, happened along and spared his life.[77] Occasionally Piegans took heads from their slain foe, believing the latters' souls would serve them as slaves in the other world as the Shoshonis believed their dead Piegan foe would do likewise.[78]

---

[76]Johnson, *Flathead and Kootenay,* 195.

[77]T.C. Elliott, "Introduction to David Thompson's Narrative: The Discovery of the Source of the Columbia," 44.

[78]When Thompson's Nor'Wester colleague, Alexander Henry, met some Crow Indians, they offered from their stock of slaves a "handsome slave girl" of about twelve years in exchange for a gun, a hundred balls and powder to fire them. Coues, *Henry-Thompson Journals* 2, p. 399.

Like the Flatheads, the Crows were on good terms with Americans. Helping initiate the high regard which Americans developed for Flatheads was the fact that Lewis and Clark had peacefully passed through their lands en route to the Pacific. This image remained untarnished by ministrations of the Reverend Peter De Smet, S.J. (with American connections), who, in the early 1840s, established Saint Mary's Mission on their lands (near present-day Missoula, Montana). A medievalist in spirit, De Smet watched his Flathead parishioners war against Blackfeet as though they were Christian crusaders fighting the infidel. He wrote that in 1845 in two Flathead-Kalispel skirmishes with Blackfeet, the latter lost twenty-one warriors after which Crees carried off a large number of their horses and scalps, massacred fifty families, and led one hundred-sixty women and children into captivity and slavery while sacrificing others to their fallen warriors. De Smet, *Oregon Missions,* 242.

A half-century after Sacajawea returned to her Lemhi Shoshonis, the Mormons of the Church of Jesus Christ of Latter-day Saints established its Lemhi Mission (present-day east-central Idaho). For an account of this mission, see Ruby and Brown, *Indians of the Pacific Northwest,* 161. Despite its abandonment due to troubles with the Shoshoni-Bannocks, its Salt Lake City-based mission retained a permanency not enjoyed by many such groups in the Pacific Northwest. The Mormon program was said to have initially spurred the practice of slavery, but eventually, to have brought about its demise among area Paiutes, Utes and other Shoshoneans who sold slaves to Spaniards to the south. The strong Mormon foothold in Utah enabled its legislature to pass laws regulating slave purchases so as to provide Indians the amenities of a free people by calling for the eventual discontinuance of slavery. Carling Malouf and A. Arline Malouf, *The Effects of Spanish Slavery on Indians of the Intermountain West,* 434. One law passed in 1850 prohibited sales of guns and ammunition to Indians entering Utah from Mexico. This legislation was aimed at keeping guns out of outsiders' hands to lessen pressure on area tribes to surrender their slaves to those threatening to take them with guns as those obtained from Spaniards. With fewer guns in hand area tribes would have been less successful raiding other tribes for slaves. Carling and A.

Sorting out the causes for the decline of slavery, in various Plateau tribes, it should be noted that their declining numbers and those of the buffalo reduced their conflict with Plains tribesmen. This helped doom slavery as did efforts of Catholic missionaries who sought to reduce strife among their Indian parishioners on proposed Paraguayan-type reductions. During the President U.S. Grant Peace Policy of the 1870s, church-sanctioned agents sought virtually the same goals for reservation Indians.[79]

The importance of horses which provided quick-striking Plateau tribesmen the means of acquiring slaves cannot be overstated; neither can be overstated the value of these animals as property with which their owners purchased slaves to heighten their own status. Nowhere was this truer than among Klamath Indians, who had few peers in the Pacific Northwest in the practice and extent of slavery and especially, its trade.

Arline Malouf have pointed out the importance of Mormon presence in the Salt Lake valley as deterring the slave traffic which once flourished along the Old Spanish Trail. Ibid. See also L.R. Bailey, *Indian Slave Trade in the Southwest.* Slaves were also traded out of the Plateau into the Plains, but apparently in no great numbers.

About the time negotiations began for removing Flatheads to a reservation, violence erupted on the southern Plateau and northern Great Basin during the Civil War as youthful braves along the Immigrant Road, in the absence of federal troops, attacked and killed westerly moving settlers. The return of troops after the war could not have been too soon for the editor of the *Montana Post* of Virginia City in southwestern Montana. Seymour Dunbar and Paul C. Phillips, have included his June 10, 1865, editorial in "A Caucasian Opinion of the Red Race." In his editorial, titled "Indian Troubles," he stated:

> ...On the general score we cannot help saying that, were it not too serious a subject for a jest, that we might smile at the Democracy [the Democratic party] that is so righteously and so severely exercised at the idea of tyranny in the shape of game laws, and forced tithings in the old countries, and yet enforces them so stringently on behalf of the copper-colored banditti, who, scorning useful labor, make pack horses of their own women, ravish and enslave all of ours they can lay their hands on, and dry the scalps of our plundered and murdered people in that nest of abominations, an Indian wigwam.

The return of troops and the hand of the government in the form of Indian agencies served to check the incursions and slavery to which the editor of the *Post* alluded. Passage of the Thirteenth Amendment (December 1865), the year the editorial appeared, may have had some impact on the demise of slavery among red men as it did among those who were black.

[79]For a commentary on Grant's Peace Policy. See Ruby and Brown, *Indians of the Pacific Northwest,* 229-37.

9

The Klamath Slave Cluster

The slave trade was zealously pursued by Klamath peoples of the southern extent of the Plateau. Once fairly isolated and less prone than other Plateau peoples to trade, they entered into the practice in historic times with such fervor that social stratification began to emerge in the tribe before the demise of the practice.. The inception and development of slavery among the Northern Indians, which took centuries to develop, followed conditions which first permitted an aristocracy. The Klamath stratification nidus resulted within a couple decades following the introduction of the practice of slavery from which they derived their wealth.

Klamath peoples, living in the highlands of south central Oregon at settlements at places such as Klamath Lake, Klamath Marsh, the Williamson and Sprague rivers, were relatively isolated until well past contact times. Surrounding tribes adopted the horse culture nearly a half-century earlier than they. Consequently, they were victims of raider-poachers seeking their territory and women. Later the Klamaths acquired mounts and discovered two important things: slave captives were in demand, and they could meet that demand by adopting an equestrian culture. With ensuing accelerated raidings made possible by use of horses they also discovered they could more ably subdue and wreak vengeance on foes than could other peoples less responsive to horse culture. Thus, they were assured acquisition of even more horses, goods and captives. By shortening travel time northward to places such as The Dalles and the Willamette Valley as a result of the use of the horse, these Klamaths increased their merchandising in human commodities at such places. An important consequence was increasing wealth and social stratification which separated the wealthy from the poor and the enslaved. The Klamaths found The Dalles, particularly, a good outlet for the merchandising of slaves from southern Oregon and northern California. At The Dalles they met other Plateau tribesmen who had come there to trade. Among them were the Cayuses, who acquired horses c. 1730. The Nez Percés, Yakimas, and Spokanes to the north acquired horses about the same time. The horse was soon spread among other Plateau tribes, but it by-passed the Klamaths whom pedestrian Paiutes separated from aggressive equestrian Shoshoni-Bannocks.[1] From roughly the beginning of the 16th century when horses were introduced into the New World, it took over three centuries for mounts to reach the Klamaths.

The history of the Klamaths is closely intertwined with that of their neighbors, the Modocs. In the early 1870s a newspaper man, Samuel A. Clarke, described the landscape of these Modocs as "clothed in desert attire" where "ponies fared bountifully on the bunch grass and on the luxuriant meadows..."[2] Horses provided the Modocs a means by which to vent their aggressions. The same applied to the Klamaths after acquiring horses on a trading journey. The acquisition also created, or at least intensified, their animosities against Shoshonean "Snakes" (most likely, Paiutes) whom they raided. An elderly Klamath subchief, Chal-o-quin, the son of a chief living at a place called Oux-y at the northern end of Klamath Marsh, told Clark:

---

[1]The Spanish introduced the horse to the New World. From their Santa Fe colony (founded 1609) horses spread to the Plains where the tribes quickly adapted them to their roving life style. This adaptation gave these tribes an advantage over horseless peoples in war and in the chase. Through raids, horses spread on a northern route which bifurcated: one route east of the Continental Divide to the Plains, and another to the West. By the latter 17th and early 18th centuries the horse had spread north into the Great Basin where Shoshonis of the Snake River country obtained them at about the same time. Despite the Klamath's relative closeness to San Francisco to their south and their nearness to Shoshonean peoples to their east, the Klamaths did not acquire horses until a full century later. Harold E. Driver and William C. Massey, *Comparative Studies of North American Indians*, 284-87; Francis D. Haines, "The Northward Spread of Horses Among the Plains Indians," 429-37.

[2]Samuel A. Clarke, *Klamath County Museum Research Papers no. 2*, pp. 1, 4.

> When the Snakes made war on us that made us keen to fight other
> Indians and we made war without provocation on the Pitt River,
> Shastas and Rogue Rivers, but they never made willing war on us.
> These wars lasted a great many years. We found we could make
> money by war, for we sold the provisions and property captured for
> horses and other things we needed. It was like soldiers nowadays
> who fight for money. We made war because we made money by it
> and we rather got to like it anyhow. The Snakes provoked us to
> make war on them.[3]

Chal-o-quin recalled a fight with the Snakes from which
his Klamaths returned home with the scalp, hands and heart
of a Snake chief, Patkotk.[4] Returning from similar journeys
the Klamaths danced five nights and days around the grisly
tokens of their conquests which were suspended from high
poles.[5] After an interlude of two or three "snows" they again
became involved in conflict with the Snakes. As Chal-o-quin
told it, the Klamaths attacked before daybreak, killing nearly
all the Snake men and some women (which he confessed was
by mistake), and returning with the remainder to enslave.
During peaceful times they released some prisoners and kept
or sold others to various tribes as slaves. Captured Shastas
and Rogue Rivers were never returned and only some of the
Snakes.[6]

In retaliation tribes surrounding the Klamaths from Pit
River northwesterly to the Umpqua fought back against
them, attacking one spring when these Klamaths and Modocs were abroad digging roots. A small boy carried the
alarming news back to the camp, spurring it to hastily orga-
nize a force to beat off the invaders.[7] Now more than ever the
two tribes were forced onto the defensive against the
avengers. From Klamath-Modoc campsites they dispatched
lookouts to high prominences to scan in all direction and
alert their people to their foes. Otherwise, they could have

---

[3]Ibid., 10, 11.
[4]Ibid., 9.
[5]Ibid.
[6]Ibid., 10.
[7]Ibid., 10, 11.

lost their property, their women and even their very lives. They also kept night watches to warn their sleeping camps of danger.[8]

It was not until 1835 that French-Canadian fur traders introduced European goods to the Klamaths.[9] Changes thus wrought in their lifestyle may be said to have begun in earnest after the Hudson's Bay Company trader, Peter Skene Ogden, visited them in 1826. He discovered that they had but one horse[10] with which to counter Nez Percé-Cayuses riding up central Oregon's Deschutes River valley seeking to enslave them.[11] From the time that French-Canadian trappers escorted Klamaths to The Dalles, their travel to that place increased.[12] Exposed to many native traders with a diversity of goods, the Klamaths sought a new commercial lifestyle, despite the fact that, like their predecessors for generations, they had survived amply on their lands which were well-watered and rich in game and other food resources.

---

[8]A.N. Armstrong, *Oregon: Comprising a Brief History and Full Description of the Territories of Oregon and Washington*, 120.

[9]Leslie Spier, *Klamath Ethnography*, 7.

[10]T.C. Elliott, "Editorial Notes on the Peter Skene Ogden Journal of Snake Expedition, 1826-7," p. 210.

Anthropologist Thomas N. Layton places the horse in the Rocky Mountains near the end of the 17th century, and its western spread, by the end of that century. He does not accept the available evidence that Klamaths were late in adopting and using horses or the assertion that the tribe's trading in the southern Plateau occurred as recently as the second or third decade of the 19th century. He does cite Ogden's report of seeing one horse among Klamaths in 1826, but believes the tribe had hidden many of its horses. Layton speculates and imagines that the Klamaths "became indirectly articulated" before 1800 in a north-south trade route linking the passage of slaves between California and The Dalles. Yet, his specific citation is the trek of Indians from northern places going to trade in California in 1844. His belief in the 1800 Klamath trade is based on the fact that Samuel A. Clarke interviewed Klamaths who told him of having seen such. Although Clarke did not give the age of those he interviewed, Layton assumes they were sixty-five years of age, when they might well have been forty years younger. Layton, "Traders and Raiders: Aspects of Trans-Basin and California-Plateau Commerce, 1800-1830," *Journal of California and Great Basin Anthropology*, 127-130. Layton fails to substantiate his assertions, and his speculation is unconvincing. Horses were necessary for the Plateau trade in slaves, but there is no evidence that Klamaths traded them at The Dalles before well past the third part of the 19th century. And it is unlikely they would have hidden their horses had they possessed and used that animal. Had Klamaths been prominent in the trading system, they surely would have been as well known as other Pacific Northwestern tribes who were active and prominent in the trade.

[11]Theodore Stern, "The Klamath Indians and the Treaty of 1864," 412; Elliott, "Editorial Notes on the Peter Skene Ogden Journal of Snake Expedition, 1826-7," 210, 211.

[12]Theodore Stern, *The Klamath Tribe, A People and Their Reservation*, 22.

In an article in *The Overland Monthly* (June 1873) Stephen Painter described the Klamaths' involvement in slavery:

This nation were even worse than the Modocs in the rapacity and cruelty with which they prosecuted the slave-trade. To secure a supply of slaves, they generally made war on the timid and peaceful Indians of Pit River. Of the captives taken, they retained as many as they wished for their own service, and sold the remainder to the tribes about The Dalles and Des Chutes. It was by means of this barter that they first obtained a stock of ponies, which their northern neighbors had learned to use before themselves. These slaves, like all other property, were sacrificed upon the death of the owner, though the practice is now discontinued.[13]

The impetus to acquire horses enabled the Klamaths to overcome the isolation which had previously kept them off the major paths of communication. Classified culturally as the outermost Plateau tribe, their horizons broadened, especially, as noted by Painter, northward to The Dalles in order to conduct trade in many items, not the least important of which were slaves.[14] The Deschutes Valley, down which they transported their slaves, soon became a much used avenue for trading at The Dalles.

The Klamaths also branched westerly into the Willamette watershed, traveling down the North Fork of the Santiam River on what became known as the western branch of the Klamath Trail,[15] one of their routes to wealth. It took them through villages of the Upper, or Northern Molalas with whom they were generally on good terms, and on to villages of Kalapuyas along the upper mid-Willamette River, then to the Willamette Falls trading mart. In 1843 a missionary at that place wrote that "a large party of the Clamath tribe, fierce and warlike, from the South, came in with about twenty slaves, and sold most or all of them. Some, I was informed were sold for three horses each, some cheaper."[16] Among

[13]Powers, "The California Indians," 541.
[14]Spier, *Klamath Ethnography*, 24.
[15]Stern, "The Klamath Indians and the Treaty of 1864," 413.
[16]Robert Carlton Clark, *History of the Willamette Valley, Oregon* 1, p. 56.

tribes in the lower Willamette Valley with whom the Klamaths dealt were Clackamas Indians from whom they bought slaves.[17]

The Klamaths continued trading in the Willamette as well as in one of their favorite markets, Yainax ("The Mountain"), a pleasant valley east of the southern end of Upper Klamath Lake in the Sprague River valley north of the Oregon-California border. Witnessing the trading there in the latter 19th century, Clarke described how properties were exchanged. Now, however, the Klamaths had a new item not only with which to trade, but, to wager. Wrote Clarke: "Horses were freely lost and won and when excitement of the game grew high it might be that a favorite slave or captive was put up as a stake to win all back or leave him lovelorn at her loss as otherwise impecunious."[18]

Yainax bustled with the noise of human activity—trading interspersed with foot and horse races, archery contests and other gaming and dancing. When the trading and the noises were over, the valley returned to its original silence to await another gathering of the tribes. With its short but intense spurts of seasonal activity, Yainax lacked the "international" flavor, continuity, and variety of goods found at The Dalles. The Klamaths continued trading at both The Dalles and in the Willamette. They also turned east and south to trade with the Shoshoneans, and to the south to trade with the Pit Rivers—the Achomawis and Atsugewis of northern California.

The Achomawi Pit Rivers lived in the watershed of the river bearing their name from near Montgomery Creek in Shasta County to Goose Lake just below the Oregon border, except on lands used by Atsugewi Pit Rivers in Burney and other northern California valleys. The Klamath-Modocs also picked on the Achomawis, but were not alone in doing so, for tribes as Paiutes, Shastas, Wintuns, Yanas and Maidus

<hr>

[17]Curtis, *The North American Indian* 9, p. 75.
[18]Clarke, *Klamath County Museum Research Papers*, 27.

did likewise.[19] The Achomawis and Atsugewis were the armorers of their day, possessing bows of yew and sinew. Of these Clarke wrote that none used by the English ever rivaled them, "not even those wielded by bold Robin Hood and his merry archer men."[20] They stole from the rich and not so rich, but unlike the outlaws of Sherwood Forest, had no thought of giving their booty to the poor. Unlike the arrows of Robin Hood and his men, theirs were tipped with poison.[21] Effective as were their weapons, they could not hold off bold attacks of the Klamaths who raided them for slaves and the superior weapons which they both traded and used. Despite their mercantilism and aggressions, the Klamaths did not acquire guns as readily as they did horses. The fact that they acquired few firearms before mid-19th century[22] did not dull their aggressiveness, for with their aboriginal weapons they did quite well in increasing their supply of slaves by annually raiding tribes as the Pit Rivers who had but few, if any, firearms. An anonymous manuscript, dated 1873, entitled, "The Shastas and Their Neighbors," stated that the Pit Rivers were not strong enough to retaliate against the Modocs, who enslaved their women and children and killed their men.[23]

Klamaths and Modocs combined to raid for slaves.[24] Of this partnership Stephen Painter noted that they "attained of

[19]Curtis, *The North American Indian* 13, p. 236. The Achomawis and Atsugewis were originally classified as of a single stock under the name Palaihnihan, an eastern branch of Shastan stock, but were later placed under the widely-spread Hokan family.

[20]Clarke, *Klamath County Museum Research Papers*, 26.

[21]Curtis, *The North American Indian* 13, p. 236.

[22]The only gun the Klamaths had when fighting Rogue River tribes was one they captured as booty from the enemy. That fight during which Klamath Chief Lalakes lost his brother, probably occurred prior to the middle of the 19th century. Clarke, *Klamath County Museum Research Papers*, 11. Theodore Stern writes: "...even by midcentury they had only one firearm among them." *The Klamath Tribe*, 22. Stern also writes: "Items [acquired by the Klamaths] from the alien [Euro-American] culture, such as firearms, do not appear, nor do horses, which are late additions to Klamath culture." "Some Sources of Variability in Klamath Mythology," 136. In 1826 the Klamaths told Peter Skene Ogden they had no guns. T.C. Elliott, "The Peter Skene Ogden Journals," 210-11.

[23]Erminie Wheeler-Voegelin, *Pitt River Indians of California*, 119.

[24]Verne F. Ray, *Primitive Pragmatists: The Modoc Indians of Northern California*, 134.

old to a great infamy as slave-dealers, their principal victims being the timid, simple, joyous races in California, and especially those of Pit River, though now the latter have forgiven the ancient crime, and heartily wish them well in their fight [the Modoc War] with the American."[25] Verne Ray discusses the role of "Leaders" in Modoc society. They were a modifying force who attempted to provide their tribesmen a measure of peace by urging them to seek reconciliation with their foes. Among other means, they suggested sending to the adversaries the slave wives of Modoc husbands to talk peace. Yet, when Pit Rivers were being raided for slaves, their requests for peace with offerings of money and maidens were refused by the Modocs.[26] Working against efforts of Modoc leaders was the economic importance of taking and selling slaves. Their alliance with Klamaths benefitted the latter more than it did them, since slave purchases by the Klamaths from the Modocs allowed the Klamaths to amass more wealth in trade than that of their ally.[27]

Until the California gold rush of the late 1840s, there were few whites to challenge raidings of the alliance partners. The whites considered the warfare primarily an Indian matter. Among those who observed Klamath aggressions in acquiring slaves from Shastas and other natives in 1841 were members of the United States Exploring Expedition.[28]

It would appear that an increasingly strong motive for Klamath-Modoc slave raiding was less murder than money, which propelled them into commercial prominence as entrepreneurs of the interior, placing them in strong control in the pricing of slaves and horses. One anthropologist, however, minimizes the importance of their raidings against Pit Rivers, suggesting that

> Their raiding of the Achomawi of Pit River has also been exploited. That they were the better warriors is indisputable. But if they

[25]Powers, "The California Indians," 536.
[26]Curtis, The North American Indian 13, p. 130.
[27]Ray, Primitive Pragmatists, 138-39.
[28]Charles Wilkes, U.S.N., Western America, Including California and Oregon, 100.

had conducted annual raids, slaughtering the men and dragging the women and children off to sell at The Dalles, the Achomawi would long since have ceased to exist instead of being found by the Americans a fairly numerous and resistant tribe in a rather adverse habitat, and being to-day one of the most populous groups in California. It is probable that the Klamath and Modoc were stimulated to their raiding warfare, unusual in the California region, by their northern affiliations, which early provided them with an abundance of horses and offered a lucrative market for captives who otherwise would have been killed. In fact, investigation may reveal that the slave raiding consisted of only two or three incidents, and these perhaps indirectly brought on by the changes of conditions caused by the advent of the whites, whose imagination magnified some temporary events into a custom. The basis of all the clashes may have been a mere vengeance feud such as sooner or later embroiled almost all Californian groups. Thus it is known that while the Modoc fought certain Achomawi groups of villages, they remained friendly with others.[29]

Investigation of other sources makes it appear that the foregoing underestimates the prevalence and impact of Klamath-Modoc slave raiding of the Pit Rivers, despite the fact that much of the intense raiding with horses was telescoped into a short period of time.

The Klamath-Modocs usually raided Achomawi Pit Rivers in the spring and summer. Ray estimates that those involved in battle mode could expect losses of from five to ten percent. He states that most captives were not taken in such warfare, but in small-scale raids.[30] Sometimes Modocs raided Pit Rivers on their own in summer and fall. In late August 1857 California Indian agent E.A. Stevenson, reported finding a large number of Klamaths under their Chief Lalakes in the Pit River country seeking to steal "squaws" and

---

[29]Kroeber, *Handbook of the Indians of California*, 319-30. On the other hand, Spier, supporting a general contention, states: "For their part the Klamath were stimulated by the lucrative traffic in slaves established with the Columbia river tribes, and the majority of captives were by all accounts Pit River people." *Klamath Ethnography*, 25.

[30]Ray, *Primitive Pragmatists*, 142. The Modocs practiced euthanasia, killing their comrades left by the enemy, states Ray. He also states that Modoc wives were taken along on slave raids to control captured women and children and to steal enemy property, ibid., 135-36, 143.

children to take north into Oregon to sell as slaves.[31] Shastas also raided Pit Rivers on snowshoes, creeping into their pit houses to take them unawares. Living in higher elevations, these Shastas would have been adept at getting around in wintry conditions. The Achomawi Pit Rivers delayed their retaliations until spring.[32] Modocs annually raided their more feared Californian Shasta foe from whom they captured children to trade to Cayuses and Teninos to the north for horses in order to build up their own herds and wealth.[33] On the other hand, the Shastas treated Pit River captives less like slaves than like adoptees into their own families.

Upon reaching their majority, slave children of Shastas were allowed to marry into the lower free Shastan class. Shastan bands nearer Rogue River frequently clashed with Athapaskan-speaking Dakubetedes (Applegates) and Taltushtuntudes (Galice Creeks).[34] The Klamaths were not spared Shastan attacks. Traveling in open country along the Klamath River, these invaders crossed that stream near Klamath Falls or by a little island to launch a surprise attack on a village on the east bank. The Shastas in turn were raided by Oregon Klickitats and others from the Columbia River. A half-Shasta and half-Modoc, Johnny Bullhart, in about 1908 told how his people were caught off guard by these northern tribesmen in a raid from which he was taken to near Fort Vancouver and freed in the late 1850s.[35] Klamaths also captured Shasta and Rogue River women, selling them in the North to Nez Percés and Cayuses.[36]

Latgawas (Upland Takelmas) raided tribes of southwestern Oregon and northwestern California including Lowland Takelmas, Taltushtuntudes and Dakubetedes for food, valu-

---

[31]Wheeler-Voegelin, *Pitt River Indians of California*, 90.

[32]Curtis, *The North American Indian* 13, pp. 130-31.

[33]Ruby and Brown, *A Guide to the Indian Tribes of the Pacific Northwest*, 134; Curtis, *The North American Indian* 13, p. 234.

[34]Ibid., 106, 232.

[35]Spier and Sapir, *Wishram Ethnography*, 222.

[36]A.N. Armstrong stated that the Klamaths plundered white immigrants crossing their territory, killing some and capturing their women since the latters' relatives, falling victim to the Klamaths, were unable to protect these women. *Oregon*, 114.

ables and slaves. They sold the Dakubetedes to neighboring Klamaths to the east.[37] With ambivalence characteristic of intermingling tribal war and peace the Upland Takelmas, perhaps as late as mid-19th century, wiped out a Klamath party of five or six. The only one spared was a lad who arrived footsore at Klamath Marsh with news of the tragedy. Gathering the bodies of their slain the Klamaths discovered that the foe had dismembered them, taking parts of bodies home as trophies. In revenge the Klamaths killed a woman whom anthropologist Leslie Spier claimed to be "perhaps a slave" of the Upper Takelma chief. In the continuing retaliation LaLakes recruited braves from several small tribes to fight their common Takelman foe. Crossing the mountains on foot

> they found the Takelma encamped in Molala territory at the head of Rogue river. They attacked as the Takelma rose at dawn, scalping and carrying off women and children. Among those killed was…[the Takelma chief], whose hands and heart they took. After the man was shot,…[Lalakes] lanced him through the throat…[Then Lalakes] invited all the Klamath to a huge scalp dance at Klamath marsh. During the dances a wife of …[the grandfather of Coley, the recorder's informant] danced about with the heart in her teeth. The captives were dragged by their arms and forced to dance close to the fire.[38]

Rather than taking out their aggressions against more easterly Pit Rivers, the Klamath-Modocs struck their Pit River kin in northern California's Hot (later, Warm) Springs and Big valleys. In an 1857 raid fifty-six natives of these places were enslaved and sold at the Columbia River for Cayuse ponies, one woman being exchanged for five or six horses, and a boy exchanged for a horse. Although largely on the defensive from other tribal raidings, the Pit Rivers conducted predatory sorties against white emigrants passing through their lands. Because of such raidings General George Crook was dispatched to subdue them in his 1867

---

[37]Edward Sapir, "Notes on the Takelma Indians of Southwestern Oregon," 252.
[38]Spier, *Klamath Ethnography*, 29.

campaign in the so-called Snake Wars (1864-1868).[39] One Pit River chief said that Fort Crook (established in 1857 and completed in 1860) protected local Indians since Modocs equipped with firearms were threatening them with extinction.[40]

When successfully fighting other tribesmen, the Pit Rivers held victory dances in which their women beat sticks in celebrating their men's return home. The Klamaths were not the first to have incurred upon Pit Rivers, for the latter suffered from raids of Paiutes who, unlike other aggressors, took no slaves, but according to Curtis, mutilated young girls from whom they cut breasts, carrying them off and eating them. They also crushed their male victims with large stones.[41] As described by Curtis, Pit River victory celebrations appear to have been like those of natives around Fort Walla Walla who had been described by Alexander Ross (see above). In these celebrations Pit River men and women

> formed in a circle with the captives among them and danced to their left, those who had taken scalps holding their trophies aloft. Then they formed in a line and sang, while the prisoners in pairs were forced to endure the disgrace of dancing along the line with the scalps of their slain tribesmen. If they refused, or were unable to dance, they were likely to be killed; and even weeping might call for the same fate. The victory-dance was performed daily for about a week.[42]

Klamath cruelty to Pit Rivers was mitigated by the fact that those not passed on in trade after capture enjoyed the same rights as their Klamath captors.[43] They suffered no abuse and even married into the Klamaths.

The Klamaths reportedly put slaves to death on the demise of prominent persons.[44] White settlers intervened when Klamaths were about to kill a number of slaves at the

---

[39]Albert Samuel Gatschet, *The Klamath Indians of Southwestern Oregon*, vol. 2, pp. 1x, 1xi.

[40]Ernest R. Neasham, *Fall River Valley*, 202.

[41]Curtis, *The North American Indian* 13, p. 130.

[42]Ibid., 143.

[43]Ibid., 238.

[44]Powers, "The California Indians," 541.

death, from burns, of a daughter of their (Klamath Lake) Chief Kiluampch, "Old Brave," or "Captain George." Prominent in mid-19th century tribal affairs, he opposed whites immigrating through Klamath-Modoc country.[45]

Modoc treatment of captives was reminiscent of that of Northwest Coast Indians. Before their own deaths Modocs were forbidden to distribute their properties. Except for slaves and horses, these were burned. Sometimes slaves of the deceased were designated to "honor" their owners' premature deaths by being cremated with the owners. They could, however, escape incineration by being sold to one of the mourners.[46] Modocs were not alone among tribes in the practice of cremation. If Albert Parker Niblack was correct in his "The Coast Indians of Southern Alaska and Northern British Columbia," slaves among Tsimshians "sacrificed at funerals were chosen long before the death of their master and were supposed to be peculiarly fortunate, as their bodies attained the distinction of cremation, instead of being thrown into the sea." Homes of deceased Modocs were often burned. Modoc men also often specified the inheritors of their slaves and horses, but without such instructions adult sons received these properties. Widows retained horses for minor sons until they reached manhood, and were there no sons, retained and passed along slaves at their own deaths. Slavery by inheritance was a permanent state, but free born male youngsters taken captive when adults, could free themselves by marrying free Modoc women.

Inheritance practices varied among tribes. In some tribes men assembled their people to distribute possessions of the deceased, leaving a small share for male family members of the dead thus rendering females destitute to become slaves.

According to Boas slaves of the Northern zone were lumped with items of substantial worth such as canoes, coppers, (kerfed) boxes and covers belonging to chiefs and

---

[45]Ibid.
[46]Modoc slaves dying a natural death were also cremated. Modoc slaves were probably the only ones routinely disposed of by some method other than being thrown out as refuse. Ray, *Primitive Pragmatists*, 113.

nobles. It may be assumed that with no report to the contrary slaves not killed at the time of their masters' deaths were inherited as were other chattel. According to Murdock small objects of personal property of deceased Haidas were given to various family members, but all important properties went to younger brothers who married the widows of the deceased. Were there no younger brothers, nephews inherited properties of the widows. Women left their property to sisters only in default of daughters.[47]

It behooved Modocs and especially Klamaths to remain on good terms with northern Oregon tribes such as Teninos and Wascos, both better known as "Warm Springs Indians" after removal to their reservation. The two tribes stood astride the vital slave route down the Deschutes River Valley which Klamaths, extending their middlemen role, continued traversing to The Dalles. In his interview with Clarke, Chal-o-quin cited his peoples' friendship with Warm Springs peoples: "We were always friendly with the Warm Springs Indians and sold them the women we had captured of the nations around us and they also bought all our skins, and sold us in return many things we needed, blankets, beads, clothing, axes, spears and fish hooks."[48] Trade ties had been forged not only at The Dalles, but at Yainax. Chal-o-quin stated that Columbia River tribesmen had come to this latter trade site with "all the airs of experienced foreign traders."[49] After mid-19th century Warm Springs Indians also traded horses to Pit Rivers mostly for clam-shell beads, exchanging one horse for a fathom of this wampum. They also traded for Pit River bows which firearms had not replaced and for furs during that trading era.[50]

After what must have been an initial awkward period of

---

[47]Niblack, "The Coast Indians of Southeastern Alaska and Northern British Columbia," 252; Ray, Primitive Pragmatists, 113, 133, 145; Elijah White, *Ten Years in Oregon*, 277; Boas, *The Social Organization and the Secret Societies of the Kwakiutl Indians*, 416; George Peter Murdock, "Kinship and Social Behavior Among the Haidas," 367.

[48]Clarke, *Klamath County Museum Research Papers*, 10.

[49]Ibid., 26.

[50]Curtis, *The North American Indians*, 13, p. 131.

Dalles trading, the Klamaths literally learned the tricks of the trade, bolstered by an awareness that they were the premier traders of interior Oregon. Combat with the Paiutes against whom the Klamaths were aligned with Warm Springs Teninos and Wascos, complicated the Klamath's trading. The Klamaths had much to gain by keeping trade channels open to The Dalles since Paiute aggressions threatened not only their trading at that place, but their very lives. The Warm Springs Reservation was barely established in 1859 when Bannock-Paiutes, "stealthy as the fox and fierce as the wolf," raided it. This prompted the reservation's frantic agent to request military aid to retaliate against the incursions which continued into the 1860s.[51] Not content to steal only horses, the Bannock-Paiutes captured women and children. During the Snake wars Warm Springs Indians scouted for the United States army which capitalized on their lingering hatred of their perennial foes. Their contract with the military helped them wreak vengeance on the enemy. This may have been their primary motive for scouting, although monetary reward was surely a factor. On January 7, 1867, they attacked a Paiute camp killing three persons and enslaving two children primarily for their economic value.[52] On their reservation the following year the Warm Springs held one hundred-fifty captives which they sought to enslave according to ancient practice. Oregon Superintendent of Indian Affairs J.W. Perit Huntington issued an order forbidding the practice.[53]

An agreement was finally reached with Paiute Chief Ocheo that if he removed to the Klamath Reservation all

---

[51]Bvt. General W.S. Harney, Comdg. Military Dept., Oregon, to James W. Nesmith, August 15, 1859. *Records of the Oregon Superintendency of Indian Affairs, 1848-1872. Letter Book F: 10;* Edward R. Geary, Supt. Indian Affairs (Washington and Oregon), to A.B. Greenwood, Commr. of Indian Affairs, October 1, 1860, *Annual Report, Secy. Interior, 1860,* Serial 1078, p. 400.

[52]Keith Clark and Donna Clark, "William McKay's Journal, 1866-67; Indian Scouts" Pt. 1, p. 149.

[53]J.W. Perit Huntington, Oregon Supt. Indian Affairs, to Lindsay Applegate, Special Indian Commr., November 18, 1868. *Records of the Oregon Superintendency of Indian Affairs, 1848-1872, Letter Book I: 10.*

Paiutes "now held in bondage by the tribes as slaves," would be returned to him from any tribe with which the government had treaties. Like Huntington, Alfred B. Meacham who succeeded him declared that slavery would no longer be tolerated. Dr. William C. McKay (pronounced McKai) was dispatched with scouts in 1871 to round up Paiutes held as slaves even among tribes in Washington Territory, and to deliver them to Yainax, now a Klamath subagency. In Meacham's words the task proved difficult because of the Indian custom of moving slaves from tribe to tribe.[54]

In 1867 the Warm Springs scouts surprised a Paiute band in a narrow canyon of the small fork of central Oregon's Crooked River, killing all seven of its men and capturing fourteen women and children.[55] On December 18 the *Dalles Mountaineer* reported that in the fall of 1866 the scouts had taken, among other trophies, thirty-six scalps and, in the spring of 1867, forty-three more and about twenty women and children.[56] The conflict had indeed been long and desultory; a decade earlier the government had dispatched a company of fifty-three armed Indians to recover cattle and horses stolen from the Warm Springs with orders to kill or enslave the purloiners. In doing so, the government potentially involved itself in slavery. Possibly its officials permitted the taking of slaves to placate the scouts who regarded such action as a reward for their efforts. Those dispatching the scouts must have known they could not recover the livestock without the prospect of a fight. Following orders the scouts pounced on two Paiute lodges up the John Day River, a tributary to the Columbia, killing men and capturing women and children.[57] Such attacks did not stop Paiute raids, for they

---

[54]A.B. Meacham, Oregon Supt. Indian Affairs, to Dr. Wm. McKay, Physician, Warm Springs Reservation, June 24, 1871; Meacham to T.J. McKenney, Wash. Supt. Indian Affairs, June 26, 1871; Meacham to Lindsay Applegate, Commissary, Klamath Agency, Yainax, November 5, 1871, *Records of the Oregon Superintendency of Indian Affairs, 1848-1872. Letter Book I:10.*

[55]Clark and Clark, "William McKay's Journal, 1866-67," 329.

[56]*Dalles Mountaineer,* December 18, 1867.

[57]A.P. Dennison, Indian Agent, Eastern Dist., Oregon, to Supt. Edward R. Geary, July 14, 1858. *Annual Report, Secy. Interior, 1859,* Serial 1023, p. 801.

continued not only on the Warm Springs Reservation, but on the Umatilla to the east.

According to Meacham, who chronicled the event, the most daring and disastrous Paiute raid on the Warm Springs was the kidnapping of a daughter of a Warm Springs chief in broad daylight and inside the line of white settlement. As a reward for anyone recapturing her, the chief offered her rescuer the right to marry her. Donald McKay, who led the Warm Springs Scouts during the Snake War, took special interest in his work, for his wife, Zuletta, had been a Paiute slave for three years.[58]

Slave raiding on the Warm Springs did not break off cleanly. Neither did slavery on that confine since its tribes continued purchasing slaves from the Klamaths. In 1869 the Wascos were reported to be holding eighteen Pit River slaves which Klamaths had sold them some years before.[59] Tenino slaves were nearly always captured Paiutes. Others were obtained in trade from the Klamath country, and some were part Modoc, but usually, Pit River Achowawis and Atsugewis.[60] "Most slaves," writes Murdock, "whatever their provenience, were passed on in trade to the north, through the Wishram, but a few were retained." He states that informants

> estimated the number of slaves kept by the Tenino themselves in the immediate precontact period at about twenty-five, three being the largest number held by a single owner. Captured slaves were exclusively women and children, for male war captives were invariably slain. Adult female slaves were neither married nor kept as mistresses. Children were accepted as members of the household. When they grew up, they married Tenino and became free, though they never fully lost the stigma of their slave origin. Debt slavery was not practiced.[61]

As among other tribes, Klamath chieftains were beneficiaries of slavery and its trade. In forays against neighboring

[58]Alfred B. Meacham, *Wigwam and War-Path; Or the Royal Chief in Chains,* 213-14.
[59]David French, "Wasco-Wishram," 388.
[60]Murdock, *Culture and Society,* 215-16.
[61]Ibid., 216.

tribes their wealthy and powerful Chief Lalakes actively engaged in capture and subsequent enslavement of several Indians including at least a half-dozen slave wives. Mention has been made of the exploits of subchief Chal-o-quin whose interview with Clarke was scarcely a modest reminiscence of his past. These leaders helped develop among Klamaths an incipient stratified society composed of the wealthy, the prestigious, the free and the enslaved. Displays among the wealthy may have been an emergent potlatch veneer.

Ownership of horses to transport themselves and their slaves and symbolize their owners' wealth was as important to Klamaths as were canoes to coastal peoples. Important as were slaves in Klamath-Modoc wealth, they did not surpass horses in propelling their owners toward an aristocracy. Christopher Miller states:

> Horses did not constitute wealth in the European sense, but they did resemble modern capital in some significant ways. First, horse herds were highly visible, so one's relative standing in the community was constantly on display. Second, herds grew in direct proportion to their initial size, so the more one had to begin with, the faster one could produce more. Finally, horses were directly inheritable. Aided by these characteristics and the fact that the horse continued to be a widely valued commodity until well into the current century, those who possessed large herds came to form an aristocracy.[62]

Miller states that the new aristocracy, by gaining control of local government positions, was enabled to gain power. Their position was further enhanced by intermarriage within chiefly families, resulting in strong leadership capabilities.[63] This trend is confirmed by Theodore Stern, a student of the

---

[62]Miller, *Prophetic Worlds: Indians and Whites on the Columbia Plateau*, 39.

[63]Ibid. As Miller points out, the society of an emerging aristocracy (which in the case of the Klamaths has been a laboratory study for anthropologists since it occurred roughly in historic times) involved the rise of war chiefs from obscure positions in pre-horse and pre-gun society. After contact chieftains' war exploits became a means of ascending in social rank. Property in earlier times was largely communal, all tribal members sharing food gathering places. With the new animals which required more care, however, ownership was in individual control. Also, what property persons acquired more likely became their personal possessions.

Klamaths, who states that "The almost endemic condition of warfare and the enlarging scale of operations, together with the lucrative trade in booty, brought about the emergence of a chiefly class, the members of which based their power upon eminence in war and possession of wealth, including slaves... In the growing eminence of the new leadership hereditary principles may have been operative."[64]

Government officials helped centralize tribal power by dealing with hand-picked spokesmen, a policy contrary to the former deliberative nature of discussing tribal affairs. Under government pressure this policy also shifted the power center of individual bands to that of tribes. The most successful chiefs were now those who could most ably communicate and cooperate with government officials. These officials could not have but noted the movements of powerful tribal leaders. Agent Stevenson noted that in 1857 Lalakes had been down in Pit River country stealing women and children which were taken to sell at The Dalles.[65] In 1860 Lieut. Alexander Piper, 3d U.S. Artillery, commanding Fort Umpqua, while in the upper Klamath country to establish a camp near the South Immigrant Road, wrote Maj. W.W. Mackall, adjutant of the Military Department of California, that Chiefs Lalakes, George (Kiluampch?), and Kumtuckney were on an expedition to The Dalles to trade "some squaws & horses lately taken from the Pitt River Indian."[66]

Considering the sensitive relationship between the Indian Office and the military, the latter would have hesitated to interfere with actions of chiefs in fear of stepping on toes of Indian agents whose province it was to look after Indians in matters of slavery and other practices. Not the least of these was the coalescing of Indians by the government to better control them. A good example of this policy involved Nez Percés, whom Special Subagent Elijah White in 1844 had talked into establishing for the first time a (temporary) head

---

[64]Stern, *The Klamath Tribe*, 24.
[65]Jack D. Forbes, *The Indian in America's Past*, 94.
[66]Alexander Piper, "Reports and Journal," 245.

chieftaincy of their numerous bands. A similar coalescing was applied to Klamaths in their October 14, 1864, treaty (ratified by the U.S., July 2, 1866 and proclaimed, February 17, 1870) in which their roughly 700-member tribe along with 339 Modocs and 22 Yahuskin Paiutes were to be brought under the blanket of the Klamath Reservation.[67] In a February 1864 council in Yreka, California, Elijah Steele, Superintendent of Indian Affairs for the Northern District of that state, told Modoc chiefs not to enter Pit River Indian country to fight nor, to steal women and children with intent to enslave and sell them. The chiefs agreed to the order.[68]

There was no provision in the Klamath treaty freeing slaves. The government order to do so was delayed several years. This was possibly due to opposition by powerful chiefs whom officials wished to placate in their efforts to establish the Klamath Reservation. All of this was despite the fact that the chiefs in council with Steele agreed to no longer sell women (mainly for prostitution) and children to whites or to other tribes.[69] Lalakes and others voiced opposition to an 1865 proposal to free the slaves by declaring in the words of Agent Lindsay Applegate "that if such was to be the case, they would kill all of the Pit River Indians among them or run them off to other places to trade for horses."[70]

In his *The Klamath Indians of Southwestern Oregon*, Albert Samuel Gatschet states, as does Leslie Spier in his *Klamath Ethnography*, that the treaty ended Klamath raidings and thus, their slave trade.[71] In reality, the treaty was but one step, albeit an important one, toward ending these practices. In 1868 the government still sought to gather Klamaths, Mod-

[67]Ruby and Brown, *Indians of the Pacific Northwest*, 206.

[68]Wheeler-Voegelin, *Pitt River Indians of California*, 99.

[69]Gatschet, *The Klamath Indians of Southwestern Oregon*, lix; Lieut. Col. C.S. Drew, *Official Report of the Owyhee Reconnaissance, Made by Lieut. Colonel C.S. Drew 1st Oregon Cavalry*, 17. Slaves on the Klamath Reservation were freed by order of an agent in 1869. See Philleo Nash, "The Place of Religious Revivalism in the Formation of the Intercultural Community on Klamath Reservation," 408.

[70]Stern, *The Klamath Tribe*, 77.

[71]Gatschet, *The Klamath Indians of Southwestern Oregon*, lix; Spier, *Klamath Ethnography*, 40.

ocs and Yahuskin Paiutes onto the reservation. Once there, they were to elect a chief acceptable to them. Unlike others there by treaty, the Pit Rivers were disqualified from the selection process because of their previous enslavement. Klamath Subagent John Meacham in 1871 arranged for slaves to elect a representative to the tribal councils and courts.[72]

An 1881 breakdown of populations on the reservation revealed that its southern or lower end was composed of a small number of freed slaves living there with Klamaths.[73] When advancement became open to all Indians of the reservation, ex-Pit River slaves were said to have become "quite prosperous and energetic, having learned how to work while slaves for the Klamaths."[74] Such a one was Skedaddle, formerly belonging to Chief Lilu (not Lalakes), who was employed at the agency. During the Modoc War (1871-1872) he enlisted as a scout under the name Henry Jackson, and in 1883 returned to the Yainax Subagency as an interpreter. He also cut hay for agency cattle and split rails for whites, taking half his pay in cash and the other half in cattle until amassing a sizeable herd of his own, capping off his accomplishments by marrying the daughter of a Modoc chief. Former slaves such as he not only contributed to the Klamath community in an economic way, but in a social way as well. One doing so was Pit River Charley, who returned from his people in 1873 with new rites which were added to the (first) Ghost Dance which came to the Klamaths at about that time.[75]

Once scorned as marriage partners, some slaves during the reservation era were able to marry free persons. Even Chal-

---

[72]Stern, *The Klamath Tribe*, 79.   [73]Ibid., 95.
[74]David W. Matthews, Klamath Indian Agent, to Commr. Indian Affairs, August 4, 1891. *Annual Report, Secy. Interior, 1891*. Serial 2943, p. 372. Matthews reported a number of Pit River Indians on the reservation who, when children, had been captured and enslaved by the Klamaths many years prior to 1891.
[75]Stern, *The Klamath Tribe*, 70; Spier, *Klamath Ethnography*, 41 and n. The Ghost Dance referred to here was the first such dance (1862-1872) begun by the Paiute, Wodziwob. The better known second Ghost Dance (1889-1892) resulting in the infamous Wounded Knee massacre was led by the Paiute, Wovoka.

o-quin married a Shasta slave,[76] but perhaps because of the lingering stigma of such a marriage partner, made no allusion to it when interviewed by Clarke. Slave youngsters growing up with their masters' children, however, formed bonds not easily broken in later life. One slave willed his property to his master's son with whom he had grown up;[77] yet, tribal members were aware of those who had descended from slaves and those who had not. On the reservation in 1905 there were 59 Pit Rivers, mostly ex-slaves it may be presumed, joining its 755 Klamaths, 223 Modocs and 112 Yahuskin Paiutes.[78]

Acquisition of slaves and horses had permitted the Klamaths to ride out of their isolation literally and figuratively on the backs of both their horses and slaves. Wealth gained from the purchase and sale of these animate possessions helped to begin the stratification of their society. One might speculate that had such strata grouping been allowed to continue unabated it might have approximated that of the Northwest Coast; but willing and unwilling compromise with white men blocked their path more surely than had natives theretofore, and their traditional lifestyle was threatened with change.

Down the Klamath River from the Klamaths were the Yuroks of the California slave cluster who had an established slave owning society in their lower Klamath River homelands. Klamath society was not a copy of Yurok society. Had it been so, considering the Klamath propensity to quickly acquire a slave-owning society, they would have done so sooner. The emerging commerce in live chattel was dissimilar to that of the Yuroks, whose wealth lay in land ownership and control of harvests, an old, established system benefitting the upper classes. Yurok land ownership concepts were more rigid than that of other Pacific Northwest tribes. Lucy Thompson, a descendant of the wealthy Yurok class wrote in

[76]Stern, *The Klamath Tribe*, 99.
[77]Ibid.
[78]Horace Wilson, Agent, to Commr. Indian Affairs, September 1, 1905, *Records of the Klamath Indian Agency, Letter Book May 1, 1905-October 31, 1905.*

1916 that her people at the coming of white men were

a very large tribe, there being several thousand of them. It taxed every resource of the country in which they lived for all of them to obtain a subsistence; therefore everything was owned in the same way that it is now owned by the white man. The land was divided up by the boundaries of the creeks, ridges and the river: all open prairies for gathering grass seeds, such as Indian wheat, which looks similar to rye, besides other kinds of seed; the oak timber for gathering acorns, the sugarpine for gathering pine nuts, the hazel flats for gathering hazelnuts and the fishing places for catching salmon...[79]

Yurok slave couples were permitted to marry, but lacking material possessions, they exchanged foodstuffs in lieu of more valuable items. They were treated ambivalently by their owners. Some were taken to doctors when ill while others receiving care were left to suffer and die. Near the end of the slavery period Yurok slaves could purchase their freedom. Similarities of Klamath and Yurok slavery, however, did occur in the post-slavery period. Once free, some Yuroks, like Klamaths, took advantage of the right to own property, utilizing the work ethic to accumulate estates. And like Klamaths, they lorded it over their former owners.

Abandoning what had been their own Edenic-like garden homeland which had supplied their aboriginal needs, Klamaths were enticed into seeking more material things, though land ownership was not one of them. As narrated by Chal-o-quin, a Klamath subchief named Link River Joe, seeking what he believed to be the higher things in life, journeyed

to the Columbia River [where] good men [possibly Methodists who had established their Wascopam Mission at The Dalles] told him about the Holy Spirit that was to come to the whole world and visit its remotest parts. When he came back from The Dalles he told his people about it but found them groping in perfect darkness. They were killing and murdering each other and he tried to tell them about the mission of the Holy Spirit preached by the white men, who, they said, would bring peace on earth among all men. They would not believe him and told him that he lied. He had waited long for the coming of the Holy Spirit and had never doubt-

---

[79]Lucy Thompson, "Reminiscences of a Yurok Aristocrat," *The Californians* (November-December, 1992), 21, 28-29.

ed that he would see him. He had heard Mr. [A.B.] Meacham [Oregon Superintendent of Indian Affairs] talk for many days and had looked steadily into his eyes thinking that he would get tired if he was like other men, but now he saw that he was not like other men and knew that he must be the Holy Spirit come at last to bring gracious gifts for all tribes. For his own part he wanted a new wagon and "hiyou ictas," which last [in the Chinook jargon] means *lots of things.*[80]

Missionaries believed that as far as Link River Joe and his people were concerned the ultimate proof of the beneficence of the Great Spirit was in providing them the material things they coveted and which they believed were not to be found through mystic communion with some distant heaven, but at a specific place on earth—The Dalles of the Columbia River.

---

[80]Clarke, *Klamath County Museum Research Papers* 21-22.

10

The Dalles Marketplace:
Slaves for Sale

The greatest Pacific Northwestern native slave market involving trade between peoples of the interior and those of the coast was at The Dalles of the lower Columbia River, where waters surged beneath frowning cliffs, spirals and monuments. In historic times slaves and blankets of foreign manufacture replaced shells (especially dentalia) at that location as the most valued commodity. At The Dalles waters drained from the Plateau were mixed before rushing through the Columbia Gorge to meet the ocean, just as were products of many cultures of coastal and interior peoples. The delicately balanced trade process was disrupted with the entry of foreign goods brought by Russian, Spanish, British and American traders. The tastes of native peoples were thus excited and within a century their accustomed pleasures and values were disrupted, and social systems were replaced in a leveling process.

The Dalles received its name from the flatness of the rocks located in the rapids. These cataracts were called by French-Canadian fur men, *Les Dalles,* the Place of Flat Rocks. Here lived the Upper Chinookan Wascos and Wishrams and the Sahaptin Teninos who hosted natives coming there from distant places and from a distant past to trade and socialize. At The Dalles the babel of human tongues mingled with the never silent roarings of the river churning its way westward as though in a hurry to reach the sea. Just as the waters swept by The Dalles in a brief instant, so did slaves brought there remain but briefly before being whisked away to unwanted places. Some were destined for the north, passing through several hands in exchange for items of the North until they came to British Columbia markets. Leslie Spier and Edward Sapir, who made a study of Wishram peoples, are indeed correct in stating that the trade in slaves was "heavier at the Dalles than probably any other place in the northwest."[1]

The Dalles attracted traders since it was a geologic-cultural breaking point stimulating the exchange of goods. Routes converged here on an east-west axis between Pacific Coast and Plateau and between watershed streams of the Columbia such as the Yakima, Snake, Umatilla, Klickitat and White Salmon to the east and north, and the Deschutes and John Day to the south. Visitors' camps were established on the Columbia right bank at the head of Five Mile Rapids (the Long Narrows), giving local Wishrams and their guests ample space to work and play.[2] Also on the right bank at the head of the Rapids, and immediately upstream from The Dalles, was Wishram Village, a main entrepôt for commercial enterprises which, as described by Nattali in 1846, were methodically and systematically conducted. "It is to this place," he wrote,

> that the tribes from the mouth of the Columbia repaired with the fish of the sea coast, the roots, berries, and especially the Wappatoo, gathered in the lower parts of the river, together with goods and trinkets, obtained from the ships which casually visited the coast. Hither also the tribes from the Rocky Mountains brought down horses, beargrass, quamash [camass], and other commodities of the interior. The merchant fishermen at the falls acted as middlemen or factors, and passed the objects of traffic as it were cross-handed, trading away part of their wares received from the mountain tribe, to those of the river and the plains, and *vice versa:* their packages of pounded salmon entered largely into the system of barter, and being carried off in opposite directions, found their way to the savage hunting camps far in the interior, and to the casual white traders, who touched upon the coast.[3]

The Dalles trading season usually extended from August

---

[1]Spier and Sapir, *Wishram Ethnography*, 221.
[2]For a history of The Dalles and its people see Robert Boyd, *People of The Dalles*..
[3]Nattali, *The Oregon Territory*, 56, 57.

Celilo Falls of the Columbia River where Indians speared, hooked and netted,
then preserved salmon to trade at The Dalles, about ten miles downstream. The
falls are now submerged beneath waters of The Dalles Dam, built in 1957, ending the once prosperous, busy fishery, the greatest on the Columbia. Salmon
from Celilo and slaves from interior Oregon, northern California and the
Northwest Coast were principal items of trade at The Dalles. *Courtesy, Thelma
Roberts photo, The Dalles, Oregon. Neg. #1296.*

through October after the larger salmon runs when local
natives processed their own winter stores of salmon and
those left over for trading. This activity plus fishing and processing kept its semi-sedentary natives busy in most seasons.
There was no single slave mart or block here; instead, visiting
tradesmen went from camp to camp and from house to house

bartering with their people. Items not exchanged on an even par were once purchased with strings of dentalia.[4] Transactions involving slaves were typical time-consuming hagglings for such tradesmen as the Klamaths, who in 1857 sold their fifty-six Pit River women and children at The Dalles.[5]

Another important village was on the Columbia right bank at Celilo Falls six miles upstream from Five Mile Rapids. Across the Columbia on the left bank in Tenino lands salmon of good quality were taken by the thousands. Living most of their life cycle in the sea and migrating up to their parent streams, these fish were the most important single food of coastal and lower riverine peoples.[6] Although salmon were a most vital food to peoples of the upper Plateau, they found game important for their subsistence during poor runs of the silvery migrants. These northern natives came down annually to The Dalles to purchase pulverized salmon, a form more easily transported back to their homes. Among other items which Plateau peoples traded at The Dalles were lush peltries from cold wintering places. Middle Fraser River jade celts also passed southward in the trade as did mountain sheep horns, basketry and soft, painted rabbit skin robes.

The large number of salmon taken at The Dalles and other Columbia watershed fisheries such as those at Kettle Falls below the Canadian border, Rock Island and Priest rapids further south on the Columbia, and Salmon Falls on the

---

[4]Murdock, *Culture and Society*, 202.

[5]Spier and Sapir, *Wishram Ethnography*, 222.

[6]Salmon were caught at The Dalles with scoops, nets and hoops attached to long poles skillfully maneuvered by natives who were dangerously perched on platforms over the roaring river. As leaping salmon fell backwards vainly trying to clear the falls, the natives clubbed them and threw them aside for women to quickly gather, disembowel and skin. The meat would then be sliced into long thick pieces and hung like flannel-red rags on scaffolds to dry. The dried meat would be pounded with stone or wood packers. The result was a fine mealy substance which was pressed into cured salmon-skin-lined, cord-tied funnel-shaped baskets, or into bales in matting for export. About a foot in diameter and two-feet-long, these bales and baskets were secured by cords at one end which were passed through holes in the edges for tying. The women then bundled these roughly two-pound bales into a dozen parcels and placed perhaps as many as seven of them on the bottom and five above so they would not tip over. They were then stacked to dry with corded ends up and covered with matting.

upper Snake, was a source of wonderment for white observers. One of them, the Reverend DeSmet, described native fishing at The Dalles when Indians and their slaves in toe flocked

> thither from different quarters of the interior, to attend, at this season of the year, to the salmon fisheries. This is their glorious time for rejoicing, gambling, and feasting; the long lent is passed; the have at last assembled in the midst of abundance—all that the eye can see, or the nose smell, is fish, and nothing but fish. Piles of them are lying everywhere on the rocks, the Indian huts abound with them, and the dogs are dragging and fighting over the offal in all directions.[7]

Male Wishram fishermen and female processors were busy at fishing times. A mostly sedentary, peaceful people, the Wishrams were content to purchase their slaves rather than fighting to obtain them. The wealthiest of the tribe owned perhaps up to ten slaves, and other upper class persons, from two to three. Although standing at the bottom of Wishram society without wealth and means these bondsmen were treated kindly and amply sustained by their masters.[8] They ate in their masters' houses, although apart from them therein.[9] Female slaves performed such daily tasks as root digging, berry picking, fish, wood and water carrying while males paddled their masters' canoes, fished, hunted and carried wood. At the scene of their labor De Smet wrote: "At the dalles you enter a barren region, where drift wood is brought into every encampment by the Indians, for which they gladly receive a piece of tobacco in return."[10]

In The Dalles area slaves lived much like poor freemen. Sapir and Spier state that "the largest single element of their lives that distinguished them from poor Wishram was uncer-

[7]De Smet, *Oregon Missions*, 282-83.
[8]Curtis, *The North American Indian* 8, p. 88. In Wishram social strata there were chieftain families, the rich, the poor and the slaves. War leaders, grouped among the chiefly class, served not necessarily because of their wealth, but for their supernatural powers of invulnerability to their foe, and for their bravery; nevertheless, they had great influence. French, "Wasco-Wishram," 363.
[9]Curtis, *The North American Indian* 8, p. 88.
[10]De Smet, *Oregon Missions*, 258.

tainty."[11] When Wishram did make occasional war, they thought it a high honor to capture sons, brothers, or other relatives of tribal chiefs. In their new servility once haughty ones suffered the humility of inferior status and should they run away their masters used the punishment of mutilating the soles of escapees' feet by burning and lacerating them.[12]

Very much a part of The Dalles trading complex were the Wascos of the Columbia left bank. With Wishrams they occupied the upper end of the Chinookan-speaking arc which extended downstream from Celilo Falls to the sea. A cross-cultured people, these two tribes used the canoe of river and coast and the horse of the Plateau to move about. Traveling before the 19th century as far south as Klamath country, they took slaves in wars against Paiutes and Modocs and sometimes joined Klamaths in warring against Shastas, scalping and killing their male foe, but keeping captured women and children as slaves.[13] Sometimes they carried to the Klamaths beaver skins obtained from Rocky Mountain tribes. Like Wishrams, Wascos did not enslave their own people for debt, and hence, had no issue of slaves from among them.[14] Like Sahaptin, Salishan and Waiilatpuan speakers, the Wishram and Wascos had a long-standing hatred of Paiutes whom they often raided, taking boy and girl captives, some of whom they traded on to Yakimas for six or seven horses or one good slave for a good canoe. Not sparing adult Paiute males, the Wascos seemed bent on proving they could match Paiute brutality body for body and scalp for scalp, exhibiting trophies of their revenge for all to see.[15] During the Warm Springs Reservation period Wascos and Teninos were continuing targets for revenge-seeking Paiutes

[11]Spier and Sapir, *Wishram Ethnography*, 223.
[12]Ibid.; Curtis, *The North American Indian* 8, p. 89. The Illinois warred against their southern and western neighbors to carry off slaves, some of whom Hernando De Soto found toiling on southern farms. Some had mutilated feet as did Iroquois slaves. Hodge, *Handbook of American Indians North of Mexico* 2, pp. 599-600.
[13]McWhorter, "Paiute-Wasco Indian Tribal Warfare." Ms. 1538.
[14]Spier and Sapir, *Wishram Ethnography*, 221; French, "Wasco-Wishram," 344-47.
[15]McWhorter, "Paiute-Wasco Indian Tribal Warfare." Ms. 1538.

who stole upon them in broad daylight, killing elderly males
and capturing women and children.[16] The Paiutes would
have found these captives burdensome on their peregrina-
tions about the Plateau. An Indian informant of the historian of the Yakimas, Lucullus V. McWhorter, recounted an
incident in which Paiutes were supposed to have skewered
children with sticks which they thrust up their victims'
abdomens to their mouths, and then, as a final act of cruelty,
staked them around campfires and cooked them.[17]

During the 1840s white emigrants ended their overland
journey from the States at the Wasco village breaking point
from which they took barges down the Columbia to the
Willamette settlements. Wascos took a liking to the emigrants' European style clothing as did other natives when
first encountering these garments. Seeing natives wearing a
variety of clothing prompted De Smet to describe The
Dalles as a "kind of masquerading thoroughfare, where emigrants and Indians meet..."[18] In exchange for the clothing
the Indians provided their guests horses, canoes and guides.
The Indians wanted the emigrants' clothing not only to wear,
but to turn around and trade since a good man's or woman's
outfit could purchase a slave.[19] Remaining outside the
exchanges, Wasco slaves continued as destitute of such goods
as ever.

Like Wascos, the Teninos also met the white travelers and
participated in activities at The Dalles, not the least of which
was trade. Through the many long years of friendy co-min-
gling in play and trade, the two peoples freely used each
other's hunting, gathering, fishing and trading areas.[20] The
Teninos clung close to The Dalles, their traditional wintering grounds where they kept busy trading dried salmon, fish

---

[16]Lucullus V. McWhorter, "Incidents in Tribal Indian Warfare," 16. Ms. 1538, Item 15.

[17]McWhorter, "Paiute-Wasco Indian Tribal Warfare." Ms. 1538.

[18]De Smet, *Oregon Missions*, 284.

[19]Ruby and Brown, *Indians of the Pacific Northwest*, 98.

[20]Murdock, *Culture and Society*, 203.

oil and furs in exchange for dentalia, baskets, bows and slaves. Occasionally their activities at The Dalles were interrupted by continued retaliation against the Paiutes against whom, except for a war with Molalas and a minor conflict with Klamaths, they were in perpetual conflict.[21] Other McWhorter Indian informants told of incidents involving Paiutes.[22] When four Tenino males wanted a Paiute girl, they settled by cutting her to pieces.[23] Adult females, whom they captured or purchased, could not marry within Tenino society. However, coming of age, captive children were permitted to marry Teninos and gain their freedom, and like slaves in other native communities, could shake off the shackles of bondage more surely than they could the shame of it.[24]

Fewer slaves came to The Dalles from the upper Plateau than from most other quarters in the Pacific Northwest. Among native commodities circulating on the upper Plateau well after contact, and which had come from great distances via Lower Chinookans at the coast were enslaved peoples of Northern tribes who had been traded south and easterly. Products such as eulachon and fish oil from distant tribes far to the north also moved in the same direction as did the slaves. Other goods brought by or moved through Lower Chinookan hands were berries, decorative olivella shells and dentalia, the important medium of exchange traded from tribe to tribe down the coast and across Cascade Mountain passes into the northern Plateau.[25] The flow of slaves and

---

[21]Ibid.

[22]McWhorter, "Incidents in Tribal Indian Warfare." Ms. 1538, Item 15.

[23]Ibid.

[24]Murdock, *Culture and Society*, 216.

[25]After 1790 the Lower Chinookans traded at the mouth of the Columbia an increasing number of items of Euro-American manufacture obtained directly or indirectly from white maritime traders: metals, looking glasses, foods and tobacco, beads and other highly saleable products such as axes, knives, traps, fish hooks, kettles, thimbles, and pots and pans. With the inland fur trade, natives from around present-day Oregon City along the Willamette River, and Vancouver and Sauvies Island on the lower Columbia brought similar products, and like coastal tradesmen, many slaves. They had guns sought by natives at The Dalles, but perhaps not as eagerly as might be assumed since they continued firing arrows from bows more rapidly and efficiently than bullets from cumbersome muzzle loading muskets.

goods in and out of The Dalles was not only by way of the
Pacific Coast, but from inland along the Willamette Valley-
Puget Sound trade trough and inland to the east and over the
Rocky Mountains.

Items which Klamaths and other southern and lower interior tribes brought to trade at The Dalles were mostly native
to their homelands. These included not only Snake, Modoc,
Pit River and Shasta slaves, but dressed antelope, bear meat,
skins, robes, sheeps' horns, hemp and highly nutritious
processed roots. Nez Percé-Cayuse tradesmen to the east
brought horses and products from more easterly tribes to
exchange for salmon.[26] Molalas brought tanned elk hides to
trade for fur bedding. Non-aggressive Paiute bands of the
lower Oregon desert brought deerskins to exchange for horses to bolster their small herds. Umatillas from just east of
The Dalles also brought items obtained from more easterly
regions.[27] These items of Plains culture from across the
Rocky Mountains which passed through several hands to
reach The Dalles, included dried buffalo meat, furs of all
descriptions, dressed skins and rope. There were also among
these goods gaily colored skin lodges and matting which
found a new breed of consumers in those who found horses
and horse-borne tipis suitable to their expanding mobility.

Among the lowly, like slaves themselves, yet vital in The
Dalles trade, were roots. Dr. William McKay, a long-time
resident among the Indians, identified these as "Looks,
Kouse, Saweat, Nonas, Kamas, Queya, Semane, Itollo and
Wocas," the latter a most important food among Klamaths
and their neighbors.[28] Natives also brought all sorts of berries
such as the mountain whortle, the blue berry, sarvis and rasp-
berry, salal, salmon and strawberry, currants and cherries all
dried for proper storage.

The importance of horses in The Dalles trade cannot be
overstressed, for they enabled their riders to travel widely with

---

[26]Arneson, "Property Concepts of 19th Century Oregon Indians," 418.
[27]Murdock, *Culture and Society*, 203.
[28]William Cameron McKay, "Early History of The Dalles," 11.

many items to trade, as well as to subsist themselves and deco-
rate their persons. Slave-trading for most owners was not the
lucrative business that it was for seaboard peoples, since the
topography and climate of their lands forced them to move
about to subsist, thus rendering them unable to accumulate
excess properties including slaves. Only after tribes like the
Cayuses began accumulating large herds of horses at the
beginning of the 19th century could they trade more widely
and set prices on slaves and other commodities.[29]

The overland route of Cayuses to westerly places such as
The Dalles took them through grassy hill country of the
Wallawallas and Umatillas past towering lava buttes and also
barren windswept banks of the Columbia lined with fishing
settlements. Among those traveling the relatively close distance to The Dalles were the Nez Percés, Klickitats, Yakimas, Palouses, Umatillas, Wallawallas and Wanapams.
Mingling with them at The Dalles were Salish speakers from
northern river, hill and plateau countries. All of these people
in turn mingled with coastal natives who bought and sold
slaves, wore capes and skirts of matted grass and smelled of
fish. Lewis and Clark in 1805 noted that most peoples of the
Plateau came to The Dalles area in early times despite the
contention of some scholars that they had not.[30] The horse
made such jouneys possible. Alvin Josephy describes the
polyglot Dalles assemblage as a place of "Dozens of temporary camps, boisterous with dogs and children and foul with
the stench of mounds of decaying fishheads [which], lined
the rocky shores above the turbulent river...busy with festivi-
ties and with constant visiting" to nightly "dancing, gambling, and the telling of stories, and during the day gossiping
and trading."[31]

Like other native trading places, medieval fairs and mod-

---

[29]For an account of the Cayuses' acquisition of the horse and their ensuing horse culture,
see Ruby and Brown, *The Cauyse Indians.*

[30]See Teit, *The Salishan Tribes of the Western Plateaus;* James K. Hosmer, ed., *History of
the Expedition of Captains Lewis and Clark 1804-5-6,* II, 506.

[31]Alvin M. Josephy, Jr., "Origins of the Nez Perce People," 10.

ern supermarkets, The Dalles was relatively stationary unlike the products exchanged there which, having passed through many hands, fluctuated in value from time to time. In like manner, its traders rose or fell in prominence to be replaced by others. It seems unusual that during recorded times the Klamaths did not appear at The Dalles until quite late. On one occasion in 1859 they sold two children there for five horses along with several buffalo skins and some beads, measuring the value of slaves not so much in dentalia or other commodities as in horses.[32]

A half-dozen years after Lewis and Clark, fur men began traversing the area. Few other white men came there until 1838 when Methodists established their Wascopam Mission among area Wasco and Wishram Indians. The missionaries found their task of saving Indian souls difficult since excessive merchandising, plus slavery, shamanism, polygyny and gambling were practiced there. In his *Sketches of Mission Life Among the Indians of Oregon*, which Zachariah Mudge edited there appears the account of Indian, Sciats, who, "having become important in his own eyes," set out from The Dalles for the Klamath country seeking to exchange two horses for two slaves. In response to the missionary's remonstrances not to take the journey, Sciats, a "whipper" among his people, threatened to ply his profession on the cleric. When he returned from his journey his two slaves ran away whereupon the missionary whipped him, a common practice among both Indians and white men of that day.[33]

A Wascopam missionary, the Reverend Henry K.W. Perkins, recorded an incident involving a slave lad of an important Wasco chief. When about five or six years old the lad was captured by Klamaths and sold to the chief who wanted him as a companion for his son. The two boys became inseparable friends, hunting rabbits, snaring wildfowl and fishing in streams. When the chief's son died, the

---

[32]Spier and Sapir, *Wishram Ethnography*, 223-24.
[33]Zachariah Mudge, ed., *Sketches of Mission Life Among the Indians of Oregon*, 152-54.

grieving father wanted the slave boy to accompany his son in death as he had in life. The lad was dutifully taken to the house of the dead, a roughly fifteen by thrity-foot mausoleum on a rocky island in the Columbia River. De Smet described such burial structures as "little huts made of pieces of split cedar, frequently covered with mats and boards; [where] great care is taken to hinder birds of prey, or the rapacious wolves, with their hyena stomachs and plundering propensities, from breaking in upon the abode of the dead."[34] The structure was sod-banked except at one end where an aperture was barely wide enough through which to pass a body and leading to a narrow passage separating bodies stacked on either side.

Slaves targeted for death were sometimes strangled with cords or stabbed by other slaves after which their bodies were canoed to the Columbia island mausoleum. In this instance it was decided to place the lad in the death house to starve. Tightly bound with strong bark-cord he was placed face to face with his dead companion, in the missionary's words, "till the very lips met...nestled down into his couch of rottenness, to impede his breathing as far as possible, and smother his cries." His shrieks and screams, wrote the minister, were "so agonizing that a tear stood in the eye of even his master" who was insufficiently moved to rescue the child from "heaps of hideous, festering dead; the cold, clammy reptile crawling over his quaking flesh, as it toiled to and fro in its feast of loathsomeness, choking with the hot, fulsome, putrid vapors of his ghostly bed."[35] Some scholars consider this report as a melodramatic passage written for consumption of eastern abolitionists; however, it was written in the histrionic mode of the day. Apprised of the situation, the missionary went to the tomb to discover that "insensible and almost breathless," the boy had kicked loose from the pile all scarred and beaten. He survived to be taken to the Methodist Mission near present-day Salem, Oregon, in the Willamette valley.[36]

[34]De Smet, *Oregon Missions*, 282.
[35]White, *Ten Years in Oregon*, 262.   [36]Ibid.

In another account, possibly the same incident, the father of the slave boy's companion had died. The successor chief, the brother of the dead leader had come under the influence of the Reverend Alvan Waller of the Wascopam Mission. According to this account the slave boy was bound to the dead chief's body. After three days of pleading, Waller received the successor chief's consent to remove the boy from the tomb. From there he was reportedly taken to the Reverend Josiah Parrish at the Clatsop Mission where he remained until 1849 when he went to work in the California gold diggings.[37] Another Methodist, and also Indian agent, Dr. Elijah White, revealed yet another atrocity at The Dalles involving a blood-feud in which males from two families were chopped to pieces after which the wife and two daughters of one victim were to be sold as slaves.[38]

The short-lived Wascopam Mission was abandoned partly, at least, because of Indian troubles erupting in the 1847 Whitman massacre and the ensuing Cayuse War, leaving Catholic clerics at The Dalles to minister to Indians from their Saint Peter's Mission, established in 1848. Subsequently, Indian Office and army personnel dealt with Indians of the area. With the establishment of reservations, Indians often returned from them to The Dalles to fish. They did so, but without two important things: the ease with which they had come there in former times—and, without slaves to buy and sell.

---

[37]Minto, "The Number and Condition of the Native Race in Oregon When First Seen By White Men," 301.
[38]White, *Ten Years in Oregon*, 277.

11

Of Human Bondage:
Measurable Consequences

Before the demise of slavery many Pacific Northwestern natives lost their identity, freedom and humanity, and indeed, their very lives to the whims and caprice of wealthy and aristocratic natives. During early historic times the percentage of disenfranchised peoples satisfying the vagaries of their owners accounted for as much as a quarter of native tribal populations in many areas, attesting to the enormity of slave numbers and the extensity and intensity of their use as chattel.

These human consequences of Indian slavery can be quantified only in cold statistics coming down primarily, although tenuously, from white men in the contact and post-contact periods. Wealthy, aristocratic tribal persons with much of their resources in slaves were aware that sudden changes in the delicate balance in ratios of free men to bondsmen could jeopardize the upper class socio-economic status quo. With the eventual post contact erosion in native economies, brought on primarily by the advent of white men in the region, attempts of upper classes to control slave-non-slave ratios failed several decades before the 20th century and eventually became impossible with the demise of the practice. There are few sources of tribal slave numbers. Exact enumerations were impossible. A few times a census was made of some tribes in occasional years by agents of fur posts and by travelers. Demographers have extrapolated possible quantifications of slave holdings by various tribes.

Among the Chinooks with whom we began this study,

292 INDIAN SLAVERY IN THE PACIFIC NORTHWEST

22.6% of their 1825 populations were slaves.[1] Among their Clatsop neighbors, slave numbers have been rendered as high as 47.4%.[2] Taking issue with this figure is anthropologist Herbert Taylor, Jr., who believes it to have been a 25% maximum.[3] Close to this figure, however, were Chinookan speakers from the mouth of the Columbia River to its Cascades, whose slave numbers Governor Simpson in 1824-1825 reported as near 24.3%.[4] Along this stretch of the river, unlike many other regional areas, male slaves outnumbered female slaves 395 to 275.[5]

In 1838 the population of three Chinook villages had dropped to 288 of which 21% were slaves.[6] A census the following year revealed 290 Chinooks of which 20% were slaves.[7] There were about the same number of Clatsops and slaves. By 1851 Chinook slave populations remained constant at 21.1%, while among Clatsops, who succumbed even more severely to disease, liquor and other excesses of "civilization," the slave population fell to 10%.[8] In 1854-1855 that of mixed Chinooks and Chehalis peoples in the vicinity of Shoalwater Bay at the immediate northern end of the Chinook slave vortex stood at 23%.[9] As reported by Dr. Tolmie at Fort Nisqually there was on and near Puget Sound in 1844 a 6.14% slave population. Among tribes in his report were: Squaxins, 2.98% slaves; Nisquallys, 6.37%; Puyallups, 3.8%; Skokomishes, 5.6%; Suquamishes, 12.21%; Snoqualmies, 2.15%; Lummis, 9.14%; and Snohomishes none.[10] Gathering accurate population statistics of Indians living in white

[1]J.C. Craig, Archivist, Hudson's Bay Company, to authors, February 4, 1971.
[2]Ibid.
[3]Herbert C. Taylor, Jr., "Aboriginal Populations of the Lower Northwest Coast," 160.
[4]Merk, *Fur Trade and Empire,* 170.
[5]Ibid.
[6]Nellie B. Pipes, "Journal of John H. Frost, 1840-43," 59.
[7]Strickland, *History of the Missions of the Methodist Episcopal Church,* 139-40.
[8]Robert Shortess, Subagent to Anson Dart, Oregon Supt. of Indian Affairs, February 5, 1851. *Records of the Oregon Superintendency of Indian Affairs, 1848-1872. Letter Book B:10.*
[9]William H. Tappan, Agent, to Isaac I. Stevens, Washington Supt. of Indian Affairs, January 18, 1855. *Records of the Washington Superintendency of Indian Affairs, 1853-1874, No. 5, Roll 17.*
[10]Dennis, "Indian Slavery in Pacific Northwest," 110.

communities was difficult; in Indian communities it was doubly so. Discrepancies in numbers reported were not unusual. The traveling Achilles De Harley, for example, reported in 1849 an 8% slave population among Snohomishes, but for 1845-1846 the British engineers H.J. Warre and M. Vavasour reported a 2.3% population for that tribe. For neighboring Skagits they reported 3.3%; and for Clallams, 2.17%.[11]

De Harley's figure of 232 slaves in eight tribes and tribal groups of Sound and Strait (excluding four tribes for which apparently no slave statistics were available) was 4% of the area native population. His figures, published in the *New York Tribune*, January 11, 1850, appeared fifteen days later in the *Friends' Review. A Religious, Literary and Miscellaneous Journal*, as well as in Henry Rowe Schoolcraft's *Historical and Statistical Information Respecting the History, Condition and Prospects of the Indian Tribes of the United States*.[12] In the early 1850s George Gibbs reported that slaves composed 10% of Puget Sound tribal populations[13] which figure was 6 percentage points higher than that of De Harley.[14]

In reporting a census of coastal tribes from 45°n. latitude, including Tillamooks to the south, Warre and Vavasour listed 5,146 slaves from a total population of 79,847, or roughly 6.44% of their numbers. These figures did not include those of Tlingits north of 54°n. latitude and for some reason included none among Chinooks, Clatsops and Tillamooks. South of the Tillamooks Warre and Vavasour provided only general population figures with no mention of slaves to n.

---

[11]*New York Tribune*, Jan. 11, 1850; Joseph Schafer, ed., "Documents Relative to Warre and Vavasour's Military Reconnaissance in Oregon," 61.

[12]Schoolcraft, *Historical and Statistical Information Respecting the History Condition and Prospects of the Indian Tribes of the United States* 5, pp. 700-701; "The Oregon Indians and Their Slaves," 297-98.

[13]Gibbs, Tribes of Western Washington and Northwestern Oregon I, Pt. 2, p. 189.

[14]Anthropologist Donald H. Mitchell, an authority on slave census, writes, "One point...to consider...when discussing the Puget Sound data, is that the 'census' to 'census' variation in slave percentages is mostly a product of wildly varying 'counts' of the free population. There cannot actually have been such swings in so short a period (a 17 year span). Under those circumstances, if there is no reason to consider one more reliable than the other, averaging the figures is justified." Letter to authors, Feb. 4, 1993.

latitude 42°, and no figures for tribes of the Columbia Plateau, an area of lesser concern to them.[15] Leland Donald writes that demographic data on the Nootkas was poor, but that in the villages a quarter were title-holders; one-half, commoners; and a quarter, slaves.[16] In 1838 the Hudson's Bay Company had reported among Bella Bellas 47 slaves, or 2.99% of their 1,573 number. That same year Southern Kwakiutl groups had totaled 37,381 persons of which number 1,430 or 3.83% were slaves. The Company reported population figures for two groups of Salish speakers of the Strait of Georgia; for the Comox north of the Strait, 1,960, a hundred of which were slaves, or 5.1%; and for the Klahuse (also Clahose, classified by some as a Comox subdivision) of whose 2,490 people 40, or 1.6% were slaves.

Fifteen years later a Hudson's Bay Company census of

[15]Martin, *The Hudson's Bay Territories and Vancouver Island,* 80-82. Martin described these figures as estimates of H.J. Warre and M. Vavasour of native populations including the coastal area from the Oregon-California border up to the southern tip of Alaska, the southern boundary of Russian land claims to their north. Their estimates omit for the most part the Tlingits living in the Alaskan panhandle, and, except for this omission, cover the slave-holding coastal areas and other parts of the Pacific Northwest. From thirty-four groups of Wakashan speakers in Canada John Work, in an 1836-1841 census, listed 1,526 slaves from a total population of 39,472, or roughly 2.5%. See Work's census cited in Curtis, *The North American Indian* 10, p. 303. Work's figures of the Kwakiutl are considered bogus.

One writer described these figures as "the nearest approach to accuracy of the number of inhabitants in any of the north-west regions..." Martin, *The Hudson's Bay Territories and Vancouver Island,* 80. Several tribes listed in the Warre-Vavasour report as non-slave-holding, did, in fact, hold them.

The difficulties of ascertaining slave populations are obvious and numerous. Simpson had reported slaves among the Northern Indians as constituting "one full third of the large population of this coast..." Simpson, *Narrative of a Journey Round the World* 1, p. 211. Differences in slave numbers in Simpson's report and those of Warre and Vavasour may be credited not only to the time differential in their tallys, but also possibly to the Superintendent's burgeoning of figures in attempting to equate them with the excesses of slavery in the northern quarter. His estimates are above those rendered not only by Taylor, but by MacLeod who, on the basis of observations of others who were among those Indians, termed them as "perhaps, rather exaggerated," stating that from about 1836 to 1841 Tlingit numbers were one slave out of seven, but those of Southern Kwakiutls and tribes of the Oregon coast, but one out of twenty. Taylor, "Aboriginal Populations of the Lower Northwest Coast," 160; MacLeod, "Economic Aspects of Indigenous American Slavery," 638-39. By contrast, Yurok slaves of northern California in the less intense southern, or lower, end of the slave belt represented roughly one percent of that tribe's population. Elmendorf and Kroeber, *The Structure of Twana Culture,* 319n.

[16]Leland Donald. "Was Nuu-chah-nulth-aht (Nootka) Society Based on Slave Labor?" 112.

combined Tsimshians and Haisla (a portion of the Northern Kwakiutal Bella Bella) revealed 4,538 persons of whom 196, or 4.32% were slaves. Following its merger with the North West Company, the Hudson's Bay Company took a periodic census of various tribes. Some of its figures were solid enumerations; others were estimates. An 1845 survey listed 4,791 Tlingits of whom 652, or 13.61% were slaves.[17] In an 1861 census of Kaigani, the Russian Ivan Petroff listed this Haida summer village of 758 as having 198 slaves, or nearly 26.1% of their population. Among Tlingits he listed 630 slaves from among 7,831 persons, or a slave population of 8%.[18] Another Russian census the same year by P.A. Tikhmenev enumerated 6,594 Tlingits, of whom 513 were slaves which was 7.78%, thus very close to Petroff's census. These estimates reveal a drop in slave percentages from 1845. The sixteen-year variation of Tlingit slave percentages from nearly 13.61% in 1845 to 8% in 1861 was due to an increase in the free population, making a relative decline in slaves whose figures remained fairly stable.[19] Gilbert Malcolm Sproat reported in 1864 that the Opetchists, a Nootkan group, held only 3 slaves, or 6.4% of their population of 47.[20]

Behind these cold, albeit declining, slave statistics were human beings seeking what for them must have been the nebulous goal of freedom. With the near 20th century demise of slavery, its victims were finally unshackled, but not suddenly or completely as the scars of stigma remained with them into the future.

In later times the matter of slave ancestry, discussed in hushed tones in Indian communities, occasionally broke into the open. A case in point began around 1870 when a group of Haidas from present-day Kasaan, Alaska, fought natives in the area of Victoria, British Columbia. In all likelihood the latter were Coast Salish speakers who traded to the Tom Will

[17]Donald Mitchell, "A Demographic Profile of Northwest Coast Slavery," 231.
[18]Ivan Petroff, "The Population and Resources of Alaska, 1880," 99.
[19]Mitchell, "A Demographic Profile of Northwest Coast Slavery," 228-33.
[20]Sproat, Scenes and Studies of Savage Life, 108-09.

family two Haida captives, one a male of approximately twenty-five years, and the other, a young girl, who escaped in a waiting canoe. The young man was given the name Tom Ting, meaning to "ask for something," or "to beg."[21] On the Lummi Reservation he married Julia Roberts, another Haida slave. They raised a family, although she had a daughter from a previous marriage. Since Puget Sound tribes had signed treaties in the mid-1850s to relinquish slavery, the government treated as free individuals all reservation Indians under these pacts. Thus, in the absence of overt slavery on the reservation, Ting, as a "Lummi," on December 31, 1884, was allotted a trust patent for 160 acres.[22]

Nearly a century later the Alaska Native Land Claims Settlement Act of 1969 was submitted to Congress to recommend legislative settlement for native Alaskan claims for land and resources of that state. Senate bill 3702 (approved, December 18, 1971, becoming Public Law 92-203 (85 Stat, 688) called for funding $462,500,000 to settle the claims.[23] Aware of the slave background of Tom Ting and Julia Roberts, their descendants revealed their backgrounds to declare their Alaskan native ancestry in a Bellingham, Washington, district court. When it was ordered that the defendants remain on the rolls of Alaskan natives under the Alaska Native Land Claims Settlement Act, the government took the case to the Department of Interior Office of Hearings and Appeals, which, after a hearing rendered in 1979 a judgement favorable to the Ting descendants.[24] They were able to share in the claims settlement.

---

[21]Wayne Suttles, *Affidavit*, May 4, 1877. Mary L. Durant, Notary Public, Photocopy in possession of authors; *United States of America, Contestant* v. *Frank Abbott, et al, Contestees.* Feb. 1, 1979 U.S. Department of the Interior, Office of Hearings and Appeals, Hearings Division, Arlington, Virginia.

[22]*U.S.A.* v. *Frank Abbott, et al; The Alaska Native Times*, March, 1979.

[23]To receive financial benefits under the Settlement Act one had to be a U.S. citizen, with some Alaskan Indian, Eskimo, or Aleut blood, or a combination of such. The Act specifically included Indians whose adopted parents were not Alaskan natives.

[24]*U.S.A., Contestant* v. *Frank Abbott, et al.* After the precedent setting, successfully acted upon petition of the first group of ten Ting descendants in 1977 to file for enrollment under section 5 of the Alaska Native Claims Settlement Act, Maxine Faye Hanks Stremler filed a

Overriding any embarrassment the defendants might have had regarding their slave ancestry, the judgement in their behalf was of greater satisfaction to them since justice had finally been done. Confirming this was Wayne Suttles who had done anthropological work among the Lummis in 1949. Wrote Suttles: "I was pleased to have played a role in what seemed like a wonderful instance of the triumph of justice."[25]

---

petition which also received a favorable decision after appealing at first an adverse decision. Following this, several others petitioned for enrollment under ANCSA as descendants of Ting, and received their share of settlement. Several others of similar descent were too late in petitioning the government under the deadline set by the Act. Maxine Faye Stremler interview, Lynden, Washington, Jan. 31, 1989; Stremler, Maxine Faye, *Final Decision*, Enrollment Coordinator, Anchorage, Alaska, March 14, 1980; Stremler, *Petition*, Enrollment Coordinating Office, Anchorage, Alaska, July 25, 1979.

[25]Suttles to authors, Oct. 31, 1988.

12

Demise and Delivery

Despite futile efforts to end the Pacific Northwestern native slave trade through treaties and injection of moralist counteractions, it was actually the introduction of capitalistic merchandising at contact by Euro-Americans that eventually brought the system to its knees following a period of expansion. The aboriginal economic system supporting an aristocracy gave way to a free enterprise social leveling which rendered the holding of potlatches impossible in the usual and customary fashion.

Missionaries and others sought to eliminate slavery. Americans sought to force its abolition among coastal tribes through treaties even prior to the manumission of blacks in the American South. The clergy, and fur traders in an abating enterprise, sought to emancipate native slaves and abolish slavery in the waning years of the 19th century. Yet, slavery did not end through their efforts, but of its own weight under a trade system in a changing social-economic environment which no longer supported that practice. The last of the slaves disappeared by attrition.

In the latter 19th century Hudson's Bay Company officials, helped by Americans and Russians, sought to eliminate slavery among the Northern Indians. No such effort was made simultaneously by Bay Company officials in the American Pacific Northwest simply because that firm by then had lost position and influence in this American region. For that matter, earlier in the century most mariner-traders appear to have been unconcerned about the practice, although Company officials were aware of it since they reported slave numbers. What appears as Chief Factor McLoughlin's earlier low-key response to slavery may have been an attempt to avoid disruptions which interference might have brought to the fur trade. Moreover, the humanitarianism he extended Protestant and Roman Catholic missionaries might have discouraged them from criticizing his failure to end slavery. Unlike the Anglican Reverend Beaver, American Protestant missionaries though they criticized the practice of slavery they made no effort to abolish slavery amongst the Indians despite words of pro-mission advocate, Zachariah Mudge, that "religious teachers were the means of preventing, in many cases, such cruelty; and by making the dark mind of the Indian understand the law of love, they were the instruments of the abolition, in a measure, of this system of slavery."[1]

That "measure" appeared small considering the missionaries' absence of abolitionist zeal. As evidenced in their journal, the *Friends' Review,* the Quakers, who led the denominations in condemning slavery in eastern and southern portions of America and in Africa, South America and Asia, were silent concerning the plight of Indian slaves in the Pacific Northwest. What might appear as indifference was more likely ignorance of the slavery existing in the region, since these Quakers had no missionaries there to observe and report it. Reference to slavery in the *Missionary Herald,* the organ of the American Board, appeared only incidentally for reasons on which one can only speculate. Perhaps more important than the Biblical recognition of bonded and free persons was the fact that in northeastern America from which their missionaries came, abolition had opponents ranging from those who believed it would split the Union to those who owned northern mills which processed southern cotton.

Where native slave and free women may have appeared indistinguishable to American Board missionaries, such lack of discernment would not have held for black American slaves with whom they were more familiar. Along the Pacific Coast it would appear that the shock of the natives' flattened heads left little room in the missionaries catalogue of abhor-

---

[1]Mudge, *Sketches of Mission Life Among the Indians of Oregon,* 72.

rent things for them to recognize that those whose heads were round suffered more than those whose heads were flat. Ironically, John Beeson, who came to Oregon in 1853 to champion the cause of red men (described in his *A Plea for the Indian...* as cowering "like a miserable slave") with missionary zeal during the Indian wars, overlooked the fact that the plight of their slaves made his statement less simile than reality. To him the Indians' problems were caused by evil white men when, in fact, at least their slavery was largely a product of their own race.[2] In similar vein a leading Indian rights publication, *The Council Fire,* which began publication in Philadelphia in 1878, in citing wrongs committed by whites against Indians, scarcely alluded to this self-imposed Indian slavery. Like Beeson, its concern was for the larger body of Indian problems.

Unfortunately the plight of Indian slaves got caught up in Anglo-American contests for ownership of the Oregon country. In this struggle patriot-spokesmen of both nations found a handy vehicle with which to denigrate the other's claim to the region. Provisions in the 1854-1855 treaties abolishing slavery and its trade had not solved the problem. Nearly a quarter-century later, in August 1868, Superintendent McKenny reported that slavery was still "clung [to] with great tenacity, even [among] those whose treaty stipulations forbid it."[3] Among Twana treaty signatories the Reverend Myron Eells in the 1870s admitted the presence of slaves, quickly pointing out that they enjoyed "considerable liberty." Moreover, he claimed that slavery among Twanas was waning due to the treaty stipulations and the passing of intertribal warfare. As a missionary he exerted a humanitarian influence against slavery. His Indian agent brother, Edwin, exerted a legal one. On one occasion when attending a pot-

---

[2]John Beeson, *A Plea for the Indians; with Facts and Features of the late War in Oregon,* 80. Beeson also wrote, p. 99: "What they [the Indians] need is a religion of love, and beauty, and peace, and freedom, and harmony, and civilization; but they have received one of hatred, and violence, and harshness, and slavery, and war, and misery, and retrogradation."

[3]McKenney to Taylor, August (n.d.), 1868. *Annual Report, Secy. Interior, 1868,* Serial 1366, p. 549.

latch it was reported to Edwin that a slave was attending the ceremonial. He ordered his immediate release.[4] In a vocabulary which Myron Eells compiled for an 1877 publication the word "slave" was noticeably absent.[5] Perhaps because of its late (1882) foundings among nearby Squaxin Indians, the Indian Shaker Church did not stress anti-slavery as it did anti-drinking, gambling and other vices.

During the Oregon territorial and early statehood periods, white settlers were more concerned with black American slavery than with that among its red men. Even had early-day whites been sympathetic to the plight of Indian slaves, they would have been too busy or tired from hacking farms from the wilderness to espouse the cause of Indian emancipation. This is not to say there was no white impact on Indian slavery, but its waning was due less to any kindness on the part of both whites and Indians than to the fact that Indian slave owners had to treat their subjects more humanely under the impact of expanding white culture. With this impact bondsmen decreased in number which resulted in their becoming less disposable and hence, more valuable. Most whites not only had little time or inclination to concern themselves with Indian slavery, but had little understanding of the culture in which it existed. The phenomenon has to be examined within the general context of native mores, a process whites were unwilling or unable to probe and understand. Life was indeed harsh in native societies whose people, unlike those in modern ones, were not buffered from the

---

[4]Myron Eells, "The Twana Indians of the Skokomish Reservation in Washington Territory," 103; Edwin Eells Papers, "Autobiography." Dictation by Edwin Eells March 11, 1914, p. 29. Supplement Folder 19-A, Box 1. Typescript copy of ms. in Washington State Historical Society, Tacoma.

[5]Eells, "The Twana Indians of the Skokomish Reservation in Washington Territory," 93-98. In the same publication, p. 107, Eells wrote: "There are a very few slaves; but as there has been no war for a long time, slavery is dying out, and the few which there are are not treated as harshly as they formerly were." In 1887 he wrote: "Slavery is dead." *The Twana, Chemakum, and Klallam Indians, of Washington Territory,* 615. Eells' output of detailed accounts of Puget Sound Indian life was prolific with the obvious exception of allusions to slavery. He was either unaware of this once important aspect of native life or he chose to minimize it as did other early-day missionaries like the Whitmans, and even the Lees, who made scant comment about it.

law of the survival of the fittest. In Aristotelian fashion, Indians regarded slavery as a natural condition. Under missionary influence the sins to which converts confessed were individual, not corporate or institutional. Slavery was noticeably absent in their confessions, for they regarded human bondage as neither aberrant nor abhorrent.

There was, in essence, no manumission of Pacific Northwestern Indian slaves in the traditional sense of the word except in a few treaties effected by Governor Stevens and in a few written and verbal orders of Indian agents. As noted, there were cases of individuals released from bondage by masters,[6] but the practice was not general. Like some slaves in the post Civil War era there were some Indian slaves who, unprepared for freedom, chose to remain with their masters. Slavery finally ended by socio-economic default when former wealthy families lost their rationale for acquiring slaves and their ability to hold and trade them. Despite its millstone grinding slowness, the decline time of slavery was short when compared with the long period of its existence.

On more remote Indian reservations proponents of slavery fought a rear-guard action to retain it. On the Klamath where the economic structure collided with requirements of a new era, its agent in 1869 issued orders to stop the practice. On the Warm Springs its Presbyterian agent, Captain John Smith, in a January 31, 1881 letter to the editor of the *Council Fire* wrote that "Upon my [1877] advent...there were many slaves who had been taken as captives in war, or purchased from other tribes of Indians. The first thing I did was to issue a general *emancipation proclamation,* and set them at liberty." Smith stated that his order was "extremely unpopular" at the time.[7]

Preventing a clean break with Indian slavery was not only Indian recalcitrance to end it, but the untimely arrival of hordes of miners, lumberjacks and other laborers pouring

---

[6]*Christian Advocate & Journal,* August 19, 1836; Robert Moulton Gathke, "The First Indian School of the Pacific Northwest," 71; Lee and Frost, *Ten Years in Oregon,* 132-33.

[7]John Smith, Capt., Agent, Warm Springs Res. "Letter to the Editor." 52.

into the region, some of whom abused Indian women in the manner of slaves. This new type of bondage could not always be distinguished from the "old time" variety which died a slow death especially in the North. Thomas Crosby told of girls who came to a mission house at midnight to plead with a missionary for help. One girl pleaded. "please will you not take me in. They are going to sell me as a slave, and I don't want to go."[8]

In no society did slavery die a sudden death. Among Indians discussed herein the stigma of slavery took much longer to die, keeping alive the memory of an evil institution. As elsewhere in America and other industrialized nations, Indians and white men were in a sense enslaved in the maws of an industrial revolution managed by a new breed of entrepreneurial masters.

In a Hobbsean sense, of all men, slave lives were indeed solitary, poor, nasty, brutish and short. The gap between the free and those in one form of bondage or another may never close, but despite the hazards and pitfalls besetting mankind, it is hoped that especially for the descendants of those of this study the gap of injustice can at least be narrowed.

---

[8]Thomas Crosby, *Among the An-ko-me-nums or Flathead Tribes of the Pacific Coast*, 63.

Bibliography

UNPUBLISHED MATERIALS AND MANUSCRIPTS

Averkieva, U.P. "Slavery Among the Indians of North America, U.S.S.R. Academy of Sciences, Moscow-Leningrad, 1941." Trans. by G.R. Elliott, Victoria College, Victoria, B.C., 1957. (Rev., 1966). Typescript copy of ms., Northwest Coll., Univ. of Wash. Libraries, Seattle.

Bishop, Charles. "Commercial Journal Copy's of Letters and Accts. of Ship Ruby's voyage to the N.W.T. coast of America and China, 1794, 5, 6. Typescript copy of Ms. A/A/20.5/R.82B, Provincial Arch., Victoria.

Clark, Helen W. "Chips From an Old Block." Typescript copy of ms. in possession of authors.

Eells, Edwin. Papers, "Autobiography." Dictation by Edwin Eells March 11, 1914. Supplement Folder 19-A, Box A. Typescript copy in Wash. State Hist. Soc., Tacoma.

Finlayson, Roderick. "The History of Vancouver Island and the Northwest Coast." Ms. P-C 15, Bancroft Library, Univ. of Calif., Berkeley.

Furgerson, Samuel. "Journal of a voyage from Boston to the North-West Coast of America, in the Brig Otter, Samuel Hill Commander. Kept by Samuel Furgerson, Ships Carpenter, March 31, 1809 to March 24, 1811." Ms. 207, Beinecke Library, Yale Univ., New Haven.

Gatschet, Albert Samuel. "The Molale tribe raided by the Cayuses." Ms. 2029, National Anthropological Arch., Smithsonian Inst., Washington.

Hancock, Samuel. "Journal Whidbey Island, W.T. February 17, 1860." Typescript copy of ms., Special Coll. Div., Univ. of Wash Libraries, Seattle.

Heglar, Rodger, "A Racial Analysis of Indian Skeletal Material From the Columbia River Valley." 1957. Thesis 813030, Univ. of Wash. Libraries, Seattle.

Hinds, Richard Brinsley, "Journal, 1838-1842." Ms. in British Museum, London. Ms. 1524. Microfilm Reel 2, Oregon Hist. Soc., Portland.

Hoskins, John. "The Narrative of a Voyage to the North West Coast of America and China on Trade and Discoveries by John Hoskins Performed in the Ship Columbia Rediviva 1790, 1791, 1792 & 1793."

Typescript copy of Ms. 119.1 G77 H82, Ayers Coll., Newberry Library, Chicago.

Johnson, Philip C. "Private Notes of Philip C. Johnson, Jr. on Board U.S.S. Active 1855-56." Typescript copy of ms., Northwest Coll., Univ. of Wash. Libraries, Seattle.

Lee, Jason. "Journal of Jason Lee, Written at Mission House, Willamette, March 15, 1841." 12 vols. Carton 2 of 2 AIA 2/6 Box 22. Typescript copy of ms., Clarence Booth Bagley Coll., Arch., Univ. of Wash. Libraries, Seattle.

"Log-Book of the Brig Lydia on a Fur-Trading voyage from Boston to the Northwest Coast of America 1804-1805 with the Return Voyage by way of the Sandwich Islands and Canton Aboard the Ships Atahualpa and Swift 1805-1807." Ms. S-213, Beinecke Library, Yale Univ., New Haven.

McKay, William Cameron. "Early History of The Dalles." William Cameron McKay Papers, Umatilla County Library, Pendleton, Ore.

McWhorter, Lucullus V. "Chief Owhi's Only Crime." Ms. 1530. Lucullus V. McWhorter Papers, Holland Library, Wash. State Univ., Pullman.

_____. "The Chiefs of Some of the Columbia River Tribes." Wasco Jim Interview. Ms. 1535, Item 6, McWhorter Papers.

_____. "Chief William Spencer's Foray Against the Rogue River Tribe." Ms. 1548, McWhorter Papers.

_____. "The Dreamer Religion of the Yakima Indians." Ms. 1519, no. 1, McWhorter Papers.

_____. "Incidents in Tribal Indian Warfare." Caesar Williams, Interview, Ms. 1538, Item 15, McWhorter Papers.

_____. "Incidents of the Piute War 1878." Kate (Mrs. Caesar) Williams, Interview, Ms. 1542, McWhorter Papers.

_____. "Origin of Yakima." George Olney, Interview. Ms. 1518, McWhorter Papers.

_____. "Paiute-Wasco Indian Tribal Warfare." Wasco Jim, Interview. Ms. 1538, Item 6, McWhorter Papers.

Meeker, Ezra, Family. "Notebooks," no. 2. Arch. Univ. of Wash. Libraries, Seattle.

Minto, Martha Ann. "Female Pioneering in Oregon." Ms. P-A 51, Bancroft Library, Univ. of Calif., Berkeley.

Oak, Henry L. "Notes on Indian Wars in Washington Territory, 1855-1856." Ms. P-B 69, Bancroft Library, Univ. of Calif., Berkeley.

Oglesby, W.W. "The Calapoyas Indians." Ms. P-A 82, Bancroft Library, Univ. of Calif., Berkeley.

Parrish, Josiah L. "Anecdotes of Intercourse with the Indians." Ms. P-A 59, Bancroft Library, Univ. of Calif., Berkeley.

Ramsdell, T.M. "Indians of Oregon." Ms. 852, Oregon Hist. Soc., Portland.

Redington, Col. J.W. "Honest Chief Egan." Ms. 175. Lucullus V. McWhorter Papers, Holland Library, Wash. State Univ., Pullman.

Roberts, George B. "Recollections of George B. Roberts." Ms. P-A 83, Bancroft Library, Univ. of Calif., Berkeley.

Smith, A. Wesley Papers. "Neah Bay Indian Agency 1876-1909." Microfilm copy, Wash. State Library, Olympia.

Suttles, Wayne. *Affidavit*, Portland, Oregon, May 4, 1977, Mary L. Durant, Notary Public. Photocopy in possession of authors.

Whealdon, Ben. L. "On Whealdon Hill (Ilwaco, Wash.) Eve of July 16, 1860." Ms. 50, Oregon Hist. Soc., Portland.

Willoughby, Charles. "Indians of the Quinault Agency, Washington Territory." In *Papers on the Indians*, Newberry Library, Chicago.

Yoakam, John. "Coos Bay, Notes on" Vol. I. Ms. P-A 85, Bancroft Library, Univ. of Calif., Berkeley.

BOOKS, MONOGRAPHS, PAMPHLETS AND GOVERNMENT DOCUMENTS

Alvord, Benjamin. *Military Report* (34 Cong., 3 sess. House Exec. Doc. No. 76), Serial 906. Wash., D.C., 1853.

Andrade, Manuel J. *Quileute Texts. Columbia University Contributions in Anthropology* 12. New York, 1931.

Annual Report of the Secretary of the Interior for the Years 1852, 1857, 1859, 1860, 1871, 1891. Wash., D.C.

Armstrong, A.N. *Oregon: Comprising a Brief History and Full Description of Oregon and Washington.* Chicago, 1857.

Bailey, L.R. *Indian Slave Trade in the Southwest.* Los Angeles, 1973.

Bancroft, Hubert Howe. *The Works of Hubert Howe Bancroft*, 39 vols.

_____. *History of the Northwest Coast.* XXVIII. San Francisco, 1886.

_____. *The Native Races of the Pacific States on North America. Wild Tribes* I. New York, 1875.

Barnett, Homer Garner. *The Coast Salish of British Columbia*, Eugene, Ore., 1955.

_____. *Culture Element Distributions: IX, Gulf of Georgia Salish.* Anthropological Records I, no. 5. Berkeley, 1939.

_____. *Culture Element Distributions: VII, Oregon Coast.* Anthropological Records I, no. 3. Berkeley, 1937.

Beach, W.W., ed. *The Indian Miscellany: Containing Papers on the History, Antiquities, Arts, Languages, Religions, Traditions and Superstitions of the American Aboriginies.* Albany, N.Y., 1877.

Beckham, Stephen Dow. *The Indians of Western Oregon: This Land Was Theirs.* Coos Bay, Ore., 1977.

Beeson, John. *A Plea for the Indians; with Facts and Features of the Late War in Oregon.* New York, 1957.

Boas, Franz. *The Social Organization and the Secret Societies of the Kwakiutl Indians, Report of the U.S. National Museum for the year ending June 30, 1895.* Wash., D.C., 1897.

_____ and George Hunt. *Kwakiutl Texts, Memoirs of the American Museum of Natural History,* Vol. 5, New York, 1905.

Boyd, Robert. *People of the Dalles: The Indians of the Wascopam Mission.* Lincoln. In preparation.

Brabrant, Augustin Joseph. *Vancouver Island and Its Missions, 1874-1900.* New York, 1900.

Brackenridge, Henry Marie. *Journal of a Voyage Up the River Missouri, in 1811.* Vol. VI in Reuben Gold Thwaites, *Early Western Travels 1748-1846.* 32 vols. Cleveland, 1904.

Burland, Cottie. *North American Mythology.* London, 1970.

Canse, John M. *Pilgrim and Pioneer Dawn in the Northwest.* New York, 1930.

Carlson, Frank. *Chief Sealth. The Bull. of the Univ. of Wash. the State Univ.* Series III, no. 2, Seattle, December, 1903.

Castile, George Pierre. *The Indians of Puget Sound: The Notebooks of Myron Eells.* Seattle, 1985.

Chevigny, Hector. *Russian America: The Great Alaskan Venture, 1741-1867.* New York, 1965.

Chittenden, Hiram Martin and Alfred Talbot Richardson. *Life, Letters and Travels of Father Pierre-Jean De Smet, S.J. 1801-1873.* 4 vols. New York, 1905.

Chittenden, Newton H. *Hyda Land and People—Official Report of the Exploration of the Queen Charlotte Islands for the Government of British Columbia.* Victoria, 1884.

Churchill, Claire Warner. *Slave Wives of Nehalem.* Portland, 1933.

Clark, Ella E. *Indian Legends of the Pacific Northwest.* Berkeley, 1963.

Clark, Robert Carlton. *History of the Willamette Valley, Oregon.* 3 vols. Chicago, 1927.

Clarke, Samuel A. *Pioneer Days of Oregon History.* 2 vols. Portland, 1905.

_____. *Klamath County Museum Research Papers No. 2.* B.K. Swartz, ed. Klamath Falls, Ore., 1960.

Clerke, Charles. "Extract from Officers' Journals," vol. 3, pt. 2. In J.C. Beaglehole, ed., *The Journals of Captain James Cook on His Voyages of Discovery,* Cambridge, 1967.

Cleveland, Richard J. *A Narrative of Voyages and Commercial Enterprises.* London, 1842.

Codere, Helen. *Fighting with Property: A Study of Kwakiutl Potlatching and Warfare 1792-1930.* Seattle, 1972.

Cohen, Felix S. *Handbook of Federal Indian Law.* Albuquerque, n.d.

Collins, June McCormick. *Valley of the Spirits: The Upper Skagit Indians of Western Washington.* Seattle, 1974.

Colson, Elizabeth. *The Makah Indians: A Study of an American Tribe in Modern American Society.* Minneapolis, 1953.

Cook, James. *A Voyage to the Pacific Ocean; Undertaken by Command of His Majesty, for Making Discoveries in the Northern Hemisphere.* 4 vols. London, 1784.

Cook, Warren L. *Flood Tide of Empire.* New Haven, 1973.

Corney, Peter. *Early Voyages in the North Pacific, 1813-1818.* Fairfield, Wash., 1965.

Costello, J.A. *The Siwash: Their Life Legends and Tales Puget Sound and Pacific Northwest.* Seattle, 1895.

Coues, Elliott, ed. *New Light on the Early History of the Greater Northwest: The Manuscript Journals of Alexander Henry, Fur Trader of the Northwest Company, and of David Thompson, Official Geographer and Explorer of the Same Company, 1799-1814.* 3 vols. New York, 1897.

Cox, Ross. *Adventures on the Columbia River.* 2 vols. London, 1831.

Coxe, William. *Account of the Russian Discoveries between Asia and America, to Which are Added, the Conquest of Siberia, and the History of the Transactions and Commerce between Russia and China.* New York, 1970.

Crosby, Thomas. *Among the An-ko-me-nums or Flathead Tribes of Indians of the Pacific Coast.* Toronto, 1907.

Curtis, Edward S. *The North American Indian.* 20 vols. New York, 1907-1930.

Dawson, George Mercer. *Report on the Queen Charlotte Islands, 1878.* Montreal, 1880.

Densmore, Frances. *Nootka and Quileute Music.* Smithsonian Bureau of American Ethnology Bulletin 124. Wash., D.C., 1939.

De Smet, Peter J., S.J. *Letters and Sketches: With a Narrative of a Year's Residence among the Indian Tribes of the Rocky Mountains.* Vol. XXVII in Reuben Gold Thwaites, *Early Western Travels 1748-1846.* 32 vols. Cleveland, 1906.

_____. *Oregon Missions and Travels over the Rocky Mountains, 1845-46.* Vol. XXIX in Reuben Gold Thwaites, *Early Western Travels 1748-1846.* 32 vols. Cleveland, 1906.

Drew, Lieut. Colonel, C.S. *Official Report of the Owyhee Reconnaissance, Made by Lieut. Colonel C.S. Drew 1st Oregon Cavalry, in the Summer of 1864.* Jacksonville, Ore., 1865.

Driver, Harold E. *Indians of North America.* Chicago, 1961.

_____ and William C. Massey. *Comparative Studies of North American Indians.* Trans. of the American Phil. Soc. N.S. Vol. 47, Pt. 2, 1957.

Drucker, Philip. *Contributions to Alsea Ethnography.* Univ. of Calif. Pubs. in American Arch. and Ethn. Vol. 35, no. 7. Berkeley, 1939.

_____. *Cultures of the North Pacific Coast.* San Francisco, 1965.

_____. *Indians of the Northwest Coast.* New York, 1955.

_____. *The Tolowas and their Southwest Oregon Kin.* Univ. of Calif. Pubs. in American Arch. and Ethn. Vol. 36, no. 4. Berkeley, 1937.

Drury, Clifford M. *Nine Years with the Spokane Indians. The Diary, 1838-1848, of Elkanah Walker.* Glendale, 1976.

Duff, Wilson, *The Impact of the White Man in the Indian History of British Columbia* 1. *Anthropology in British Columbia, Memoir, no. 5.* Victoria, 1964.

Dunn, John. *History of the Oregon Territory and British North-American Fur Trade.* London, 1846.

Edwards, P.L. *Sketch of the Oregon Territory Or, Emigrants' Guide.* Liberty, Mo., 1842.

Eells, Rev. Myron. *The Twana, Chemakum, and Klallam Indians, of Washington Territory.* Annual Report of the Regents, Smithsonian Inst. Wash., D.C., 1887.

_____. *The Twana Indians of the Skokomish Reservation in Washington Territory.* Department of the Interior, U.S. Geological and Geographic Survey. Wash., D.C., 1877.

Elkins, Stanley M. *Slavery.* Chicago, 1976.

Elmendorf, W.W. and A.L. Kroeber. "The Structure of Twana Culture with Comparative Notes on the Structure of Yurok Culture." *Research Studies. A Quarterly Publication of Wash. State Univ.* Monographic Supplement No. 2. Pullman, 1960.

Evans, Elwood. *History of the Pacific Northwest: Oregon and Washington.* 2 vols. Portland, 1889.

Farb, Peter. *Man's Rise to Civilization as Shown by the Indians of North America from Primeval Times to the Coming of the Industrial State.* New York, 1968.

Farnham, Thomas. *Travels in the Great Western Prairies, etc.* Vol. XXVIII in Reuben Gold Thwaites, *Early Western Travels 1784-1846.* 32 vols. Cleveland, 1906.

Fisher, Robin. *Contact & Conflict: Indian-European Relations in British Columbia, 1774-1890.* Vancouver, 1977.

_____, and Hugh Johnston. *Captain James Cook and His Times.* Seattle, 1979.

Fogel, Robert William and Stanley L. Engerman. *Time on the Cross: The Economics of American Negro Slavery.* Boston, 1974.

Forbes, Jack D. *The Indian in America's Past.* Englewood Cliffs, N.J., 1964.

Franchère, Gabriel. *Narrative of a Voyage to the Northwest Coast of America in the Years 1811, 1812, 1813, and 1814 or the First American Settlement on the Pacific.* J.V. Huntington, ed. New York, 1854.

Freeman, Otis and Howard H. Martin. *The Pacific Northwest: An Over-all Appreciation.* New York, 1954.

Fried, Morton H. *The Evolution of Political Society: An Essay in Political Anthropology.* New York, 1967.

Fumoleau, Rene. *As Long As This Land Shall Last: A History of Treaty 8 and Treaty 11, 1870-1939.* Toronto, 1975.

Garfield, Viola E. *Tsimshian Clan and Society.* Univ. of Wash. Pubs. in Anth. VII, no. 3, Seattle, Feb. 1939.

Gatschet, Albert Samuel. *Extracts from the Klamath Indians of Southwestern Oregon.* Dept. of the Interior, U.S. Geog. and Geol. Survey of the Rocky Mountain Region. Wash., D.C., 1890.

_____, Leo Frachtenberg, and Melville Jacobs. *Kalapuya Texts.* Univ. of Wash. Pub. in Anth. II. Seattle, 1945.

Gibbs, George. *Tribes of Western Washington and Northwestern Oregon.* Cont. to North American Ethn. Wash., D.C., 1877.

Gray, W.H. *A History of Oregon, 1792-1849.* Portland, 1870.

Green, Johnathan S. *Journal of a Tour of the North West Coast of America in the Year 1829.* New York, 1915.

Greenhow, Robert. *The History of Oregon and California.* London, 1845.

Gunther, Erna. *Indian Life on the Northwest Coast of North America.* Chicago, 1972.

INDIAN SLAVERY IN THE PACIFIC NORTHWEST

_____. *Klallam Ethnography*. University of Wash. Pubs. in Anth. Vol. 1, no. 5. Seattle, 1927.

Hines, Gustavus. *Wild Life in Oregon*. New York, 1887.

Hodge, Frederick Webb, ed. *Handbook of American Indians North of Mexico*. Smithsonian Bureau of American Ethn. Bull. 30. 2 vols. Wash., D.C., 1912.

Hodge, William H. *The First Americans, Then and Now*. New York, 1981.

Hosmer, James K. *History of the Expedition of Captains Lewis and Clark 1804-5-6*. Chicago, 1917.

Howden, Arthur D. *The Narrative of Samuel Hancock, 1845-1860*. New York, 1927.

Howison, Lieut. Neil M. *Report*, Feb. 1, 1847 (30 Cong., 1 sess., House Misc. Docs. 29), Wash., D.C., 1848.

Hulbert, Archer Butler and Dorothy Printup Hulbert, eds. *Marcus Whitman, Crusader Part Two, 1839-1843*, Vol. VII in *Overland to the Pacific*. Denver, 1939.

Humfreville, J. Lee. *Twenty Years among Our Savage Indians*. Hartford, 1899.

Hussey, John A. *Champoeg: Place of Transition*. Portland, 1967.

Jacobs, Elizabeth Derr. *Nehalem Tillamook Tales*. Melville Jacobs, ed. Eugene, Oregon, 1959.

Jacobs, Melville. *Clackamas Chinook Texts*. Pt. II. Indiana Univ. Research Center in Anth., Folklore, and Linguistics. Bloomington, 1958.

_____. *Kalapuya Texts*. Pt. 1. *Santiam Kalapuya Ethnologic Texts*. Univ. of Wash. Pubs. in Anth. II. Seattle, 1945.

Jacobsen, John Adrian. *Alaskan Voyage 1881-1883: An Expedition to the Northwest Coast of America*. Erna Gunther, trans. Chicago, 1977.

Jessett, Thomas E. *Reports and Letters of Herbert Beaver, 1836-1838*. Portland, 1959.

Jewitt, John R. *Narrative of the Adventures and Sufferings of John R. Jewitt*. Fairfield, Wash., 1967.

Johansen, Dorothy O. and Charles M. Gates. *Empire of the Columbia*. New York, 1967.

Johnson, Olga Weydemeyer. *Flathead and Kootenay: The River, the Tribes and the Region's Traders*. Glendale, 1969.

Jones, Roy F. *Wappato Indians Their History and Prehistory*. n.p., 1972.

Jorgensen, Joseph G. *Western Indians Comparative Environments, Languages, and Cultures of 172 Western American Indian Tribes*. San Francisco, 1980.

Josephy, Alvin M., Jr. *The Nez Perce Indians and the Opening of the Northwest.* New Haven, 1965.

Kane, Paul. *Wanderings of an Artist among the Indians of North America.* London, 1859.

Kelley, Hall J. *A Geographic Sketch of that Part of North America Called Oregon. The Magazine of History with Notes and Queries.* Extra Number-No. 67. Terrytown, N.Y., 1919.

Kirk, Ruth. *Tradition and Change on the Northwest Coast.* Seattle, 1986.

Krause, Aurel. *The Tlingit Indians.* Erna Gunther, trans. Seattle, 1956.

Kroeber, A.L. *Handbook of the Indians of California.* Smithsonian Bureau of American Ethn. Bull. 78. Wash., D.C., 1925.

Ledyard, John. *The Journal of Captain Cook's Last Voyage.* Chicago, 1963.

Lee, Daniel and Joseph Frost. *Ten Years in Oregon.* Fairfield, Wash., 1968.

Lewis, Albert Buell. *Tribes of the Columbia Valley and the Coast of Washington and Oregon.* Memoirs of the American Anth. Assoc. I, Pt. 2. Lancaster, Pa., 1906.

Lewis, William S. and Naojiro Murakami, eds. *Ranald MacDonald: The Narrative of His Early Life on the Columbia...and of His Great Adventure to Japan.* Spokane, 1923.

Lord, John Keast. *The Naturalist in Vancouver Island and British Columbia.* 2 vols. London, 1866.

McBeth, Kate C. *The Nez Percé Since Lewis and Clark.* New York, 1908.

Miller, Jay. *Shamanic Odyssey: The Lushootseed Salish Journey to the Land of the Dead.* Ballena Press Anthropological Papers No. 32. Sylvia Brakke Vane, ed. Menlo Park, Calif., 1988.

MacDonald, Duncan George Forbes, C.E. *British Columbia and Vancouver's Island.* London, 1862.

McFeat, Tom. *Indians of the North Pacific Coast.* Seattle, 1966.

McWhorter, L.V. *Yellow Wolf: His Own Story.* Caldwell, Id., 1948.

Mackey, Harold. *The Kalapuyans: A Sourcebook on the Indians of the Willamette Valley.* Salem, Ore., 1974.

Majors, Harry L. *Exploring Washington.* Holland, Mich., 1975.

Malouf, Carling and A. Arline Malouf. *The Effects of Spanish Slavery on the Indians of the Intermountain West.* In *The Emergent Native Americans: A Reader in Culture Contact.* Deward E. Walker, Jr., ed. Boston, 1971.

Martin, R.H. *The Hudson's Bay Territories and Vancouver's Island.* London, 1849.

Mayne, Commander Richard Charles. *Four Years in British Columbia and Vancouver Island*. London, 1862.

Meacham, Alfred B. *Wigwam and War-Path; or the Royal Chief in Chains*. Boston, 1875.

Meany, Edmond S., ed. *A New Vancouver Journal on the Discovery of Puget Sound by a Member of the Chatham's Crew*. Seattle, 1915.

_____. *History of the State of Washington*. New York, 1941.

Meares, John. *An Introductory Narrative of a Voyage Performed in 1786, from Bengal, in the Ship Nootka*. In *Voyages Made in the Years 1788 and 1789, from China to the North West Coast of America*. London, 1790.

Merk, Frederick, ed. *Fur Trade and Empire: George Simpson's Journal*. Cambridge, Mass., 1931.

Miller, Christopher L. *Prophetic Worlds: Indians and Whites on the Columbia Plateau*. New Brunswick, N.J., 1985.

Miller, Emma Gene. *Clatsop County, Oregon: A History*. Portland, 1958.

Morgan, Dale L. *Jedediah Smith and the Opening of the West*. Indianapolis, 1953.

Mudge, Zachariah Atwell, ed. *Sketches of Mission Life among the Indians of Oregon*. New York, 1854.

Murdock, George Peter. *Culture and Society*. Pittsburg, 1965.

Nash, Philleo. *The Place of Religious Revivalism in the Formation of the Intercultural Community on Klamath Reservation*. In Fred Eggan, ed., *Social Anthropology of North American Tribes*. Chicago, 1937.

Nattali, M.A. *The Oregon Territory, Consisting of a Brief Description of the Country and Its Productions; and of the Habits and Manners of the Native Indian Tribes*. London, 1846.

Neasham, Ernest R. *Fall River Valley*. Fall River Mills, Calif., 1957. In *California Indians III*, David Agee Horr, ed. New York, 1974.

Notices & Voyages of the Famed Quebec Mission to the Pacific Northwest. Portland, 1956.

Olson, Ronald L. *The Quinault Indians and Adze, Canoe, and House Types of the Northwest Coast*. Seattle, 1967.

Owens, Kenneth N. and Alton S. Donnelly. *The Wreck of the Sv. Nikolai*. Portland, 1985.

Parker, Samuel. *Journal of an Exploring Tour Beyond the Rocky Mountains*. Ithaca, N.Y., 1844.

Péron, Capitaine. *Memoirs du Capitaine Péron, Sur ses Voyages. Tome Second*. Paris, 1824.

Pettitt, George A. *The Quileute of La Push 1775-1945*. Anth. Records, Univ. of Calif. 14, no. 1. Berkeley, 1950.

Phelps, Admiral T.S., U.S.N. *Reminiscences of Seattle, Washington Territory. Puget Sound Hist. Series, no. 2.* Seattle, 1908.

Prosch, Charles. *Reminiscences of Washington Territory Scenes, Incidents and Reflections of the Pioneer Period on Puget Sound.* Seattle, 1904.

Rathbun, J.C. *History of Thurston County, Washington.* Olympia, 1895.

Ray, Verne F. *Cultural Relations in the Plateau of Northwestern America.* Pubs. of the Frederick Webb Hodge Anniversary Publication Fund, 2. Los Angeles, 1939.

_____. *Lower Chinook Ethnographic Notes.* Univ. of Wash. Pubs. in anth., VII, no. 2, May 1938.

_____. *Primitive Pragmatists: The Modoc Indians of Northern California.* Seattle, 1963.

_____. *The Sanpoil and Nespelem: Salishan Peoples of Northeastern Washington.* Univ. of Wash. Pubs. in Anth. No. 5. Seattle, 1933.

Reagan, Albert B. *Arch. Notes on Western Washington and Adjacent British Columbia.* San Francisco, 1917.

Records of the Bureau of Indian Affairs, Documents Relating to the Negotiation of Ratified and Unratified Treaties with Various Tribes of Indians, 1801-69, Microcopy T-494, Roll 5. National Archives, Wash. D.C.

Records of the Klamath Indian Agency. Press copies of letters sent to the Commissioner of Indian Affairs. Letter Book, May 1, 1905-Oct. 31, 1905. Federal Records Center, Seattle.

Records of the Oregon Superintendency of Indian Affairs, 1848-1872. Letter Books A:10, B:10, C:10, F:10, I:10. Microcopy of Records in the National Archives, Wash., D.C.

Records of the Siletz Indian Agency. Press copies of letters sent to the Commissioner of Indian Affairs, 1873-1915. Letters sent Dec. 4, 1874-Sept. 29, 1875. Federal Records Center, Seattle.

Records of the Washington Superintendency of Indian Affairs, 1853-1874. No. 5, Rolls 9, 10, 11, 13, 14, 17, 26. Microcopy of Records in the National Archives, Wash., D.C.

Reynolds, Stephen. *The Voyage of the New Hazard to the Northwest Coast, Hawaii and China, 1810-1813.* Fairfield, Wash., 1970.

Rich, E.E., M.A., ed. *The Letters of John McLoughlin from Fort Vancouver to the Governor and Committee, First Series 1825-38.* 2 vols. London, 1941.

Ross, Alexander. *Adventures of the First Settlers on the Oregon or Columbia River.* London, 1849.

_____. *The Fur Hunters of the Far West.* Kenneth A. Spaulding, ed. Norman, 1956.

Ruby, Robert H. and John A. Brown. *The Cayuse Indians: Imperial Tribesmen of Old Oregon.* Norman, 1972.

_____. *The Chinook Indians: Traders of the Lower Columbia River.* Norman, 1976.

_____. *A Guide to the Indian Tribes of the Pacific Northwest.* Norman, 1986.

_____. *Indians of the Pacific Northwest.* Norman, 1981.

Sauter, John and Bruce Johnson. *Tillamook Indians of the Oregon Coast.* Portland, 1974.

Schoolcraft, Henry Rowe. *Historical and Statistical Information Respecting the History Condition and Prospects of the Indian Tribes of the United States.* 6 vols. Philadelphia, 1851-1857.

Sellin, Johan Thorsten. *Slavery and the Penal System.* New York, 1967.

Selwyn, Alfred. *Geographical Survey of Canada Report of Progress for 1878-79.* Montreal, 1880.

Service, Elman R. *Origins of the State and Civilization: The Process of Cultural Evolution.* New York, 1975.

_____. *Profiles in Ethnology.* New York, 1963.

Simpson, George. *Narrative of a Journey Round the World, During the Years 1841 and 1842.* 2 vols. London, 1847.

_____. *Peace River. A Canoe Voyage from Hudson's Bay to Pacific, by the Late Sir George Simpson, in 1828.* Ottawa, 1872.

_____. *Simpson's 1828 Journey to the Columbia.* The Pubs. of the Hudson's Bay Record Society. E.E. Rich, ed. Toronto, 1947.

Slacum, William. *Memorial of William A. Slacum Praying Compensation for his services in obtaining information in relation to the Settlements on the Oregon River* (25 Cong., 2 sess., Sen. Exec. Doc. No. 24). Memorial, Dec. 18, 1937.

Smith, Marian W., ed. *The Puyallup-Nisqually.* Columbia Univ. Cont. to Anth., vol. 32. New York, 1940.

Snyder, Warren A. *Southern Puget Sound Salish: Texts, Place Names, and Dictionary.* Sacramento, 1968.

Spier, Leslie. *Klamath Ethnography.* Univ. of Calif. Pubs. in American Arch. and Ethn., 30. Berkeley, 1930.

_____, and Edward Sapir. *Wishram Ethnography Linguistic Relationship and Territory.* Univ. of Wash. Pubs. in Anth. III, no. 3. Seattle, 1930.

Spinden, Herbert Joseph. *The Nez Perce Indians, Memoirs of the American Anth. Assoc.,* 2 Pt. 3. Lancaster, Pa., Nov. 1908.

Sproat, Gilbert Malcolm. *Scenes and Studies of Savage Life.* London, 1868.

Stanley, John Mix. *Portraits of North American Indians.* The Smithsonian Institution. Wash., D.C., 1852.

Stannard, M. *Memoirs of a Professional Nurse.* London, 1873.

Stern, Theodore. *The Klamath Tribe: A People and Their Reservation.* Seattle, 1966.

Stoneman, Capt. George and Lt. W.H.C. Whiting to Major E.D. Townsend, July 5, 1855 (50 Cong., 1 sess., Sen. Exec. Doc. No. 165), Serial 2513. Wash., D.C., 1888.

Stremler, Maxine Fay. *Final Decision*, Enrollment Coordinator, Anchorage, Alaska, March 14, 1980.

_____. *Petition.* Enrollment Coordinating Office, Anchorage, Alaska, July 25, 1979.

Strickland, W.P., A.M. *History of the Missions of the Methodist Episcopal Church.* Cincinnati, 1850.

Strong, James C. *Wah-Kee-Nah and Her People: The Curious Customs, Traditions, and Legends of the North American Indians.* New York, 1893.

Sumner, William Graham, *Folkways: A Study of the Sociological Importance of Usages, Manners, Customs, Mores, and Morals.* Boston, 1911.

Suttles, Wayne P. *Coast Salish Essays.* Seattle, 1987.

Swan, James G. *The Indians of Cape Flattery, at the Entrance to the Strait of Fuca, Washington Territory.* Smithsonian Contributions to Knowledge 16, no. 8. Wash., D.C., 1870.

_____. *The Northwest Coast; or, Three Years' Residence in Washington Territory.* New York, 1857.

Swanton, John R. *Contributions to the Ethnology of the Haida, Publications of the Jesup North Pacific Expedition 5; Memoirs of the American Museum of Natural History* 8, pt. 1. New York, 1905.

_____. *Social Condition, Beliefs, and Linguistic Relationship of the Tlingit Indians.* Twenty Sixth Annual Report of the Bureau of American Ethnology for the Years 1904-1905. Wash., D.C., 1908.

Teit, James A. *Culture Relations in the Plateau of Northwestern America.* Pubs. of the Frederick Webb Hodge Anniv. Pub. Fund, III. Los Angeles, 1939.

_____. *The Salishan Tribes of the Western Plateaus.* Forty-fifth Annual Report of the Bureau of American Ethn. to the Smithsonian Inst. 1927-1928. Franz Boas, ed. Wash., D.C., 1930.

Thomas, Edward Harper. *Chinook: A History and Dictionary.* Portland, 1935.

Thwaites, Reuben Gold, ed. *Original Journals of the Lewis and Clark Expedition, 1804-1806.* 8 vols. New York, 1959.

Townsend, John K. *Narrative of a Journey across the Rocky Mountains, to the Columbia River.* Vol. XXI in Reuben Gold Thwaites, *Early Western Travels, 1784-1846.* 32 vols. Cleveland, 1906.

Trafzer, Clifford E. and Richard D. Scheuerman. *Renegade Tribe: The Palouse Indians and the Invasion of the Inland Pacific Northwest.* Pullman, 1986.

Tucker, Ephraim W. *History of Oregon, Containing a Condensed Account of the Most Important Voyages and Discoveries.* Buffalo, 1844.

Underhill, Ruth. *Indians of the Pacific Northwest.* Wash., 1944.

United States of America, Contestant v. *Frank Abbott, et al, Contestees.* Feb. 1, 1979, U.S. Dept. of the Interior, Office of Hearings and Appeals, Hearings Division Arlington, Va.

Vancouver, George. *A Voyage of Discovery to the North Pacific Ocean, and Round the World under the Command of Captain George Vancouver.* 6 vols. London, 1801.

Wagner, Henry R. *Spanish Explorations of the Strait of Juan de Fuca.* Santa Ana, Calif., 1933.

Waterman, Thomas Talbot and Ruth Greiner. *Indian Houses of Puget Sound,* in *Indian Notes and Monographs.* F.W. Hodge, ed. New York, 1921.

West, John. *The Substance of a Journal During a Residence at the Red River Colony, British North America.* London, 1824.

Wheeler-Voegelin, Erminie. *Pitt River Indians of California,* in *California Indians III.* David Agee Horr, ed. New York, 1974.

White, Elijah. *Ten Years in Oregon.* Ithaca, N.Y., 1850.

Wilbur, Marguerite Eyer, ed. *Duflot de Mofras, Travels on the Pacific Coast.* Santa Ana, Calif., 1937.

Wilkes, Charles, U.S.N. *The Narrative of the United States Exploring Expedition, during the years 1838, 1839, 1840, 1841, and 1842.* 5 vols. Philadelphia, 1845.

_____. *Western America, Including California nd Oregon.* Philadelphia, 1849.

Wilkes, George. *The History of Oregon, Geographical and Political.* New York, 1845.

Yarrow, H.A. *A Further Contribution to the Study of the Mortuary Customs of the North American Indians.* First Annual Report of the Bureau of

Ethnology to the Secretary of the Smithsonian Inst. 1879-'80. Wash., D.C., 1881.

ARTICLES

Amoss, Pamela. "Man and Dog on the Northwest Coast, Ancient Man's Best Friend," *Pacific Search: Northwest Nature and Life* 10, no. 2 (Nov. 1975).

Andrews, C.L. "The Wreck of the St. Nicholas," *Wash. Hist. Qtly.* 13, no. 1 (Jan. 1922).

Arneson, James. "Property Concepts of 19th Century Oregon Indians," *Oreg. Hist. Qtly.* 81, no. 4 (Dec. 1980).

Baker, Julie Philips. "Black Slavery among the American Indians," *AB Bookman Weekly*, Feb. 17, 1992.

Bagley, Clarence B. "Chief Seattle and Angeline," *WHQ* 22, No. 4 (Oct. 1931).

_____, ed. "Journal of Occurrences at Nisqually House, 1833-1835," *WHQ* 7, nos. 1 and 2 (Jan., April, 1916).

Barnett, Homer G. "The Nature of the Potlatch," *American Anthropologist* 40 (1938).

Barry, J. Neilson. "Astorians Who Became Permanent Settlers," *WHQ* 24, no. 4 (Oct. 1933).

Bishop, Charles A. "Limiting Access to Limited Goods: The Origins of Stratification in Interior British Columbia." In *The Development of Political Organization in Native North America, 1979 Proceedings of the American Ethn. Soc.* Elisabeth Tooker, ed. Wash., D.C., 1983.

Blinman, Eric, Elizabeth Colson and Robert Heizer, "A Makah Epic Journey," *Pacific Northwest Qtly* 68, no. 4 (Oct. 1977).

Boas, Franz. "The Social Organization and Secret Societies of the Kwakiutl," *U.S. National Museum Report for 1895.* Wash., D.C., 1897.

Boit, John. "John Boit's Log of the Columbia—1790-1793," *OHQ* 22, no. 4 (Dec. 1921).

Cannon, Aubrey, "Conflict and Salmon on the Interior Plateau of British Columbia." In *A Complex Culture of the British Columbia Plateau,* Brian Hayden, ed. Vancouver, B.C., 1992.

Carey, Charles Henry. "The Mission Record Books of the Methodist Episcopal Church, Willamette Station, Oregon Territory, North America, Commenced, 1834," *OHQ* 23, no. 4 (Sept. 1922).

Chase, A.W. "Siletz, or "Lo" Reconstructed," *The Overland Monthly* 2, no. 5 (May 1869).

Clark, Keith, and Donna Clark. "William McKay's Journal, 1866-67; Indian Scouts," *OHQ* 79, Pts. I and II, no. 2 (Summer 1978).

Clark, Robert C. "The Archives of the Hudson's Bay Company," *PNQ* 29, no. 1 (Jan. 1938).

Coan, C.F. "The First Stage of the Federal Indian Policy in the Pacific Northwest, 1849-1852," *OHQ* 22, no. 2 (June 1922).

Colbert, Mildred. "Naming and Early Settlement of Ilwaco, Washington," *OHQ* 47, no. 2 (June 1946).

Cole, Douglas and David Darling, "History of the Early Period." In Wayne Suttles, ed., *Handbook of North American Indians Northwest Coast* 7. Wash., D.C., 1990.

Collins, June M. "John Fornsby: The Personal Document of a Coast Salish Indian." In *Indians of the Urban Northwest*, Marian W. Smith, ed., New York, 1949.

Crosby, H.R. "The San Juan Difficulty," *The Overland Monthly* 2, no. 3 (March 1869).

Cybulski, Jerome S. "Human Biology." In Wayne Suttles, ed., *Handbook of North American Indians Northwest Coast* 7. Wash., D.C., 1990.

Davenport, T.W. "Slavery Question in Oregon," *OHQ* 8, no. 3 (Sept. 1907).

"Decapitation of Colonel Eby," *WHQ* 1, no. 1 (Oct. 1906).

Dee, Henry Drummond, ed. "The Journal of John Work, January to October, 1935," *Memoir No. 10, 1945*. Arch. of British Columbia, Victoria.

Dennis, Elsie Frances. "Indian Slavery in Pacific Northwest," *OHQ* 21, nos. 1, 2 and 3 (March, June and Sept., 1930).

Denny, E.I. "Types and Characteristics of Puget Sound Indians," *The Northwest* 12, no. 9 (Sept. 1894).

De Laguna, Frederica, "Tlingit." In Wayne Suttles, ed., *Handbook of North Americans Northwest Coast* 7, Wash., D.C., 1990.

de Widersprach-Thor, Martine. "The Equation of Copper." In *Papers from the Sixth Annual Congress, 1979, Canadian Ethnological Society*, Marie-Francoise Guedon and D.G. Hatt, eds. Ottawa, 1981.

Donald, Leland. "The Slave Trade on the Northwest Coast of North America," *Research in Economic Anthropology* 6, 1984.

_____. "Was Nuu-chah-nulth-aht (Nootka) Society Based on Slave Labor?" In *The Development of Political Organization in Native North America, 1979 Proceedings of the American Ethn. Soc.* Elisabeth Tooker, ed., Wash., D.C., 1983.

Douglas, David. "Sketch of a Journey to Northwestern Parts of the Continent of North America during the Years 1824-'25-'26-'27," *OHQ* 6, no. 1 (March 1905).

Douglas, Jesse E., ed. "Matthews' Adventures on the Columbia," *OHQ* 40, no. 2 (June 1939).

Drucker, Philip. "Rank, Wealth, and Kinship in Northwest Coast Society," *American Anthropologist* N.S. 41, no. 1 (Jan.-March, 1939).

_____. "Sources of Northwest Coast Culture." In *New Interpretations of Aboriginal American Culture History.* Wash., D.C., 1955.

Duff, Wilson. "The Fort Victoria Treaties," *B.C. Studies No. 3* (Fall 1969).

Dunbar, Seymour and Paul C. Phillips, eds. "A Caucasian Opinion of the Red Race," *The Journals and Letters of Major John Owen Pioneer of the Northwest 1850-1871.* 2 vols. New York, 1927.

"Editorial." *The Oregonian, and Indian's Advocate* 1, no. 8 (May 1839).

Elliott, T.C. "Editorial Notes on the Peter Skene Ogden Journal of Snake Expedition, 1826-7," *OHQ* 11, no. 2 (June 1910).

_____. "Introduction to David Thompson's Narrative: The Discovery of the Source of the Columbia," *OHQ* 26, no. 1 (March 1925).

_____. "The Journal of the Ship Ruby," *OHQ* 28, no. 3 (Sept. 1927).

_____. "Journal of John Work, November and December, 1824," *WHQ* 3, no. 3 (July 1912).

Engstrand, Iris H.W. "José Mariano Moziño, Pioneer Mexican Naturalist," *Columbia: The Magazine of Northwest History* 5, no. 1 (Spring 1991).

Farrand, Livingston. "Notes on the Alsea Indians of Oregon," *American Anthropologist* N.S. 3, no. 2 (April-June 1901).

Farrar, Victor J. "Diary Kept by Colonel and Mrs. I.N. Ebey," *WHQ* 8, no. 1 (Jan. 1917).

Ferguson, Brian. "Warfare and Redistributive Exchange on the Northwest Coast." In *The Development of Political Organization in Native North America, 1979 Proceedings of the American Ethn. Soc.* Elisabeth Tooker, ed. Wash., D.C., 1983.

French, David. "Wasco-Wishram." In Edward H. Spicer, ed. *Perspectives in American Culture Change.* Chicago, 1961.

Garfield, Viola E. "A Research Problem in Northwest Indian Economics," *American Anthropologist* 47, no. 4 (1945).

Garth, Thomas R. "Early Nineteenth Century Tribal Relations in the Columbia Plateau," *Southwestern Journal of Anth.* 20, no. 1 (1964).

Gates, Charles M., ed. "Defending Puget Sound Against the Northern Indians," *PNQ* 36, no. 1 (Jan. 1945).

Gathke, Robert Moulton. "The First Indian School of the Pacific Northwest," *OHQ* 25, no. 1 (March 1922).

Gatschet, Albert Samuel. "Various Ethnographic Notes. The Kalapuya People," *Journal of American Folk-Lore* 12, no. 46 (July, Sept. 1899).

Gosnell, W.B. "Indian War in Washington Territory," *WHQ* 17, no. 4 (Oct. 1926).

Grant, Col. W.C. "Description of Vancouver Island," *Journal of the Royal Geographic Society* 27 (1857).

Gunther, Erna. "The Indian Background of Washington History," *PNQ* 41, no. 3 (July 1950).

Haines, Francis D. "The Northward Spread of Horses among the Plains Indians," *American Anthropologist* 40, no. 3 (July-Sept. 1938).

Halpin, Marjorie M. and Margaret Sequin. "Tsimshian Peoples," in Wayne Suttles, ed., *Handbook of North American Indians, Northwest Coast* 7, Washington, 1990.

Harvey, A.H. "Chief Comcomly's Skull," *OHQ* 40, no. 2 (June 1939).

"Historical Notes," *Pacific Monthly* 6, no. 6 (Nov.-Dec. 1901).

Hobucket, Harry. "Quillayute Indian Tradition," *WHQ* 25, no. 1 (Jan. 1934).

Howay, F.W. "Origin of the Chinook Jargon on the Northwest Coast," *WHQ* 44, no. 1 (March 1943).

Hunt, H.F. "Slavery Among the Indians of Northwest America," *WHQ* 9, no. 1 (June 1918).

Johansen, Dorothy O. "McLoughlin and the Indians," *Beaver*, Outfit 277, no. 1 (June 1946).

Josephy, Alvin M., Jr. "Origins of the Nez Perce People," *Idaho Yesterdays* 6, no. 1 (Spring 1962).

Kane, Paul. "Incidents of Travel on the North-West Coast, Vancouver's Island, Oregon, &c., &c.," *The Canadian Journal* (July 1955).

Kopytoff, Igor. "Slavery," *Annual Review of Anth.* 11, 1982.

Kroeber, A.L. "Types of Indian Culture in California," *Univ. of Calif. Pubs., American Arch. and Ethn.* 2, no. 3, 1904.

Layton, Thomas N. "Traders and Raiders: Aspects of Trans-Basin and California-Plateau Commerce, 1800-1830," *Jnl. of Calif. and Great Basin Anth.* Vol. 3, no. 1, 1981.

Leader, Herman A. "Douglas Expeditions, 1840-41," *OHQ* 32, nos. 2, 3 and 4 (June, Sept. and Dec. 1931).

Loring, Charles G. "Memoir of the Hon. William Sturgis," *Proc. of the Mass. Hist. Soc., 1863-1864.* Boston (Aug. 1864).

Mackey, Harold. "Siuslaw Head Flattening," *OHQ* 69, no. 2 (June 1968)

MacLeod, William Christie. "Debtor and Chattel Slavery in Aboriginal North America," *Amer. Anthropologist* N.S. 27, no. 3 (July 1925).

_____. "Economic Aspects of Indigenous American Slavery," *Amer. Anthropologist* N.S. 30, no. 4 (1928).

McLoughlin, William G. "The Choctaw Slave Burning: A Crisis in Mission Work Among the Indians," *Jnl. of the West* 13, no. 1 (Jan. 1974).

Meany, Edmond S. "Diary of Dr. W.F. Tolmie," *WHQ* 23, no. 3 (July 1932)

_____. "The Indian Chief Kitsap," *WHQ* 25, no. 4 (Oct. 1934).

_____. "A New Vancouver Journal," *WHQ* 25, no. 2 (April 1914).

Meyers, J.A. "Oregan—River of the Slaves or River of the West," *WHQ* 13, no. 4 (Oct. 1922).

Miller, Beatrice, "Neah Bay, The Makah in Transition," *PNQ* 43, no. 4 (Oct. 1952).

Minto, John. "The Number and Condition of the Native Race in Oregon When First Seen by White Men," *OHQ* 1, no. 1 (March 1900).

Mitchell, Donald H. "A Demographic Profile of Northwest Coast Slavery," in *Status, Structure and Stratification, Current Archaeological Reconstruction.* M. Thompson, M. Garcia, F. Hense, eds. Calgary, 1985.

_____. "Predatory Warfare, Social Status, and the North Pacific Slave Trade," *Ethnology* 23, 1984.

Mitchell, Donald H., "Sebassa's Men," in Donald N. Abbott, ed., *The World Is as Sharp as a Knife.* Victoria, B.C., 1981.

_____ and Leland Donald. "Some Economic Aspects of Tlingit, Haida, and Tsimshian Slavery," *Research in Econ. Anth.* 7, 1985.

Morris, Col. T. "Army Officer's Report on Indian War and Treaties," *WHQ* 19, no. 2 (April 1928).

Murdock, Goerge Peter. "Kinship and Social Behavior among the Haida," *Amer. Anthropologist,* 36, 1934.

_____. "Rank and Potlatch among the Haida," *Yale Univ. Pubs. in Anth.* no. 13. New Haven, 1970.

Niblack, Albert Parker. "The Coast Indians of Southern Alaska and Northern British Columbia," *Annual Rept. of the U.S. Museum for 1888,* Washington, 1890.

Nokes, J. Richard. "Patriot or Scalawag? John Meares' Exploits on the Northwest Coast," *Columbia: The Magazine of Northwest History* (Fall, 1990).

"Old Fort Nisqually," *The Northwest* 8, no. 2 (Feb. 1890).

Oliphant, J. Orin. "A Project for a Christian Mission on the Northwest Coast of America, 1798," *PNQ* 36, no. 2 (April 1945).

"The Oregon Indians and Their Slaves," *Friends Review: A Religious, Literary and Miscellaneous Journal* 3, no. 19 (First Month 26, 1850).

Petroff, Ivan. "The Population and Resources of Alaska, 1880," in *Narratives of Explorations in Alaska*. Washington, 1900.

Piper, Lt. Alexander. "Reports and Journal," *OHQ* 69, no. 3 (Sept. 1968).

Pipes, Nellie B., ed. "Journal of John Frost, 1840-43," *OHQ* 45, no. 1 (March 1934).

––––––. "The Journal of John Work, March 21-May 14, 1925," *OHQ* 45, no. 2 (June 1944).

Powers, Stephen. "The California Indians: No. VII—The Modocs," *The Overland Monthly* 10, no. 6 (June 1873).

Ray, Verne. "The Historical Position of the Lower Chinook in the Native Culture of the Northwest," *PNQ* 28, no. 4 (Oct. 1937).

Reagan, Albert B. "Traditions of the Hoh and Quillayute Indians," *WHQ* 20, no. 3 (July 1929).

Ruyle, Eugene E. "Slavery, Surplus, and Stratification on the Northwest Coast: The Ethnoenergetics of an Incipient Stratification System," *Current Anthropology* 14, no. 5 (Dec. 1973).

Sapir, Edward. "Notes on the Takelma Indians of Southwestern Oregon," *American Anthropologist* N.S. 9, no. 2 (April, June 1907).

Schafer, Joseph, ed. "Documents Relative to Warre and Vavasour's Military Reconnaissance in Oregon, 1845-6," *OHQ* 10, no. 1 (March 1909).

Scouler, Dr. John. "Dr. John Scouler's Journal of a Voyage to N.W. America" Pt 3, *OHQ* 6, no. 3 (Sept. 1905).

Siegel, Bernard J. "Some Methodological Considerations for a Comparative Study of Slavery," *American Anthropologist* N.S. 47, no. 3 (July-Sept. 1945).

Silverstein, Michael, "Chinookans of the Lower Columbia." In Wayne Suttles, ed., *Handbook of North American Indians Northwest Coast* 7. Wash., D.C., 1990.

Smith, Captain John. "Letter to the Editor," *The Council Fire* 4, no. 4 (April 1881).

Smith, Silas B. "Primitive Customs and Religious Beliefs of the Indians of the Pacific Northwest Coast," *OHQ* 2, no. 3 (Sept. 1901).

Stern, Theodore. "The Klamath Indians and the Treaty of 1864," *OHQ* 57, no. 3 (Sept. 1956).

_____. "Some Sources of Variability in Klamath Mythology." *Journal of American Folklore* 69, no. 272 (April-June 1956).

Suttles, Wayne, "Introduction." In Wayne Suttles, ed., *Handbook of North American Indians Northwest Coast* 7. Wash., D.C., 1990.

_____. "Private Knowledge, Morality, and Social Classes among the Coast Salish," *American Anthropologist* 60, no. 3 (June 1958).

_____, and Aldona C. Jonaitis, "History of Research in Ethnology." In Wayne Suttles, ed., *Handbook of North American Indians Northwest Coast* 7, Wash., D.C., 1990.

Taylor, Herbert C., Jr. "Aboriginal Populations of the Lower Northwest Coast," *PNQ* 54, no. 4 (Oct. 1963).

Thompson, Lucy. "Reminiscences of a Yurok Aristocrat," *The Californians* (Nov./Dec. 1992).

Townsend, Joan B. "Pre-contact Political Organization and Slavery in Aleut Societies." In *The Development of Political Organization in Native North America, 1979 Proceedings of the American Ethn. Soc.* Elisabeth Tooker, ed. Wash., D.C., 1983.

Turney-High, Harry Holbert. "The Flathead Indians of Montana." *Memoirs, American Anth. Assoc.* 48 (1937).

Vayda, Andrew P. "A Re-examination of Northwest Coast Economic Systems." In *Trans. of the New York Academy of Sciences,* Ser. 2, no. 23 (1961).

Veniaminov, Innokentii. "The Condition of the Orthodox Church in Russian America: Innoentii Veniaminov's History of the Church in Alaska." Robert Nichols and Robert Croskey, eds. *PNQ* 63, no. 2 (April 1972).

West, Oswald. "Oregon's First White Settlers on French Prairie," *OHQ* 43, no. 3 (Sept. 1942).

Wheeler, Olin D. "A Day with the Queniut Indians," *Wonderland: 1897-1906.* St. Paul, 1906.

Woody, Frank W. "From Missoula to Walla Walla in 1857 on Horseback," *WHQ* 3, no. 4 (Oct. 1912).

NEWSPAPERS

Alaska Native Times. Seattle, Wash., 1979.

Catholic Sentinel. Portland, Ore., 1878.

Christian Advocate & Journal. New York, N.Y., 1836.
Daily Astorian. Astoria, Ore., 1884.
Dalles Mountaineer. The Dalles, Ore., 1867.
Mason County Journal. Shelton, Wash., 1890, 1891.
Montana Post. Virginia City, Mont. Terr., 1865.
New York Tribune. New York, N.Y., 1850.
Nugget. Chehalis, Wash Terr., 1885.
Oregonian. Portland, Ore., 1878.
Oregonian and Indian's Advocate. Boston, Mass., 1839.
Oregon Spectator. Salem, Ore. Terr., 1847.
Oregon Sunday Journal. Portland, Ore., 1929.
Port Townsend Register. Port Townsend, Wash. Terr., 1860.
Tacoma Ladger. Tacoma, Wash. Terr., 1886.
Washington Standard. Olympia, Wash. Terr., 1861.
Weekly Ledger. Tacoma, Wash., 1893.
Weekly Oregonian. Portland, Ore., 1860.

LETTERS TO AUTHORS

Craig, J.C. Archivist, Hudson's Bay Company, Feb. 4, 1971.
Dunae, Patrick A., Archivist, British Columbia Provincial Archives, June 14, 1989.
Mitchell, Donald H., Anthropologist, Feb. 4, 1993.
Owens, Kenneth H., Historian, May 7, 1987.
Richards, Kent D., Historian, Mar. 3, 1993.
Suttles, Wayne P., Anthropologist, Oct. 31, 1988.
Wutkee, Winston, Researcher, Jan. 17, 1971.
Wyatt, Victoria, Anthropologist, June 28, 1988.

INTERVIEWS

Stremler, Maxine Faye, Jan. 31, 1989.

Index